# HUMAN LIVES

# Human Lives

## Critical Essays on Consequentialist Bioethics

Edited by

David S. Oderberg

and

Jacqueline A. Laing

First published in Great Britain 1997 by
**MACMILLAN PRESS LTD**
Houndmills, Basingstoke, Hampshire RG21 6XS and London
Companies and representatives throughout the world

A catalogue record for this book is available from the British Library.

ISBN 0–333–62980–9

First published in the United States of America 1997 by
**ST. MARTIN'S PRESS, INC.,**
Scholarly and Reference Division,
175 Fifth Avenue, New York, N.Y. 10010

ISBN 0–312–16099–2

Library of Congress Cataloging-in-Publication Data
Human lives : critical essays on consequentialist bioethics / edited
by David S. Oderberg and Jacqueline A. Laing.
p.   cm.
Includes bibliographical references and index.
ISBN 0–312–16099–2
1. Medical ethics.   2. Bioethics.   3. Consequentialism (Ethics)
I. Oderberg, David S.  II. Laing, Jacqueline A.
R724.H784   1996
174'.2—dc20                                          96–9136
                                                        CIP

This book is printed on paper suitable for recycling and made from fully managed and
sustained forest sources.

10   9   8   7   6   5   4   3   2   1
06   05   04   03   02   01   00   99   98   97

Printed in Great Britain by
The Ipswich Book Company Ltd
Ipswich, Suffolk

# Contents

# Notes on the Contributors

**Cora Diamond** is Kenan Professor of Philosophy at The University of Virginia, and has also taught at The University of Aberdeen and at Princeton University. She is the editor of *Wittgenstein's Lectures on the Foundations of Mathematics, Cambridge, 1939* (Harvester Press, 1976). Her recent works include *The Realistic Spirit: Wittgenstein, Philosophy and the Mind* (MIT Press, 1991), and articles on Frege and Wittgenstein, philosophy of language, ethics, and philosophy in relation to literature.

**Nicholas Denyer** is a Fellow of Trinity College, Cambridge, a College Lecturer in Philosophy, and a University Lecturer in the Faculty of Classics. He is the author of *Language, Thought and Falsehood in Ancient Greek Philosophy* (Routledge, 1991).

**Stephen R. L. Clark** is Professor of Philosophy at Liverpool University. He is the author of *The Moral Status of Animals* (OUP, 1984), *Civil Peace and Sacred Order* (Clarendon Press, 1989), and *How to Think about the Earth* (Mowbray, 1993).

**Brian Scarlett** is Lecturer in Philosophy at The University of Melbourne, and head of department. He has lectured at The Australian National University and the Royal Melbourne Institute of Technology, and his main philosophical interests are in moral philosophy, philosophical psychology and ancient and medieval philosophy.

**Tim Chappell** is Lecturer in Philosophy at The University of East Anglia. He is the author of *Aristotle and Augustine on Freedom* (Macmillan, 1995) and *The Plato Reader* (Edinburgh, 1996), and has published articles on ancient philosophy, ethics, and the philosophy of mind.

**Grant Gillett** is a Professor of Medical Ethics at the Bioethics Centre of the Medical School, University of Otago. He is also a practising neurosurgeon. He is the author of *Representation, Meaning and Thought* (Clarendon Press, 1992) and *Reasonable Care* (Bristol Classical Press, 1989), as well as of numerous articles in general philosophy, philosophy of mind, medical ethics and philosophy of psychiatry. He is co-author of *Practical Medical Ethics* (OUP, 1992) and *The Discursive Mind* (Sage, 1994).

**John Cottingham** is Professor of Philosophy at The University of Reading, and editor of *Ratio*, the international journal of analytical philosophy. He is co-translator of *The Philosophical Writings of Descartes* (CUP, 1985–91), and author of *Rationalism* (Paladin, 1984), *Descartes* (Blackwell, 1986), *The Rationalists* (OUP, 1988), and *A Descartes Dictionary* (Blackwell, 1993). He has also published articles on moral philosophy in many journals, and is a contributor to *The Encyclopedia of Ethics* (Garland, 1992).

**Lance Simmons** is Assistant Professor of Philosophy at The University of Dallas. He has published articles in rationality theory and theoretical ethics, and is currently working on a research project in bioethics.

**J. L. A. Garcia** is Professor of Philosophy at Rutgers University. He has taught at Georgetown and Notre Dame Universities, served as Senior Research Scholar at the Kennedy Institute of Ethics, and been both Fellow in Ethics at Harvard University and Visiting Fellow in Harvard Medical School's Division of Medical Ethics. He has written numerous articles in theoretical and practical ethics, including contributions to *African-American Perspectives on Biomedical Ethics* (Georgetown U.P., 1992), *'It Just Ain't Fair': the Ethics of Health Care for African-Americans* (Praeger, 1994), and the revised edition of the *Encyclopedia of Bioethics* (Macmillan, 1995).

**Janet E. Smith** is Associate Professor of Philosophy at the University of Dallas, and formerly Assistant Professor in the Program of Liberal Studies at the University of Notre Dame. She has published on moral philosophy, with special reference to virtue theory and natural law theory, on Aquinas's analysis of the moral act, on bioethical issues, as well as on Plato and myth.

**Jacqueline A. Laing** is a Barrister of the High Court of Australia, and Barrister and Solicitor of the Supreme Court of Victoria. She has taught moral philosophy at St Edmund's College, Oxford and at The University of Melbourne, and published articles on intention and culpability and the philosophy of the criminal law. She is currently completing a doctorate in Philosophy at Brasenose College, Oxford.

**David S. Oderberg** is Lecturer in Philosophy at The University of Reading. He has taught philosophy at The University of Melbourne and at Trinity and University Colleges, Dublin. He is the author of *The*

*Metaphysics of Identity over Time* (Macmillan, 1993), and of articles on philosophical logic, metaphysics and philosophy of language.

# Introduction

The last twenty-five years have seen the emergence of applied ethics as an independent and prominent branch of moral philosophy. For much of this century moral philosophers were occupied with reflection on the nature of morality, the possibility of moral truth and objectivity, the meaning of moral language, and related metatheoretical questions. They have, however, come to recall what in previous times was always taken for granted: that if moral philosophy is not to be a guide to *practice*, it simply does not fulfil its very purpose and is thereby seriously deficient.

Moreover, advocates of applied ethics have usually been correct in the role they have reclaimed for philosophy. On one hand, even the most mundane concrete ethical problems can sometimes require complicated and abstruse reasoning in order for a solution to be reached. It is the philosopher who is uniquely trained to carry out such reasoning. (Anyone who reasons in such fashion, professional philosopher or not, 'wears the philosopher's hat'and his reasoning is to be assessed in that light.)

On the other hand, no matter how difficult a concrete ethical problem is, its solution (whatever it be) should in principle be capable of being stated simply, in language free of philosophical jargon, to the person faced with the problem (and to anyone else).

The most prominent branch of applied ethics, one which illustrates this duality of function possessed by the philosopher who seriously concerns himself with practical moral philosophy, is the discipline that has come to be known as bioethics, or the philosophical study of what might be called 'life and death' issues: euthanasia, abortion, animal welfare, genetic engineering, the morality of war and our obligations to protect and respect the natural world are but some of the more important examples. It would be fair to say that no other area of modern philosophy has risen so spectacularly to public visibility, and in so short a time. Bioethicists have been and continue to be influential at the highest levels of policy-making, many of them having a substantial input into the framing of legislation through proliferating advisory committees and reports. They act also as regular expert commentators in the media on pressing moral issues. At the same time the academic side of bioethics is flourishing, with bioethics research institutes mushrooming in the universities, and an increasing number of journals and conferences. The research institutes and allied activities are often in direct receipt of government funding (separate from ordinary university funding), which itself reflects both the increasing importance policy-makers attach to the contribution bioethicists can make to public debate and the serious responsibility the latter have to the public whom they counsel.

It should be gratifying to philosophers that, through their own advocacy, the public has become aware of the need for rigorous and intelligent discussion of many sensitive and difficult problems of everyday morality. While they should welcome the growing contribution made by their profession to social problems of an urgent and highly practical nature, however, they should at the same time lament the serious imbalance which has distorted much of the debate. For it is plain that bioethics has been dominated by a certain way of doing moral philosophy, one which in our opinion, and in the opinion of many others, has led to proposals which are not merely false, but immoral.

It is not surprising that it should be the ethical theory known as consequentialism (divided, of course, into a number of sub-theoretical species) which has dominated the practice of bioethics and so produced the imbalance noted above. Consequentialism is in many ways ideally suited to dealing with one of the central questions raised by bioethics: whether, and to what extent, life-and-death decisions are constrained by the huge advances in medical and industrial technology. First, it is a theory which can be described as objectivist or cognitivist: consequentialism promises *answers* to specific moral questions, not the sort of evasion or fuzzy thinking that is characteristic of relativist theories.

Secondly, consequentialists rightly do not leave the solution of bioethical problems merely to the actual practice of those professionals for whom the problems are most pressing: doctors, scientists, lawyers, legislators, and others. Rather, they insist on the need for professionals to be *informed* by correct philosophical thinking. By advocating a distinctive and essential role for philosophers in the resolution of bioethical problems, they have convinced a growing number of professionals that they should look outside the ethical standards developed from within the regulatory bodies to which they belong, at the *justification* for those standards in the light of rational argument. This is not to say that ethical standards can never be correct if professionals or legislators frame them independently of philosophical ratification. It is simply that the tendency has been, where there is a belief in the need for ethical regulation (the increasing popularity of the belief itself demonstrates the impact of bioethics), to regard those people whose job it is to *implement* policy (at the ethical coal-face, as it were) as perfectly capable of devising ethical standards unaided; rather, aided only by the empirical knowledge and common sense their experience has given them. Consequentialist bioethicists have been especially vigorous in bringing policy-makers to this realization.

Thirdly, consequentialists are not afraid to look directly at the costs and benefits involved in new technologies and in proposed solutions to problems of public policy. Indeed, the assessment of costs and benefits is an *essential* part of consequentialist reasoning: for all the differences between the various forms of consequentialism (e.g. act and rule, classical and modern), they are all united by belief in the first principle of maximizing benefit and minimizing cost. (How 'benefit' and 'cost' are defined, of course, is a notoriously difficult matter, and has resulted in widely differing analyses by individual theorists. Some speak in terms of the maximization of 'utility', others of 'preference satisfaction', others of 'pleasure', or of 'happiness', among other candidates.) They are also all committed to the possibility (at least theoretical if not always practical) of *calculating* benefits and costs, and hence to their *commensurability*. Indeed some writers have gone so far as to propose a common unit of ethical measurement, such as 'hedons' (units of pleasure) or the increasingly popular 'qalys' (quality-assisted life years). Contrary to the Aristotelian dictum that ethics is only as precise as its subject matter allows and therefore contains more imprecision than, say, mathematics, the consequentialist envisages a decision procedure which will generate a result, in a finite number of steps, for any given ethical question (this being an ideal theoretical limit rather than something any consequentialist has actually proposed, at least with even a semblance of reasonableness).

It can be seen, then, that consequentialists speak a language technologists and policy-makers instinctively understand, which explains why their proposals are taken seriously by these latter. And it is this third feature of consequentialism – its commitment to a cost-benefit analysis of ethical problems – which leads, in the opinion of a growing number of philosophers, to a morality which is dehumanizing and contrary to the integrity of the professions most closely involved with bioethics.

The present collection of essays is an attempt to redress the imbalance in bioethics caused by the predominance of consequentialist thinking. We aim to provide an antidote to what can truly be called the Establishment View. It is our objective to show that bioethics – and moral philosophy in general – can be done in an entirely different way, one which is antithetical to consequentialist principles, and does not reduce the status of the human being to that of a variable in a cost-benefit analysis. This way is, however, no less rational and objectivist for being anti-consequentialist.

The papers in this collection are disparate in theoretical foundation and general outlook. By no means do they agree on the proper approach to all bioethical problems. Each contributor places emphasis on different concepts which they see as central to moral evaluation: the integrity of nature; the importance of humanity as a natural kind; the value of innocence and the need to protect the vulnerable; the role of absolute moral principles; the virtues; rights and justice; the proper role of medicine; the centrality of intention in assessing moral agency; and others.

Yet all of the concepts and principles which figure prominently in this volume can be seen to interlock to some degree, and as such to constitute elements of a moral outlook at odds both with consequentialist theory and with its concrete deliverances.

From the beginning, the promotion of consequentialism has gone hand in hand with the denigration of what consequentialists condescendingly call 'traditional morality'. Familiar charges levelled at anti-consequentialist thinking involve numerous epithets. Such thinking is often described by consequentialists as 'fundamentalist', 'reactionary', 'dogmatic', or 'essentially religious'. Many of these and similar descriptions strewn throughout consequentialist literature have little meaning but as derogatory terms. Two notions, however, stand out. One is that the anti-consequentialist is perforce a moral and social conservative. The claim is absurd. Anti-consequentialism can and does involve radical criticism of socially accepted views. Among those which have, over the years, been subject to principled anti-consequentialist opposition are: belief in the permissibility of using atomic weapons; the widespread acceptance of pragmatism and ethical neutrality in politics and economics; late-twentieth-century forms of hedonism and elevation of the value of transient pleasure; various forms of economic oppression of developing nations; the culture of materialism; and so on. The list is heterogeneous, and few anti-consequentialists would agree on what its members should be. But for consequentialists to claim, after looking at what their opponents have set themselves against, that such thinking does not challenge the social consensus, and is thereby 'reactionary', is seriously to misrepresent the other side.

A second notion in the minds of many consequentialists is that there is something essentially religious about anti-consequentialist thinking. This claim too is false. As will be seen in the pages that follow, it is possible to conduct a sustained counter-argument against consequentialism without presupposing any propositions of even a vaguely religious nature. The entire debate can be transacted using all the usual conceptual tools available to the philosopher. If it is to gain assent, a moral theory, like any philosophical theory, must present itself as compelling to reason. It is no part of its plausibility that it should receive justification from this or that religious doctrine.

One further point needs to be noted. It is an unfortunate fact that some consequentialists have co-opted worthwhile causes, such as the welfare of animals, into their otherwise implausible moral theories. Criticism of those theories, however, does not entail criticism of the laudable causes with which they have become associated in the public mind. Some of the approaches outlined in this collection, for instance, allow for a philosophy of the natural world (including but by no means confined to animals) which countenances grave moral obligations to respect and protect it.

## THE PAPERS

In 'Consequentialism in Modern Moral Philosophy and in "Modern Moral Philosophy"', Cora Diamond addresses what she believes to be a major misunderstanding of what consequentialism is, a misunderstanding which has given rise to a serious misinterpretation both of John Stuart Mill and of later moral philosophers such as Ross and Prichard.

Beginning with a consideration of Elizabeth Anscombe's famous paper 'Modern Moral Philosophy', in which the term 'consequentialism' is introduced, Diamond argues that most recent debate has ignored the issues Anscombe had tried to raise. It is commonplace simply to distinguish consequentialism from so-called deontological theories, which recognize (at least prima facie) moral obligations, for example promise-keeping, which are not themselves understood as acts which necessarily produce the best consequences. Seen this way, Ross and Prichard look like anti-consequentialists.

What this simplistic distinction overlooks, however, is that even an action which is regarded as right because of the *sort* of action it is can be treated *itself* as a consequence, and hence as a possible object of maximization. Thus for some putative deontologists, even an unjust action could be objectively right if it maximized certain other things of intrinsic value (such as promise-keeping behaviour), though its injustice would have to be factored into the consequentialist calculation.

It is this overlooked point which is at the heart of Anscombe's original discussion, and which led her to conclude that the English moral philosophers from Sidgwick on do not differ significantly, but rather all share the consequentialist outlook. It also led her to conclude that Mill was not in fact a consequentialist. Diamond takes up this suggestion, and sketches a novel interpretation of Mill according to which, while he is still a utilitarian (regarding happiness as the proper end of all human action), he is a non-consequentialist because he pays heed to agent-relativity (e.g. it matters morally whether it is *you*, as opposed to someone else, who performs a right or wrong action) and to the *tendencies* of individual actions to promote happiness, irrespective of the particular circumstances in which they are performed. Both such considerations are irrelevant to consequentialist practical reasoning. Diamond thus highlights what is really at stake in the debate between consequentialists and their opponents and indicates how to identify truly consequentialist thinking.

In 'Is Anything Absolutely Wrong?', Nicholas Denyer defends the moral theory known as 'absolutism', a term used almost always in a pejorative fashion today but denoting a view of morality that was once conventional wisdom. The central idea of absolutism is that 'certain descriptions are such that any action satisfying any of those descriptions is for that reason wrong, whatever other descriptions . . . it may also satisfy.' Denyer makes the case for absolutism first by defending some of its essential features. One is its reliance on a real distinction between causing and allowing to happen, a favourite consequentialist target. Another is the distinction between intention and foresight, which is crucial to proper accounts of practical reason and of responsibility; it too has been subjected to criticism from numerous writers, consequentialists being most prominent among them. Denyer also defends agent-relativity, which is an obstacle to any theory requiring the evaluation of impersonal states of affairs as the key to morality. He then offers direct criticism of consequentialism as a rival to absolutism and propounds four arguments *for* the latter.

Stephen Clark begins his 'Natural Integrity and Biotechnology' by arguing that even consequentialists must, in practice, judge particular actions by reference to general rules and that it is either impossible, absurd or profoundly counterintuitive to devise those rules from a purely neutral standpoint – as though, for example, rape was to be counted as wrong only because it would be best, all things considered, to have rules forbidding it. Once the thorough untenability of rule consequentialism is realized, he continues, it is possible to take intrinsic objections to current or potential biotechnology more seriously. Such biotechnological interference would only be begun by people having an irrationally high opinion of their rights, and is likely to interfere with the 'natural integrity' or 'beauty' of its victims. The recognition of 'beauty', and correspondingly of 'ugliness', as things deserving moral attention is no less rational than whatever preferences consequentialists themselves profess. It follows,

Clark concludes, that modern biotechnological practice is gravely at fault, but not that we should certainly attempt to ban it.

In 'The Moral Uniqueness of the Human Animal', Brian Scarlett defends what he plausibly calls The Common View regarding animal welfare: 'non-human animals are inferior forms of life compared with us; it is permissible to kill animals for food and to use them for other human purposes; it is, however, wrong to treat them cruelly.' Against this he places the well-known views of Peter Singer, which are aimed at overthrowing The Common View. A careful comparison is instructive, because (as noted above) part of consequentialism's superficial attractiveness for many people is a result of its having been packaged by Singer and others with the noble cause of animal welfare.

For Scarlett, however, everything that is morally persuasive in Singer's view of animals is in complete conformity with The Common View. The former is consistent with a hierarchical ordering of forms of life according to physical and psychological complexity, whereby morally significant characteristics like the capacity to feel pain and pleasure are recognized in some but not other forms. Such a capacity might be a *threshold* requirement for moral consideration, so that the welfare of each sentient creature is considered; but 'beyond the equality it is all inequality', because of the manifest differences between the capacities for pain and pleasure in higher and lower animals, and most notably in man as opposed to the rest of the animal kingdom. Equality of consideration does not entail equality of treatment, as Singer acknowledges. It is only when the novel concept of a 'person', in Singer's technical sense, is introduced that his view and The Common View part company. Scarlett argues that the concept of a 'person', according to which animals are promoted because of alleged capacities and certain humans (such as infants) are demoted, does not match reality, and he offers a range of evidence in support. In any case, he concludes, even if Singerian 'personhood' *did* signify a genuine kind of entity, the importance of *potential*, which Singer so much derides, would demonstrate the human being's moral uniqueness.

Speciesism is the topic of the next contribution, by Tim Chappell. In his 'In Defence of Speciesism', he defends the thesis that 'differences of species can, do and should provide sufficient reason, in themselves, to ground major differences in moral significance, in a way in which . . . differences of gender, race, intelligence or sensitivity to pain do not and cannot ground such differences.' Chappell first challenges a claim which he sees as central to Singer's view of animals and his condemnation of speciesism, namely that something has moral significance just in case it is sentient. Considering cases of moral significance which do not seem to rely on sentience, Chappell concludes that it is the concept of *flourishing*, not sentience, which gives us our criterion of moral significance, and flourishing is a property of *kinds* of thing.

Chappell adds that Singer is also committed to the claim that pain and pleasure are commensurable across individual creatures, but that, while true, the claim is not nearly as important to moral evaluation given the centrality of the concept of flourishing rather than that of sentience. More important would be a claim about the commensurability of *flourishing* across creatures, but such a claim is manifestly false.

Chappell goes on to argue, first, that 'what counts as flourishing for a given species is dependent upon what the species is *like*'; secondly, that 'the well-being of different species can and often does conflict'; and thirdly, that man is the only species on earth which is in a position to balance the competing interests of different species. What follows from this, he concludes, is that 'the position of the human species relative to the whole of the rest of nature is a unique one: it is that of a (reverent) regulator, as and when a regulator is needed...'. Man has an inescapable role as regulator of the natural world, and the duty to promote its flourishing and that of its parts. This must involve the making of moral discriminations between species simply on the basis that they are different, and hence flourish in different ways, and must crucially involve making discriminations between humans and other species.

Grant Gillett's paper, 'Young Human Beings: Metaphysics and Ethics', explores the basic claims and commitments of consequentialism as a metaethical theory, concentrating on its counterintuitive claim that our common beliefs concerning the special regard we should show human infants are radically mistaken. For instance, a consequentialist theory centred on maximization of preference satisfaction would have difficulty excluding heinous behaviour such as child abuse, say where the child is resented by the parents, so that he or she has negative value for them.

Objectionable conclusions such as these follow readily from consequentialist theories, and Gillett locates this flaw in some of consequentialism's suspect commitments. One is Humean reductionism, to the effect that moral judgments involve the passions rather than the discernment of real factual differences between cases we habitually treat differently from the ethical point of view. This, argues Gillett, presents a false picture of the place of the reactive attitudes in moral judgment. Another commitment is methodological individualism, against which he argues on the ground that 'morally relevant properties are intrinsically relational and reflect our engagements with and attachments to one another.' Gillett presents an alternative, non-consequentialist account of ethics which does justice to our deep intuitions concerning young human lives, and places concepts such as care and nurture at the centre of our relationships with those who depend on us.

The integrity of medicine is the subject of the next two papers in the collection. In 'Medicine, Virtues and Consequences', John Cottingham scrutinizes the claim, increasingly fashionable in bioethical circles, that medicine (to quote a recent paper) 'as an activity of human devising serving human purposes is just what we make it to be, not what nature decrees it must be.' An examination of the Aristotelian concept of *telos*, counters Cottingham, demonstrates that medicine, like every profession, art or skill, 'involves reference to human evaluations and conscious human purposes; but it also depends on naturally given features of the world that were in place long before we came on the scene.' So it is that the goal of medicine is health, just as surely as the goal of bridle-making is the making of tackle that conduces to efficient horse-riding. These are conceptual truths, and they depend equally on features of the world – for example, that human beings exist and that there *is* such a thing as health for them as a natural kind, and that there are various ways in which that health can be damaged or restored.

From this it follows, argues Cottingham, that certain activities are per se not the activities of a doctor (qua doctor), and hence not of a good doctor, even if performed by a medically qualified person: one would be the administration of capital punishment on behalf of the state, and another the commission of euthanasia. Other internal features of the doctor's profession are incompatible with consequentialist reasoning in general. For instance, one of the virtues (in the sense of excellences which perfect the art) of the medical profession is the preservation of a special relationship of care and concern for one's patients, which blocks reasoning that trades off their interests against those of other people (or of the state) in a global utility calculation. Once we appreciate these internal properties of medicine, Cottingham concludes, we can see that it is virtue theory rather than consequentialism which is able to justify them and place them within a broader and coherent ethical framework.

Lance Simmons continues the discussion of the integrity of medicine, but rather than focusing on teleology he approaches similar conclusions by means of recent accounts of virtue concepts, by Bernard Williams and Alasdair MacIntyre, which do not presuppose that medicine has a primary end such as the promotion of health. Outlining first Williams's account of 'thick' concepts, Simmons argues that since 'health' possesses

the relevant markers, it too is a thick concept and so can only be adequately explicated in terms of virtue theory. Looking then at MacIntyre's
notion of goods internal to a practice, Simmons claims that health is a
good internal to the practice of medicine, which the doctor can only promote if he possesses certain virtues. The conclusion, then, is that good
doctors do not intentionally attack or destroy the health of their patients,
even if this is to promote some other end, such as enabling the patient to
pursue a certain desirable lifestyle.

Central to most non-consequentialist ethical theories is the concept of
intention. Actions which are paradigmatically worthy of praise or blame
are also those which are intentional, as opposed to merely foreseen. In
his 'Intentions in Medical Ethics', Jorge Garcia argues, first, that 'there
is a genuine psychological difference between intending something to result from one's behaviour and merely expecting it to'. Secondly, he seeks
to show 'how it can matter to whether a health-care worker acts in ways
morally permissible that she intends (and does not merely foresee) certain aspects or results of her behaviour'. And thirdly, he argues that 'we
can often have reasonable beliefs about whether an agent acted with an
intention that should disqualify a course of action.'

In the process of justifying these claims, Garcia challenges the recent
attack by Helga Kuhse on the intention/foresight distinction and gives
criteria for applying the distinction. He also responds to critics of the
idea that intention is central to the moral evaluation of particular acts,
that they beg the question. Further, he argues that there is more to the
psychological reality of intention than the mere 'redirection of one's will',
and sketches a view according to which intentions, as real and profound
mental phenomena, fit centrally into a life of planning and execution of
projects.

Consequentialism in bioethics is complicated by another, seemingly
disparate feature of much writing in the field. Many bioethicists appeal
to the principle of respect for autonomy in grounding life-and-death decision-making. As one writer defines it, 'the right to autonomy is the
right to make one's own choices, and . . . respect for autonomy is the obligation not to interfere with the choice of another and to treat another as
a being capable of choosing.' In 'The Pre-eminence of Autonomy in
Bioethics', Janet Smith examines the principle of respect for autonomy
and locates the source of its elevation in contemporary scepticism about
ethics. Moral pluralism now dominates most ethical thinking: there is a
multiplicity of traditions and viewpoints, historically and ideologically
conditioned, resulting in a lack of consensus over even the most basic
principles which should govern individual behaviour and public values.

More disconcerting, however, is the widespread view, among both philosophers and the public at large, that it is not even *possible* to reach consensus, because there is no truth to be had in ethics. Smith quotes the bioethicists Beauchamp and Childress, who state that 'it is doubtful that moral statements have truth values and that truth is a category that should appear in moral theory.' Beauchamp and Childress also, however, give great weight to the principle of respect for autonomy as one which 'runs as deep in common morality as any other principle', which for them makes the principle more secure than if it were a product of philosophical theory.

To complicate matters further, Beauchamp and Childress are avowedly consequentialist, asserting that 'the prohibition of killing expresses important moral principles and attitudes whose loss... could have major negative consequences... Before we undertake any major changes [to such a prohibition], we need more evidence... that the changes are needed in order to avoid important harms or secure important benefits and that the good effects will outweigh the bad effects.' Smith takes Beauchamp and Childress to be fairly representative of current thinking, and thereby she has implicitly identified a major dilemma: how is it that many modern bioethicists can be consequentialist, and yet elevate respect for autonomy to the status almost of an absolute value, and yet further underlay their theorising with moral scepticism, subjectivism and relativism? Until the disparate philosophical threads informing much modern bioethics can be disentangled, there will be cause for regarding a large part of current theory as an ad hoc device for 'justifying' pre-formed bioethical proposals.

As one of the most prominent consequentialist bioethicists, Peter Singer has received substantial publicity for his support of euthanasia, genetic engineering, abortion, infanticide and other controversial causes. While his views achieve increasing respectability in academic and political quarters, his lectures have also been the subject of vigorous protest by disabled people and others opposed to his views, and conferences have had to be suspended owing to threats of disruption. Singer claims that he has been seriously misunderstood. In 'Innocence and Consequentialism', Jacqueline Laing explores Singer's influential writings in order to see whether they have been misinterpreted.

The central principles of his bioethics are examined: the distinction between persons in the ordinary sense and 'persons' in Singer's technical sense (rational, self-aware beings), where only the latter have moral value; his rejection of the moral significance of potentiality; his rejection of the importance of commonness of kind; and his apparent repudiation of restrictions on the reasonableness of third party desire. It is noted, first, that these ideas do indeed lead logically to precisely the sorts of proposals which so many people have found disturbing, and even seen the need to protest against in public. Secondly, inconsistency and equivocation in Singer's philosophy are identified, which raises the question of the extent to which he *relies* on precisely the notions he seeks to eliminate from moral theory. For instance, close inspection of what he says about potentiality suggests that he does give it moral significance. He equivocates over whether desires in a preference utilitarian scheme ought to be taken at face value or subject to rational criticism. He also appeals to important moral attitudes, such as those of care and protection, in order to rule out some practices which even he appears to regard as repellent, while rejecting their importance when admitting other practices which seem equally to undermine those attitudes. It is concluded that central to Singer's philosophy is an attack upon the value of innocence, but that no plausible moral theory can do without this value.

Voluntary euthanasia is the subject of the final paper, by David Oderberg. 'Voluntary Euthanasia and Justice' sets out to answer the question: Does a person who kills another at the latter's request commit an injustice against that person? Defining justice in terms of rights, it is argued that, since the right to life is inalienable, voluntary euthanasia is always an injustice by the killer against the killed. The justification for the claim that the right to life is inalienable comes in three parts. First, it is shown that there is nothing peculiar in the concept of an inalienable right, and that even the theory most hostile to rights – consequentialism – must recognize at least one inalienable right. Secondly, some examples of inalienable rights are considered which are likely to convince most sceptics, despite the hold which the doctrine of the paramountcy of the will has over moral theory. Further, a purported refutation of inalienability, based on the analogy with property rights, is dismissed. Thirdly, a positive account is outlined, according to which the right to life is seen as fundamental in a theory of human good. From this it follows that voluntary euthanasia is always an attack upon the good protected by that right.

It is a prelude to public recognition of the threat posed by consequentialism that an alternative way of looking at bioethics, one that preserves respect for the human being, be elaborated. Such an alternative has been conspicuously absent from modern moral philosophy. We hope that this collection of papers goes at least some way towards remedying this defect.

*The Editors*

# 1 Consequentialism in Modern Moral Philosophy and in 'Modern Moral Philosophy'
## Cora Diamond

## 1. CONSEQUENTIALISM AND G. E. M. ANSCOMBE'S THIRD THESIS

Consequentialism is an issue for bioethics because bioethics is concerned with justification, with giving reasons; and consequentialism provides an understanding of what we shall be led to if we take seriously that commitment to reason-giving. In this essay I consider how, within the context of modern moral philosophy, we see and how we do not see consequentialism. My discussion is meant to cast light on the questions, underlying many disagreements within bioethics, about what we are led to by taking reason-giving seriously.

In explaining the third thesis of her essay 'Modern Moral Philosophy', G. E. M. Anscombe introduced the term 'consequentialism'.[1] The thesis was that English moral philosophers from Sidgwick on do not differ among themselves in any significant way; they share 'consequentialism', and are in that respect significantly different from earlier philosophers, including utilitarians like J. S. Mill. In the years since the term was introduced, it has taken on a life of its own, almost entirely detached from Anscombe's third thesis. J. S. Mill, not a consequentialist on Anscombe's view, is frequently described as holding a form of consequentialism. And W. D. Ross and H. A. Prichard, whom Anscombe takes to be consequentialists, are often thought of as not consequentialists. The distinction between those who hold and those who reject consequentialism is sometimes simply identified with the distinction between those who accept some form of teleological ethics and those who accept some deontological theory.[2]

The distance between what Anscombe meant by 'consequentialism' and what the term has come to mean may be hard to see for a number of reasons. One is that Anscombe's own short statement of what conse-

13

quentialism is can very easily be misread when her third thesis is not borne in mind. Here is the sentence in which she first characterizes the view she takes to be widely shared:

> In Moore and in subsequent academic moralists of England we find it taken to be pretty obvious that 'the right action' means the one which produces the best possible consequences (reckoning among consequences the intrinsic values ascribed to certain kinds of act by some 'Objectivists').[3]

Suppose we remove from that sentence the first seventeen words, and replace them by 'Consequentialism is the view'; and suppose we simply remove the parenthetical clause at the end. Suppose we forget that Anscombe intended to make a distinction between Mill's theory and consequentialism. We are left with Anscombe's *words*; but the words detached from their context can be understood in various ways. So far as we ourselves are affected by the consequentialist climate of thought which she was describing, we are likely (this is indeed her point) to see as significant certain distinctions which are relatively unimportant, and to fail to see a significant distinction. So far, that is, as we are ourselves affected by the consequentialist climate of thought, we are likely to take her words and use them to make a distinction obliterating the one to which she was trying to draw attention.

In the next two sections, I look in more detail at the shifts in the usage of 'consequentialism': at the narrowing of the term to exclude Ross and Prichard and at the broadening of the term to include Mill. It will be useful here to bear in mind the difference between keeping the concept meant by some term the same, while our beliefs about what falls under it change, and changing what concept the term is used to mean. In the latter case, the concept meant in the later usage will have, in Frege's sense, different characteristic marks. The characteristics, or characteristic marks, of a concept are its 'logical parts'. They are the properties which an object must have if it is to fall under the concept.[4] Thus we might have come to think of Mill as a consequentialist either because we disagreed with Anscombe about whether he had the properties which people must have in order to be consequentialists, or because we had a different idea of what properties people must have in order to be consequentialists – in other words, because we were making use of a different concept. I start with the relatively simpler case of Ross and Prichard.

## 2. OXFORD OBJECTIVISM

Consequentialism is frequently defined as the view that *only* consequences count in determining the rightness or wrongness of actions. Ross and Prichard are held not to be consequentialists because they believed that consequences were frequently irrelevant to the rightness or wrongness of actions. How can there be a question, then, about their classification?

Anscombe very briefly discusses the views of Ross and others, explaining why she takes them to be consequentialists, and why she takes their differences from out-and-out consequentialists like Moore to be superficial. She notes that the Objectivists distinguish between 'consequences' and 'intrinsic values', but their 'intrinsic values' are in fact treated as consequences. She points out that 'they do not hold that the gravity of, e.g., procuring the condemnation of the innocent is such that it cannot be outweighed by, e.g., national interest', and she concludes that their distinction is of no importance.[5]

In order to see the kind of thing she has in mind when she says that these philosophers treat certain values as consequences, we might note, for example, that Ross repeatedly explains what constitutes the objectively right action in terms of the production of the greatest balance of prima facie rightness over prima facie wrongness. Thus an unjust action might on some occasion be the objectively right action. The unjust action would have various effects and thus various aspects, one of which is the aspect of its being unjust; and, as having that aspect, it would be prima facie wrong. It might nevertheless, because of its other effects and thus other aspects, be the action with the greatest balance of prima facie rightness over prima facie wrongness, and, if it did, it would then be the objectively right action.[6]

Anscombe's argument has been almost wholly overlooked. Here is some further evidence that it has been ('further'evidence, in that the general willingness to treat Ross's sort of deontological view as a typical kind of anti-consequentialism is itself evidence that Anscombe's argument was missed). Amartya Sen has put forward a form of consequentialism which takes respect for rights and violation of rights directly into account in calculating the value of situations.[7] It is thus unlike traditional welfarist utilitarianism which treats respect for rights as of mere instrumental value; it allows serious concern for rights into a fundamentally consequentialist structure. Anscombe had pointed out an analogous kind of possibility in her remarks on Oxford Objectivists, and yet Sen's view has been described as a 'conceptual innovation', capable perhaps of 'breaking the impasse' between consequentialism and its deontological critics.[8] But the term 'consequentialism', as explained by Anscombe, had from the start been intended to include critics of out-and-out consequentialism taking views like Sen's. Treating Sen's view as a new and significant move in the debate about consequentialism shows only that the debate had never been about the issues Anscombe had tried to raise.[9]

Consideration of the question how to classify Ross and Prichard should help us to see that what is at stake is two different concepts (Anscombe's *consequentialism* and that of most later moral theorists), with different characteristic marks, in Frege's sense. When Ross and Prichard are treated as non-consequentialists, consequentialism is taken to be incompatible with holding such things as that an action may be right because it is a keeping of a promise. Anscombe makes clear that an action's being a keeping of a promise may, in some moral theory, play the role of a consequence. If there are two different concepts for which 'consequentialism' is used, this is because 'consequence' itself may be used for different concepts. If we use the word as Ross, for example, does, we shall get the appearance of a significant difference between Ross and those whom he criticizes for basing their account of rightness on consequences; if we use the word as Anscombe does, that difference will appear superficial, and Ross himself will count as a consequentialist.

## 3.  J. S. MILL AND CONSEQUENTIALISM

Consider next Anscombe's view of Mill. She treats him as not a consequentialist; this is because he does not hold, of acts like murder or theft, that they might on occasion, because of their good consequences, be permissible or even required. There is nevertheless, she argues, serious objection to his theory: he does not deal adequately with the problem of multiple possible descriptions of actions.[10]

Discussions of consequentialism in the years since the publication of 'Modern Moral Philosophy' have led to the development of distinctions within consequentialism. It might therefore be argued that Mill is a consequentialist who holds a more complex kind of consequentialist theory than any which Anscombe had in mind, and indeed that remarks of his about the significance of consequences in moral theory are incompatible with any blanket denial that he is a consequentialist.[11]

Anscombe's denial that Mill is a consequentialist was based on his view that, when an action falls under only one of the secondary principles of morality (these being principles which are grounded on utility), one is not to attempt to calculate its consequences to see whether it is allowable or required in the particular case, despite being a kind of action which is generally prohibited, like stealing (or to see whether it may or must be omitted in the particular case, despite being a kind of action which is generally required, like promise-keeping). But many moral philosophers writing during the thirty-some years since Anscombe's article would hold that various kinds of consequentialist theories would yield the same result: that one should not, or should not normally or in many kinds of case, attempt to calculate consequences in deliberating about what to do. Thus an argument that Mill was a consequentialist might rest on the ascription to Mill of one of these more complex kinds of consequentialism.

First, he might, arguably, be a rule-consequentialist. Rule-consequentialism is understood on the model of rule-utilitarianism; and Mill has frequently been read as a rule-utilitarian. Rule-consequentialism holds that the rightness or wrongness of an action depends, not on *its* consequences, but on its being in conformity with, or violating, some moral rule, the rules themselves being justified by the consequences of their being generally accepted and adhered to.[12]

Secondly, Mill might, arguably, hold a version of indirect act-consequentialism. Such theories do not identify right actions with those in accordance with rules meeting some test; they do hold that actions with good consequences will most reliably be performed, and utility maximised, if agents develop traits of character like honesty (which will lead them not to see dishonest actions as serious options), and if they are trained also to adhere to such principles as those enjoining promise-keeping and prohibiting theft. The idea is that restricting deliberation in various ways (eliminating it altogether in some cases, or training agents to deliberate without calculating consequences) is the best policy for securing that the value aimed at by the moral system is realised to the greatest possible extent. On this sort of view the connection between the aims and character of deliberation, and the rightness of action, is indirect. Anscombe's third thesis, that there are no significant differences between English moral philosophers from roughly Sidgwick on, would not exclude theories of the sort I have just described merely because they give an account in which deliberation itself is not directly consequentialist.

The interpretation of Mill as some sort of consequentialist is usually a result of the assumption that utilitarian views *are* consequentialist. But it was just that assumption that Anscombe questioned. Her explanation of her third thesis was meant to draw attention to a *difference* between Mill and later English moral philosophers. If we read Mill as some kind of indirect consequentialist, we may be showing merely that we ourselves do

not see, or do not take seriously, the difference to which Anscombe had
sought to draw attention. Mill's remarks about the importance of rules
make it possible to read him as some kind of indirect consequentialist,
but the persuasiveness of such a reading may reflect our failure to see that
any other kind of reading is possible, given his utilitarianism and his rejection of direct appeal to consequences in deliberation.

What the post-Anscombe discussions of consequentialism have shown
is that there can be forms of utilitarianism which depend on a consequentialist conception of action and value, but which reject the idea that
we should appeal directly to consequences in deliberation. So it is not a
sufficient condition for a moral theorist to be *not* a consequentialist that
he should reject that idea. Mill's rejection of that idea thus does not show
that he is not a consequentialist; but this leaves open the question
whether Anscombe was correct in taking Mill's conception of action
and value to place him at a distance from those later philosophers whom
she called consequentialists. Here I am suggesting that the issues raised
by Anscombe can be seen more clearly if we drop her treatment of *allowing direct appeal to consequences in deliberation* as a characteristic mark
of consequentialism.

We saw that Anscombe treated Oxford Objectivists as consequentialists because they treated certain values (which they did not call consequences) in a fundamentally consequentialist way. If Mill is *not* a
consequentialist, it will be because, for him, justice (for example) is not
treated as a consequence *in that way.* So what is *the way* Sidgwick, Moore,
Ross, Prichard, Hare, Smart and later moral philosophers like Jonathan
Glover and Peter Singer treat consequences? And is there some *other*
way to treat them, to be found, possibly, in Mill?

## 4. ROBERT GRAVES AND THE IRISH SERGEANT

The next three sections are meant to make clear a contrast between two
ways of treating consequences, illustrated by two ways of thinking about
the case of the Irish sergeant in Robert Graves's *Goodbye to All That.* In
this section I sketch a consequentialist approach; Section 5 develops a
non-consequentialist reading of Mill; in Section 6, I return to the case of
the Irish sergeant and look at a possible Millian approach to it. Here is
Graves's description of the case:

> Brigade appointed me a member of a field general court-martial that
> was to sit on an Irish sergeant charged with 'shamefully casting away

his arms in the presence of the enemy'. I had heard about the case un-officially; the man, maddened by an intense bombardment, had thrown away his rifle and run with the rest of his platoon. An army or-der, secret and confidential, addressed to officers of captain's rank and above, laid down that, in the case of men tried for their life on other charges, sentence might be mitigated if conduct in the field had been exemplary; but cowardice was punishable only with death, and no medical excuses could be accepted. Therefore I saw no choice be-tween sentencing the man to death and refusing to take part in the pro-ceedings. If I refused, I should be court-martialled myself, and a reconstituted court would sentence the sergeant to death anyhow. Yet I could not sign a death-verdict for an offence which I might have com-mitted myself in similar circumstances. I evaded the dilemma... I found [one other officer in the battalion] willing enough to take my place. He was hard-boiled and glad of a trip to Amiens, and I took over his duties.[13]

Graves says that he could not sign a death-verdict for an offence which he might have committed himself in similar circumstances. He does not explicitly say that he took the death-verdict, in the circumstances of the sergeant, to be unjust. In discussing the case, I take Graves to have thought that the combination of shell-shock plus exemplary prior con-duct (if the sergeant's prior conduct had been exemplary) *would* make ex-ecution an unjustly harsh punishment, and that any court procedure ruling out consideration of the medical excuse was therefore unjust.[14] (Graves's own reasoning, quite realistically in the circumstances, ex-cludes any idea that, if he refuses to sign, it might encourage others in fu-ture to refuse to act unjustly; to simplify discussion, I for the most part exclude the qualifications to the argument which would be necessary to take such effects into account.)

I want now to construct a consequentialist argument about this case, to illustrate one way of thinking about consequences.

Graves's concern about signing the death-verdict is either a concern for the sergeant as victim, or a concern for himself (a concern that he not be an agent of injustice, a concern that he 'keep his hands clean'), or a concern for both the sergeant as victim and himself as agent. But what is going to happen is: the sergeant is going to be executed. The sergeant will be the victim of unjust treatment regardless of what Graves does. Graves either treats him unjustly or, by refusing to participate or refusing to sign, he sets in motion a chain of events in which someone else treats the sergeant unjustly. The consequences for the sergeant of either action on Graves's part are the same. Since Graves knows that the consequences for the sergeant will be the same whatever he does, it cannot be concern about the injustice *to the sergeant* which leads Graves to say that he could not sign the death-verdict. It is rather concern that he, Graves, shall not have acted in an unjust way, concern to keep his own moral account book clear. Or, possibly, his inability to sign might simply indicate that he is incapable of freeing himself from the effects of his upbringing; he cannot distance himself from the powerful but irrational feeling that signing is ruled out.

That consequentialist argument makes it seem as if the badness of doing injustice can be a reason for Graves only in so far as it is tied to his wish to avoid being the person who does the injustice. It looks as if that must be what Graves cares about, because the action (of his signing the death-verdict) affects only his own moral accounts, and is known in advance to have only such consequences. He may want people not to be treated unjustly, but (on the consequentialist argument) there is no room for that concern to enter his reasoning about whether he could sign the death-verdict, if he knows that he cannot change at all whether the sergeant will be the victim of injustice (and if he does not see his own refusal as having any desirable effects in preventing future injustice).[15]

I have given the consequentialist argument as it might refer to the reasons available to Graves; a somewhat different consequentialist argument could be made from the point of view of the kind of indirect consequentialist theory which separates what belongs to deliberation from what belongs to the justification of actions.[16] Here the argument would be that it might be valuable, from a consequentialist point of view, to have people think as Graves does when they deliberate about unjust acts, if indeed the consequentialist payoff over many cases, taking into account indirect effects, is greatest if they do so. But the argument would still include the fundamental consequentialist move, namely that Graves does not have any reason for refusing to sign in what he would be doing *to the sergeant*, since what he will not do, someone else will.

## 5. A NON-CONSEQUENTIALIST READING OF J. S. MILL

In this section I sketch a non-consequentialist form of utilitarianism. Although I shall not try to prove that Mill was such a utilitarian, my reading could, I think, be defended by a more detailed discussion of the texts. Here I am concerned primarily to show that Anscombe was right that there is conceptual space for a non-consequentialist kind of utilitarianism, and thus for such a reading of Mill. It will be useful for me to locate at the beginning the point at which, on my reading, Mill's utilitarianism departs from consequentialism. In describing the utilitarian doctrine of responsibility, Bernard Williams writes that what matters from the utilitarian point of view 'is what states of affairs the world contains, and so what matters with respect to a given action is what comes about if it is done, and what comes about if it is not done, and those are questions not intrinsically affected by the nature of the causal linkage, in particular by whether the outcome is partly produced by other agents'.[17] In the version of utilitarianism which I ascribe to Mill, the nature of the causal linkage between a person's actions and the things that will come about if the action is done matters greatly, and in particular, in many cases, it matters whether the outcome is partly produced by other agents.[18]

Consider a well-known remark of Mill's, which has been appealed to in the argument that he was a rule-utilitarian:

> The creed which accepts as the foundation of morals, Utility, or the Greatest Happiness Principle, holds that actions are right in proportion as they tend to promote happiness, wrong as they tend to produce the reverse of happiness.[19]

In discussing this passage, J. O. Urmson commented that individual actions cannot be said to have tendencies: only action-types have tendencies. That claim seems to me wrong, and also to lead to a distorted account of Mill, since he (like John Austin) certainly held that individual actions *do* have tendencies.[20] On the view which I am ascribing to Mill, any tendency which a particular action has depends on its being of some specifiable kind. Lies generally, for example, have a certain tendency, which supposedly includes a bad effect on the reliability of communication. The tendency of lies to diminish reliability will be realized to a greater or lesser extent in the particular circumstances of particular lies. If a lie is told to a person already deeply suspicious of everything said to him, and spoken by a man who is dying, whose attachment to truth cannot any longer be weakened, the tendency of the lie to diminish reliability may be virtually entirely counteracted by those other elements of the situation.

The particular circumstances of an agent leave openings for various acts; they also enmesh each such act in a web of causal relations specific to the situation, through which the tendencies of the possible actions may be furthered or counteracted. The moral character of an action, its rightness or wrongness, is dependent on what it tends to promote, not in general on the things it may lead to in the particular circumstances of the act. That there are various things in the circumstances which will further or interfere with its tendency to promote something is importantly not up to you, the agent. What is up to you is the act-with-tendency which you choose. Moral criticism of the action properly has in view what was 'up to you' in the sense just specified: your action is not in general made right or wrong by features of the situation which are independent of the act-with-tendency and dependent instead on the web of circumstances. Thus the liar has 'done what depends on him' to bring about the evils towards which lies tend to lead; he has 'acted the part' of an enemy of mankind, even if, in the circumstances, acting the part of enemy was foreseeably unlikely to lead to actual damage to the interests of mankind.

Utilitarian talk of the tendency of actions has sometimes been explained in terms of the effects of everyone's performing an action of the same kind; David Lyons, for example, explains his way of using the term this way:

> [I]n speaking of *the effects of* an act I intend to include *all* the effects; in speaking of *the tendency of* an act I intend to include *all* the effects resulting from *everyone's* doing acts of the sort specified.[21]

The point of my reference to this way of speaking is that it is not what I am ascribing to Mill. What I mean to ascribe to him is a kind of analysis of the causal relations of our actions similar to the analysis we may give of the causal relations of things in the world other than actions, where there is no question 'What would it be like if everyone did it?' An object set in motion has a tendency to continue to move in the same direction at the same velocity. If it stops suddenly, its trajectory can be explained by considering both the tendency to continue to move in the original direction and the effects of whatever it was that interfered with that tendency.[22] On my view of what Mill means by the tendency of an act, we can unproblematically speak of the tendencies of actions in many cases in which 'what would happen if everyone did it' has no relevance, for example in cases of making a law; thus, e.g., the act of a legislative body passing a law punishing theft with death would have as part of its tendency a decrease in the willingness of juries to convict for theft.

An act may belong to some category of acts all of which have some tendency to promote happiness or the reverse. But the action may be appropriately describable in some more specific way; and acts of the more narrowly specified category may have a stronger opposite tendency. Thus acts of returning something borrowed have some tendency to promote happiness; an act of returning a weapon to someone who has subsequently gone mad has a tendency greatly to increase the risk of the reverse. Many of the things to which an act will probably lead in particular circumstances, though, should not be treated as belonging to its tendency.

How are the tendencies of actions of various kinds discovered? This is an analytical business, and not a matter of frequencies. That is, there is a vital distinction between what some kind of action might generally lead to (because of the way it is usually enmeshed in causal relations), and what the tendency is of such acts. Thus it might, for example, be the case that tyrannical suppression of liberty frequently leads to people's prizing their liberty, and to their coming to have a better understanding of what they must do to preserve it. And let us suppose that prizing liberty and understanding how to preserve it do help to promote the end aimed at by utilitarianism (as Mill certainly thought). It would not follow that acts of tyrannical suppression of liberty have as part of their tendency a tendency to promote the utilitarian end by increasing regard for liberty (a little plus, as it were, to counterbalance somewhat the large minus). The fact that such suppression frequently leads to some good does not suffice to make it part of the tendency of acts of suppression to promote that good, in the sense of 'tendency' which I am suggesting we can see in Mill. That is to say, we have to analyse the relation between a certain outcome and the sorts of acts with which it may be associated before we can draw conclusions about what belongs to the tendency of acts of that kind, and what belongs rather to other causes in their circumstances. The result of such an analysis is that acts of suppression of liberty *get no credit* for the good which is brought about in response to such acts.[23]

We should note here the contrast between the way utilitarianism of a non-consequentialist sort can treat such effects and the way it can treat the bad effects of lying. Analysis of the latter sort of case might lead a utilitarian to treat the encouraging of lying by other people as part of the tendency of lies. (There is no general principle that everything which an act leads to through the choices of others is excluded from the tendency of an act; some such causal ramifications of actions belong to their tendency and others do not.) Collecting the tendencies of actions itself involves care and intelligence in distinguishing, among the changes in the world to which acts of some kind frequently make some causal contribution (or those to which they might make some causal contribution), those properly treated as part of the tendency of such acts from those properly treated as accidental to it and effects rather of other elements in the circumstances within which the action is frequently enmeshed.[24] This distinction would not be treated as of any significance in consequentialist versions of utilitarianism; consequentialists would indeed object to the inclusion of any such distinction within utilitarianism.[25] (Mill's recognition of the distinction is reflected, I think, in his reading of Kant. Mill says that Kant, when he attempts to derive rules of conduct from the categorical imperative, in fact shows that the consequences of the adoption of outrageously immoral rules of conduct would be such as no one would choose to incur.[26] For that to be even a minimally respectable comment on Kant, 'consequences' must be taken in a tendency sense, not in a consequentialist sense.)

When Anscombe explains the difference between earlier moral philosophers (including Mill) and Sidgwick, she focuses on the issue of the agent's responsibility for foreseen but unintended consequences of his action. She states this way a thesis which Sidgwick puts forward: 'it does not make any difference to a man's responsibility for an effect of his action which he can foresee, that he does not intend it'.[27] The kind of non-consequentialist utilitarianism which I have ascribed to Mill does not commit him to any such thesis. How exactly it would be avoided depends upon how the Millian view might treat intention – on how exactly the agent's intention should be taken to affect the appropriate description of an action, and in that way to be connected with the tendency of the action to promote this or that. The main point to be made here is that there is room in a non-consequentialist utilitarianism for cases in which an agent is not responsible for consequences foreseeably arising through the specific circumstances of his action, consequences not belonging to what the action tends to bring about, and not intended by the agent.

Mill says that we can make a direct appeal to the Utility Principle when two secondary principles conflict; and it is easy to take that view to represent at least an element of consequentialism in Mill's moral theory. But it is not obvious that it must be taken so. To appeal directly to the Utility Principle in a particular case is, for a consequentialist, to attempt to predict the outcome of the alternatives, taking into account both immediate and indirect effects, and allowing for probabilities of the different possible outcomes. But we may instead take a direct appeal to the first principle to be an attempt to determine the tendency (to promote happiness or the reverse) of the proposed action, using a new description of it. On this account of what constitutes a direct appeal to the Utility Principle, the original treatment of the action, as involving a conflict of secondary principles, would have depended on the use of two descriptions of the proposed action, each of which excluded at least one morally salient feature of the action. Even in the case of a direct appeal to the Utility Principle, there is retained the important distinction between the tendency of an action and the things to which it will probably lead through the interaction of various causes in the specific circumstances. Understood in a non-consequentialist way, direct appeal to the Utility Principle in a particular case may yield entirely different results from what we get with a consequentialist understanding.[28] As Anscombe points out, Mill does not tell us how to provide appropriate descriptions of actions;[29] and Mill himself makes clear that such cases provide openings for moral cheating.

Bernard Williams noted that 'a non-consequentialist can hold both that it is a better state of affairs in which more people keep their promises, and that the right thing for $X$ to do is something that brings it about that fewer promises are kept'. The fact that such a state of affairs is better does not, for a non-consequentialist, carry the implication that it is $X$'s 'business to bring it about'.[30] As I have explained Mill's theory, it can make a non-consequentialist distinction between what it is the agent's business to do (explained in terms of the tendencies of actions), and what would, in the circumstances, probably lead to the best state of affairs. But this immediately appears to make such a theory open to a form of the objection raised by Williams and others to rule-utilitarianism. If the aim of a moral theory is that certain sorts of states of affairs be realized, and if, in some circumstances, it appears certain (or as certain as such things can be) that such a state of affairs can be realized by the agent's doing so-and-so, how can the theory coherently imply that it is the agent's business to do something else?[31] I return to this objection in §7.

Before leaving this topic, I should note that 'tendency' thought is extremely common in ordinary discussions of moral issues. It may, for example, be said that such-and-such sorts of experiments on foetuses will tend to brutalize the experimenter. Tendency thought provides a way of viewing actions, tied to experience but not directly dependent on empirical sociological generalizations. Mill himself clearly recognized that ordinary thought about the tendencies of actions was often very vague, crude or prejudiced.

## 6. J. S. MILL AND THE IRISH SERGEANT

Instead of considering directly how a theory like Mill's can treat the case of the Irish sergeant, let us consider a simple stand-in theory: acts are right in so far as they tend to promote the Irish sergeant's *not* being unjustly treated, wrong in so far as they tend to produce the reverse.

As we saw, the consequentialist understanding of the sergeant's case takes as central the fact that, whatever Graves does, the ultimate consequences for the sergeant will be the same; no action of Graves's will promote more than any other the sergeant's not being unjustly treated. So, if Graves does aim to promote the sergeant's not being unjustly treated, that aim gives him no reason to refuse to serve.

In contrast, the theory I am ascribing to Mill enables us to make sense of this idea: if you want something *not* done to the sergeant, then you have a reason for not doing it to the sergeant, regardless of whether others will do it to the sergeant if you do not. (Your reason may not be conclusive in the circumstances, but the circumstances do not stop it being a reason.) For Graves to serve on the court-martial and to sign the death-verdict would be for him to do what depends on him to bring it about that the sergeant is unjustly treated; and that is the fundamental reason why he concludes that he cannot do it. Refusal to serve or refusal to sign, even though it foreseeably initiates a course of events leading to the sergeant's unjust treatment, has nevertheless no tendency to promote such treatment. The phrase 'what it depends on him to do' is tied to the distinction between an action-with-its-tendency and the action taken together with all the causal relations belonging to the circumstances. Suppose we redescribe the action: 'Refusing to serve on a court-martial when such refusal will foreseeably lead to someone else's serving and thus to the signing of an unjust death-verdict'. Even under that description, it is not, on the Millian view, an action which promotes or tends to promote the unjust treatment of the sergeant. The symmetry of the alternatives open to Graves, in terms of ultimate outcome, does not imply on the Millian view that there is a symmetry in what they tend to promote.

As we saw, on the consequentialist view, the only reasons a person in Graves's circumstances could have for refusal to serve would be concern to keep his own hands clean, and interest in the fate of people who might in the future be better treated as a possible result of his refusal in this case. There is not available to him, as a reason for refusal, concern that the sergeant not be unjustly treated. On the view I am ascribing to Mill, it makes perfectly good sense for someone who cares that the sergeant not be unjustly treated to refuse for that reason to serve on the court-martial, or to refuse to sign the death-verdict. Having as your aim that the sergeant not be unjustly treated does not imply that, if the sergeant will be unjustly sentenced to death even if you do not sign the unjust verdict, you had no reason not to sign (apart from keeping your own hands clean and any interest in long-term indirect effects). If, of the actions open to you, one action involves your doing your bit to bring about, so far as it lies in you to do so, the *frustration* of your aim, and some other does not, you have reason to do the latter.

It is usually thought that any moral theory which takes as its aim the promoting of some good must be consequentialist. My argument in this section has been that we can understand Graves's refusal as refusal to do what would tend to promote the sergeant's being unjustly treated. This then illustrates a non-consequentialist way of treating consequences and a non-consequentialist understanding of what it is to promote an end or aim. Such a treatment of the case of the Irish sergeant can be fitted easily into the non-consequentialist reading of Mill's theory.

Moral philosophers who have brought to attention the role given to the idea of 'better states of affairs' in consequentialism sometimes suggest that anyone who wants to reject consequentialism needs to drop the idea of ranking states of affairs so far as they realize some value. The non-consequentialist theory I have ascribed to Mill does have as a central idea that morality should aim to promote certain sorts of states of affairs. In showing how that theory can be applied to the case of the Irish sergeant, I have argued that the fact that some action, because of the kind of action it is, tends to promote the realization of such-and-such sort of state of affairs can in many cases give us a reason to act, regardless of what others are likely to do; and the reason to act is not tied to probable indirect future effects of the action or to the moral satisfaction of the agent.[32]

Those who hold consequentialist theories have devoted much attention to such questions as whether there is any justification, on consequentialist grounds, for voting in an election which is certain not to be decided by one's vote. This sort of question does not present serious difficulty for the kind of theory I have ascribed to Mill. Your voting will frequently be your doing what depends on you for the realization of some aim of yours. To vote will have a tendency to promote the realization of that aim, and that is a reason for doing it – which is not to say that such a reason will be conclusive. If, in the circumstances, your aim is virtually certain to be frustrated, that will in many cases give you a reason against doing what depends on you for the realization of the aim. In a particular case it may be a matter of judgment what the wise course is, or the decent course, or the only possible course. All I am arguing here is that the kind of non-consequentialism I ascribe to Mill does not approach such issues as consequentialism does.[33]

## 7. MODERN AND PRE-MODERN UTILITARIANISM

In this section I explore a range of interconnected objections to Mill's theory as I have explained it; my aim is to show how it differs from more modern versions of utilitarianism.

In §5, I mentioned an important and now familiar kind of objection to rule-utilitarianism. So far as rule-utilitarianism tells us to act in certain ways – even in those circumstances in which the most likely effect of acting in those ways will not be to increase utility – it appears to be incoherent or irrational. Here is part of Bernard Williams's formulation of the argument:

> If calculation has already been made, and the consequences of breaking the rule are found better than those of keeping it; then certainly no considerations about the disutility of calculation could upset that result. And, indeed, it is very difficult to see how *anything*, for a consistent utilitarian, could upset that result. Whatever the general utility of having a certain rule, if one has actually reached the point of seeing that the utility of breaking it on a certain occasion is greater than that of following it, then surely it would be pure irrationality not to break it?[34]

That sort of objection may not seem to apply to the kind of utilitarianism I have ascribed to Mill. It takes actions to be right or wrong so far as they tend to promote happiness, or to produce the reverse. If, in some circumstances, the theory tells us that some action is right despite the fact that in those circumstances some other action will in fact probably lead to greater happiness or less unhappiness, this will not be a matter of mere 'rule worship'. It might be rule worship to perform an action of a kind which usually tends to promote happiness, even though the particular action has a stronger opposite tendency (as in the returning-his-weapon-to-the-madman case), but performing an action the overall tendency of which is to promote the end aimed at, in circumstances which will counter that tendency, is not that sort of case.

But anyone who wanted to raise the original objection to rule-utilitarianism could reformulate it as an objection to the non-consequentialist theory I am ascribing to Mill. The fundamental objection to rule-utilitarianism was its irrationality. And if the Mill-theory implies some account of rationality in which it counts as rational to perform some action because it 'tends to promote' utility, even though some alternative is known to be likely to lead to greater utility, would we not be better off, from a utilitarian point of view, to give up any account of rationality with that implication? And would we not therefore be better off, from a utilitarian point of view, to give up this 'tendency to promote' talk? So far as there is any element in any version of utilitarianism which prevents the greatest realization possible of the utilitarian aim, the version in question is less satisfactory, from a utilitarian point of view, than some improved version without the element in question. The justification for a thoroughgoing consequentialist utilitarianism is that it is the best way to realize the end at which utilitarianism aims.

A related objection to the Mill-theory begins by noting that philosophers, and especially utilitarians, have held that a main function of the philosophical study of morality is to examine and criticize the fundamental assumptions and categories of commonsense morality.[35] Mill certainly believed in the importance of such criticism. The objection continues: if, in commonsense morality we take it to be rational to act in ways which tend to promote some end, even in circumstances in which that tendency will be counteracted by other factors, or in which some other action will most probably lead to some better outcome, then such a notion of rationality should not be taken for granted in our moral philosophy but subjected to criticism and possibly replaced. Either it should be shown that inculcating in people that notion of rationality, although it leads to bad consequences in many particular cases, is the best policy overall for realizing the utilitarian end (taking 'best policy' in a thoroughly consequentialist sense), or the notion should be replaced. As applied to the Mill-theory, then, the objection would be that if (as seems unlikely) the non-consequentialist notion of rationality implicit in it could be shown to have some indirect consequentialist justification, the theory should be replaced by a coherent indirect consequentialism. If the notion lacks such a justification, then the utilitarian end would be better achieved by replacing the 'tendency' conception of rightness by a thoroughgoing consequentialism, including a consequentialist understanding of what is rational.

There is a certain lack of clarity in all versions of the objection if it is directed against the theory I ascribe to Mill. The force of the original objection to rule-utilitarianism depends on the structure of the rule-utilitarian theories against which it is directed. In such theories, secondary moral rules are supposed to be justified by appeal to the Utility Principle, which itself is understood in terms of a consequentialist idea of rational choice. That structure then provides a basis for the objection that the theories are inconsistent: they combine a consequentialist First Principle of morality with an account of right actions through which the overall system is less efficient at securing the end of morality than a system with a different structure would be. Mill's theory as I have explained it is not open to the objection in that form, since the Utility Principle itself is not given a consequentialist reading. In §5, in discussing how Mill's theory allows direct appeal to the Utility Principle in cases of conflicting secondary rules, I argued that such appeals do not involve a consequenti-

alist reading of the First Principle. Similarly, the justification of secondary principles does not involve a consequentialist understanding of the
First Principle. The First Principle directs us to inquire into the tendencies of actions; it implies that we should make this or that secondary
principle a part of morality when teaching and enforcing the principle will tend to promote happiness. There is lacking here the source of
the supposed inconsistency in rule-utilitarianism, namely the presence
of a consequentialist first principle in a system which is less efficient in
consequentialist terms than some possible alternative.

In formulating the objection to Mill's theory, we need to be careful not
to presuppose a consequentialist reading of the First Principle. But if we
then argue that the theory would be improved if it were made more thoroughly consequentialist, and that utilitarian criticism of conventional
morality should not itself stop short of a theory which is through-and-
through consequentialist, the question is the source of the idea of 'improvement' central to the objection. Of course, by a consequentialist
criterion of what constitutes a satisfactory moral theory, a non-consequentialist theory will be open to objection. But it is equally true that a
Millian criterion provides a basis for objecting to consequentialist theories (as we can see by noting that such a criterion provides a basis for rejecting the consequentialist approach to the case of the Irish sergeant).
The possibility of a consequentialist objection to Mill's theory is not surprising. There is equally a Millian objection to consequentialist theories.
If the consequentialist objection is thought to be the more telling, we
should need to see why, without simply supposing that a teleological theory must rest on some consequentialist understanding of rationality.

Consequentialist thinking is not a neutral way of conceiving what it is
to seek an end. Seen from the point of view of Millian non-consequentialism, it reflects, and has itself a tendency to promote, forms of human relationship and kinds of character which impede the realization of the
aim of morality as Mill understood it. Here we reach a particularly complex issue. It is sometimes held that consequentialism concerns only
how the end at which morality supposedly aims should be achieved, and
that it is compatible with any conception of what the end is. But the assumption that consequentialism is compatible with any and every conception of the aim or end of morality is itself arguably a consequentialist
assumption, and arguably an assumption rejected by Mill. He criticized
Bentham's proto-consequentialism because it encouraged the treating of
morality in terms of trade-offs, good and bad bargains, within which the
internalizing of certain ends, and the development of certain sorts of
character, could be evaluated (if at all) only as more or less efficient

means to promote the ultimate end, itself understood in independent terms. But such a theory cannot embody an adequate conception of what human happiness may be; it rests on an inadequate conception of human nature.[36]

There are forms of human relationship (like Graves's relation to the Irish sergeant, as he understood it) and character traits (like the sense of honour, as Mill understood it) which are partly constituted by a style of practical thinking distant from consequentialism. Such forms of relationship and such character traits are, in Mill's theory, not merely in- strumentally good, but part of happiness in any adequate conception. But a consequentialist might ask why a philosophical reformer who wishes to encourage such character traits or kinds of relationship should not take a thoroughly consequentialist view of how they may best be fos- tered. The consequentialist argument here is that there is available to the opponent of consequentialism no coherent objection that we get better consequences if we give up consequentialism. The consequentialist will be willing to grant that consequentialism must be complex enough to take into account the good effects, if any, of encouraging certain non- consequentialist kinds of thinking within appropriate limits. But moral theory itself is outside those limits. And there is, it may be suggested, a further objection to Mill's theory, so far as it takes an adequate account of human happiness to have as part the importance of specific kinds of relationships and specific character traits like the sense of honour. The objection is that, if the theory treats such relationships and traits as of special value – that is to say, not merely as useful or as desired among the many things which are desired – it lacks neutrality; it imposes the the- orist's own bias towards particular satisfactions. I shall discuss only the second objection; the first objection can be reformulated as an insistence on neutrality at the level of moral theory.[37]

Modern utilitarianism, Bernard Williams points out, is supposed to be neutral between the preferences or desires which people actually have, neutral with regard to what sorts of things make people happy or what their projects are.[38] Any project, preference, desire or what-not will go into the utility calculation in the same sort of way. Mill is then exactly not a modern utilitarian. The question is whether the modernness of modern utilitarianism, its insistence on neutrality between our prefer- ences or our desires or what-not, is not itself part of the distinctive conse- quentialist cast of contemporary utilitarianism. If a utilitarian moralist takes seriously, as Mill thinks he should, the difference in human signifi- cance of different kinds of projects or desires, he may commit himself to non-consequentialist evaluation of actions and institutions.

I mentioned earlier, as an objection to Mill's theory as I had described it, that its use of a non-consequentialist notion of rationality reflected a failure in the philosophical task of criticism of accepted morality. The same objection might be directed against Mill's theory all over again, on the basis of its distance, just mentioned, from modern utilitarianism. The point might be put so: the neutrality of modern utilitarianism is essential if the theory is to be able to engage in a critical examination of accepted moral thought. Neutrality between preferences or desires prevents the theory having smuggled into it unexamined assumptions about what is good; in modern utilitarianism, any candidate for inclusion in the utilitarian end will have its credentials examined in the same way.

There is in play in that objection a modern conception of what it is for utilitarianism to be genuinely critical of received views. Mill rejects that understanding, which he saw in Bentham. Philosophical criticism of received morality is of the highest importance to Mill, but not conceived as it is in modern moral philosophy. Mill, like other utilitarians, rejects the idea of the philosophical critic as appealing to 'intuitions'; he must, though, be able to draw on experience, his own and that of others. If his own nature and circumstances have given him little understanding of human life and what enriches it, he will be ill qualified for his task. The more of human experience he can draw on, the better; the liveliness of his imagination, the quickness of his sympathies, will be of inestimable aid to him.

The issue here is not whether Mill is correct, but whether the alternative understanding of utilitarian theory and of the utilitarian as critic has consequentialism built into it. The 'neutrality' of modern utilitarianism between different sources of happiness, that is, may not be neutral at all on the issue of consequentialism versus non-consequentialism. Mill's insistence on the moral critic's need to draw on the fullest experience of human life and human nature is part of his own resistance to the proto-consequentialism – the trade-off moral style – which he took to be tied to Bentham's 'neutrality' between various kinds of pleasures. The modern utilitarian's conception of a 'neutral' stance for philosophical criticism reflects (this then is the suggestion) a consequentialist conception of what such criticism must be.

As John McDowell reads Aristotle, he provides a model of critical, reflective moral thought, in which the moral critic speaks from inside a view of human life and human nature dependent on his own moral upbringing. McDowell argues against the reading of Aristotle which sees him as recommending the cultivation of character traits such that behaviour manifesting those traits will help the agent achieve a good life, as judged by standards independendent of any specific ethical view.[39] That is, on the reading of Aristotle which he rejects, the traits to be cultivated are not to be judged through the modes of evaluation acquired through moral upbringing. My reading of Mill has strong structural analogies with McDowell's reading of Aristotle. Reflective philosophical moral thought, as Mill understands it, does not have to be undertaken from a point of view external to the modes of evaluation, the standards for judging what is genuinely rewarding in human life, acquired through one's moral education. Mill's conception of the inductive character of reflective, critical ethics includes the exercise within it of modes of evaluation the worth of which has been learned in one's own life and experience and that of others. The fact that a different pattern of past experience would not have led one to the same values does not mean that such experience must be discounted by the moral critic, or that the critic should be neutral between all the goods people might come to value through their experience and nature. If the moral critic has character traits and habitual modes of relationship with others which are tied to non-consequentialist thought, there is no implication (on the view of moral criticism which I am sketching) that he needs to make a consequentialist assessment of those traits and modes of relationship. There is nothing particularly ultimate about consequentialism. Like the non-consequentialism I have ascribed to Mill, it has ties to particular traits and forms of human relationship. It has no special credentials that make it the appropriate stance for philosophical criticism of morality. Any way of understanding the workings-out of causal relations between our actions and the rest of the world, including the actions of others, will embody some way of thinking of ourselves and our relations to others. A mode of evaluation, or a way of understanding causal relations, is not ill-suited for the philosophical critic because it reflects what the critic has come to through experience.

In the essay to which I have referred, McDowell says that enquiry 'is an intellectual activity in which we aim to make our thinking, on whatever subject matter, responsive to reasons for thinking one thing rather than another'; and he argues against the characteristically modern worry that we can achieve such responsiveness only by transcending reasons tied to the contingent facts of our historical circumstances and our particular forms of upbringing. He sees Aristotle as free from such a worry; I have been arguing that Mill, in his understanding of moral criticism, is also free of that worry.[40] The consequentialist objections to Mill which I have examined in this section seem to me to depend on that modern worry, especially in their understanding of 'bias' and of what constitutes an unbiased treatment of what it is to exercise rationality in the pursuit of our ends.

## 8. CONCLUSIONS

My aim has not been to defend the theory I have ascribed to Mill; I should not myself want to speak of morality as having an aim or end. I have been concerned rather with the fact that modern moral philosophy has either ignored the possibility of the kind of utilitarianism I have ascribed to Mill, or ruled it out by defining utilitarianism as a subcategory of consequentialism, differing from other subcategories only in its account of what is to be aimed at. But ethics with a strong teleological bent, ethics understood as drawing on human experience, need not be consequentialist. This was certainly emphasized in Anscombe's original essay, and in the treatment of Aristotle in it. In §1, I said that one reason it has been difficult to see what Anscombe meant by 'consequentialism' is that we have separated our use of the term from the thesis with which she linked it, that there is no significant difference between the English moral philosophers from Sidgwick on. But what consequentialism is, on her original understanding, is also linked to the first thesis of 'Modern Moral Philosophy', that it is not profitable for us at present to do moral philosophy because we lack an adequate philosophy of psychology. I have not explicitly tried to show the links to that first thesis; but I have tried to show that the invisibility of non-consequentialist utilitarianism is connected with a consequentialist understanding of rationality.[41]

## NOTES

1 Originally in *Philosophy* 33 (1958) 1–19; reprinted in Anscombe, *Ethics, Religion and Politics* (Oxford: Blackwell, 1981), pp. 26–42. The explanation of 'consequentialism' is on pp. 33–36.
2 For the view of Mill see, e.g., Anne Maclean, *The Elimination of Morality* (London: Routledge, 1993), p. 81; her detailed account of Mill earlier in the book is meant to support the idea of his moral theory as a good example of consequentialism, an example by reference to which the term may be explained. For the identification of deontological views with rejection of consequentialism, see Michael Slote, 'Consequentialism', in L. Becker, ed., *Encyclopedia of Ethics* (New York: Garland, 1992); also Nancy Davis, 'Contemporary Deontology',

in Peter Singer, ed., *A Companion to Ethics* (Oxford: Blackwell, 1991); also Jonathan Dancy, 'An Ethic of Prima Facie Duties', in Singer, *Companion to Ethics*. Dancy takes Ross to be a paradigmatic opponent of consequentialism.
3 Anscombe, 'Modern Moral Philosophy', p. 33. I have omitted the footnote to Anscombe's sentence; I discuss it below.
4 Gottlob Frege, 'Foundations of Geometry', I, *Collected Papers* (Oxford: Blackwell, 1984), p. 283.
5 Anscombe, 'Modern Moral Philosophy', p. 33n.
6 See W. D. Ross, *The Right and the Good* (Oxford: Clarendon Press, 1930), p. 41: 'It is obvious that any of the acts that we do has countless effects, directly or indirectly, on countless people, and the probability is that any act, however right it be, will have adverse effects (though these may be very trivial) on some innocent people. Similarly, any wrong act will probably have beneficial effects on some deserving people. Every act therefore, viewed in some aspects, will be *prima facie* right, and viewed in others, *prima facie* wrong, and right acts can be distinguished from wrong acts only as being those which, of all those possible for the agent in the circumstances, have the greatest balance of *prima facie* rightness, in those respects in which they are *prima facie* right, over their *prima facie* wrongness, in those respects in which they are *prima facie* wrong – *prima facie* rightness and wrongness being understood in the sense previously explained. For the estimation of the comparative stringency of these *prima facie* obligations no general rules can, so far as I can see, be laid down.' In the light of that quotation it is quite remarkable that Ross is so frequently taken to be an anti-consequentialist. Although he does attack the role given to consequences in theories like utilitarianism and that of Moore, the differences are (as Anscombe implies) less significant than the resemblances. See also Ross, *Foundations of Ethics* (Oxford: Clarendon Press, 1939), pp. 165 and 190.
7 'Rights and Agency', in *Philosophy and Public Affairs* 11 (1982) 3–39; reprinted in Samuel Scheffler, *Consequentialism and Its Critics* (Oxford: OUP, 1988), pp. 187–223.
8 Samuel Scheffler, Introduction to *Consequentialism and Its Critics*, p. 11.
9 But cf. Bernard Williams's discussion of the contrast between a consequentialist and a non-consequentialist treatment of the rightness of keeping promises, in 'A Critique of Utilitarianism' (henceforward referred to as 'CU'), in J. J. C. Smart and Bernard Williams, *Utilitarianism: For and Against* (Cambridge: CUP, 1973), pp. 88–89. Williams's argument leaves open the possibility of treating philosophers like Ross as consequentialists.
10 Anscombe, 'Modern Moral Philosophy', p. 33; cf. also pp. 27–8.
11 There is, for example, this: 'The morality of an action depends on its foreseeable consequences', from the essay 'Bentham', in *Dissertations and Discussions* (New York: Henry Holt, 1874) I, p. 412.
12 See, for example, the forms of rule-consequentialism discussed by Railton, 'Alienation, Consequentialism, Morality', in Scheffler, *Consequentialism and its Critics*, pp. 93–133, §7. It may be argued that there is no coherent form of rule-consequentialism; but even if there is not, it might be held that Mill had attempted to put forward some kind of rule-consequentialism.
13 *Goodbye to All That* (Harmondsworth: Penguin, 1960), pp. 197–198.
14 If Graves had said 'Yet I knew I would be unable to sign' and not 'Yet I could not sign', he would have been making a prediction, and would have been

distancing himself from the recognition that this was not something he could
do. He would then have had a dilemma of a different sort from the one he did
have, in which he takes signing to be ruled out. See Bernard Williams, 'Moral
Incapacity', *Proceedings of the Aristotelian Society* 93 (1993) 59–70.

15  My imagined consequentialist argument is meant to reflect such typical consequentialist lines of thought as that in S. Scheffler, Introduction to *Consequentialism and its Critics*, pp. 4–10. Cf. also Jonathan Glover, 'It Makes No
Difference Whether or Not I Do It', *Proceedings of the Aristotelian Society*,
Supp. Vol. 49 (1975) 171–190.

16  On this kind of attempt to separate deliberation from justification, see Williams, 'CU', p. 128.

17  'CU', p. 95.

18  On John Skorupski's reading, Mill's account of liberty of expression gives weight
to the nature of the causal linkage through which what someone says plays a role
in what happens; Skorupski does not, though, see this as a case of an application by Mill of a kind of distinction that plays a more general role in his moral
theory. See his *John Stuart Mill* (London: Routledge, 1989), §9 of chapter 10.

19  *Utilitarianism*, II, paragraph 2.

20  J. O. Urmson, 'The Interpretation of the Moral Philosophy of J. S. Mill', *Philosophical Quarterly* 3 (1953) 33–39. Urmson argues that, although drinking alcohol may tend to produce exhilaration, my drinking a particular glass
either does or does not produce it. But Mill's idea is roughly that, if drinking
alcohol tends to produce exhilaration, and if your drinking a particular glass
does not produce it, then the failure to produce exhilaration is the result of
the counteracting, by the tendency of some other cause operative in the circumstances, of the tendency of the action to produce exhilaration. Far from
its being impossible to speak of tendencies of individual actions, such tendencies are essential in explaining how the outcome in a particular situation is
brought about by interacting causes.

21  David Lyons, *Forms and Limits of Utilitarianism* (Oxford: Clarendon Press,
1965), p. 28.

22  It is perhaps worth noting that Mill's use of the expression 'the effects of' is
not the same as Lyons's. When Mill speaks of the effects of something he frequently means only those effects which it tends to produce, as contrasted with
those things to which it leads 'accidentally', through the complex causal network within which it is placed, including the tendencies of other causes operative in the circumstances. Mill has many discussions in *System of Logic* of the
tendencies through which some effect was produced; see, e.g., Book III, especially chapters 10 and 11. Mill's brief methodological remarks, in his bracketed
comments on Herbert Spencer in the second footnote to Ch. V of *Utilitarianism*, should be read with the discussions of method in *System of Logic*. See
also the fine brief summary of Mill's view in the *Autobiography* (Oxford:
OUP, 1924), pp. 135–136. Mill there uses the principle of the Composition of
Forces in dynamics to illustrate the derivation of the effect of several con-
joined causes from their individual tendencies.

23  Compare Anscombe on our not getting credit for the good consequences of
our bad acts, 'Modern Moral Philosophy', pp. 35–36.

24  Although I claimed that Mill does not mean by the tendency of an action what
would happen if everyone performed actions of the same kind, there is no rea-

son why asking such a question might not sometimes be useful in determining the tendency of an action. (Mill uses the question in that way.) But then again care and intelligence will be called for in distinguishing those things which would probably happen if everyone did actions of the kind but which are not part of the tendency of such actions from those things which should be regarded as belonging to their tendency. If everyone always broke promises when it was convenient, and promising as an institution then disappeared, some people would be deprived of the pleasure of saying 'I told you so!' when other people broke their promises; but that loss of pleasure is not properly regarded as part of the tendency of acts-of-breaking-promises-when-it-is-convenient-to-do-so. And so it is not the sort of thing we are supposed to mention when discussing what would happen if everyone broke promises when it was convenient. In many cases, then, talk of 'what would happen if everyone did such-and-such' reflects a prior idea of what should be treated as belonging to the tendency of actions of the relevant kind. Moral education includes coming to understand the particular ways in which the question 'What would happen if everyone did it?' is used in moral thinking; it is not a request merely for a prediction of things that are likely to happen if everyone did such-and-such.

25  See §7 for a discussion of some objections closely related to this one. Utilitarianism is frequently defined in such a way as to exclude the moral significance within it of the distinction with which I am concerned. From a consequentialist point of view, the attractiveness of utilitarianism (utilitarianism defined in consequentialist terms) lies in part in its not excluding from the determinants of the moral character of an action any of the causal relations dependent on the particular circumstances of the action.

26  *Utilitarianism*, I, paragraph 4.

27  'Modern Moral Philosophy', p. 35.

28  I cannot here argue for that claim; but my sketch in §6 of a Millian approach to the case of the Irish sergeant provides an illustration of how such an approach can yield a different result from what we would get through consequentialist reasoning.

29  Mill does, however, provide an example in the description of certain acts as the denial of something known to be the case, in order to withhold the facts from some individual when such withholding will save someone from great and unmerited evil, and the withholding can be effected only by denial (*Utilitarianism*, II, para. 23). In this case direct appeal to Utility would supposedly show that the good tendency of such acts outweighs their bad tendency. Social recognition of the very narrow class of exceptions and of its limits would itself have a tendency to counteract the harmful tendency which these lies share with other lies.

30  'CU', p. 89.

31  See Williams, *Morality: An Introduction to Ethics* (Cambridge: CUP, 1972), pp. 99–102. J. D. Mabbott raises the objection as an objection to Urmson's reading of Mill as a rule-utilitarian; see 'Interpretations of Mill's "Utilitarianism"', *Philosophical Quarterly* 6 (1956), 115–20. See also J. J. C. Smart, 'Extreme and Restricted Utilitarianism', *Philosophical Quarterly* 6 (1956), pp. 344–354.

32  See also Williams on the possibility of non-consequentialist theories which rank states of affairs, 'CU', pp. 88–89.

33  There are, however, forms of consequentialism for which the problem does
    not arise in the way it does for act-utilitarian consequentialists. A theory like
    Ross's might, e.g., include a prima facie duty to vote.
34  Bernard Williams, *Morality*, pp. 107–8.
35  My wording of this point is derived from Jonathan Glover, *Responsibility*
    (London: Routledge, 1970), p. 193.
36  Mill, 'Bentham'; see note 11 above.
37  The argument for the reformulation would go something like this. So far as
    the moral theorist remains within a non-consequentialist mode of thinking
    which he conceives to be tied to some character trait which he regards as of
    special value, he is writing into the moral theory certain preferences of his
    own; the theory has a bias built into it. The value of the traits can be recog-
    nized within a genuinely neutral moral theory only through testing them
    against a criterion which does not have built into it a form of thinking tied to
    the traits themselves.
38  'CU', p. 131; cf. pp. 112–113.
39  McDowell's reading is developed in various essays; my exposition draws espe-
    cially from 'Eudaimonism and Realism in Aristotle's Ethics', in R. Heinaman
    (ed.), *Aristotle and Moral Realism* (London: UCL Press, 1995), pp. 201–18.
40  McDowell also argues that we do Aristotle no favour if we equip him with a
    response to the worry; I should want to make the corresponding point about
    Mill.
41  I am very grateful for helpful comments and suggestions from A. D. Woozley.

# 2 Is Anything Absolutely Wrong?

## Nicholas Denyer

BONES: He thinks there's nothing *wrong* with killing people?
GEORGE: Well, put like that, of course... But *philosophically*, he doesn't think it's actually, inherently wrong in itself, no.
BONES (*amazed*): What sort of philosophy is that?
GEORGE: Mainstream, I'd call it. Orthodox mainstream.
(BONES *scratches his head.* GEORGE *gazes at him innocently.*)

Tom Stoppard, *Jumpers*, Act One.

## 1. WHAT ABSOLUTISM IS

Like anything else, human actions can be described in many ways. For example, this morning I put some meat out on a dish, and served the cat's breakfast; and as it happens, both these descriptions are true of just a single action of mine, for the cat's breakfast was the only meat I put out this morning. In this essay, I will discuss how the various descriptions that an action might satisfy are related to the action's being wrong or otherwise. In particular, I will explore the idea that certain descriptions (e.g. 'dismembering a baby') are such that any action satisfying any of those descriptions is for that reason wrong, whatever other descriptions (e.g. 'saving a life') it may also satisfy. This idea is called absolutism. It was once the conventional wisdom.[1]

If anything is absolutely wrong, then, I take it, murder is. Under the term 'murder' I include the deliberate killing of people who have not, by any wicked deed of their own, merited such treatment. Thus it would be absolutely wrong to kill people whose principal failing is that their deformities make them an embarrassment and a burden to others, or that they were conceived through an illegitimate sexual act like rape or incest. The more abstract arguments in this paper may seem less dry if it is borne in mind that the absolute wrongness of murder, so understood, is among the issues they address.

There is more at stake than just the status of murder. For we will examine arguments purporting to show that, with such obvious and boring

39

exceptions as 'doing something wrong', there is no description whatsoever such that actions of that description are always wrong; that things like robbery, rape, torture, or indeed murder, cannot possibly be ruled out in principle; and that each such thing would therefore, in appropriate circumstances, be permissible, and maybe even obligatory. My goal is to show that none of these arguments work, and that it is, if anything, the rival to absolutism that is incoherent.

## 2. WHAT ABSOLUTISM IS NOT

Absolutism might be confused with what Bernard Williams called 'the *whatever the consequences* position', and also with what Amartya Sen called 'the constraint-based deontological view'. It should not be. For absolutism is free from the objections that can be brought against those doctrines.

The *whatever the consequences* position shares with absolutism the thought that certain things are always wrong. However, it goes beyond absolutism by adding 'the claim that there is a type of action which is right *whatever the consequences*'; for it is the view that 'there are some actions which one should always do, or again some which one should never do, *whatever the consequences*'.[2] In other words, the *whatever the consequences* position attempts to treat both rightness and wrongness in the way that absolutism treats wrongness alone. For in holding that some kinds of action are absolutely wrong, absolutism does not hold that some kinds of action are absolutely right. It does not hold that there is (apart of course from such boring and obvious exceptions as 'doing the right thing') any description such that actions of that description are uniformly right, no matter what other descriptions they satisfy. In saying that anyone who dismembers a baby is thereby acting wrongly, I imply nothing about descriptions which always guarantee that actions are right. I do not even imply that those who are not dismembering babies are thereby guaranteed to be acting rightly, whatever other descriptions (e.g. 'disembowelling children') may apply to what they are doing. I imply at most that not dismembering babies is not absolutely wrong. For in this respect, being absolutely wrong is like being illegal: when I say that theft is illegal, I do not imply that there is any description (apart from e.g. 'legal') which guarantees that all actions to which it applies are legal; I do not even imply that any action, so long as it is not theft, is legal, even if it happens to be murder.

The constraint-based deontological view is the view whereby 'rights are treated as constraints on actions', and 'these constraints must not be violated *even if* such violation would lead to better states of affairs. Violating rights is simply wrong'.[3] Thus this view holds that you should never break into the office of some innocent party, even in a grave emergency where only thus can you get the information that will enable you to prevent a serious assault. For, unlike the assault itself, failing to take such steps to prevent it would not violate the victim's right to bodily security; whereas taking such steps would violate the property rights of the owner of the office.[4] And on this view, the violation of rights should enter our decision making, not as an evil to be minimized, but as a wrong to be eschewed, no matter what.

There are at least three respects in which an absolutist ethic need not treat rights in the manner of the constraint-based deontological view. Let us show this for an ethic holding that murder is absolutely wrong; the points to be made about this ethic will apply, *mutatis mutandis*, to absolutist ethics more generally.

First, this ethic need not derive the absolute wrongness of murder from the claim that murder always violates rights; indeed, this ethic might be better advised not to attempt such a derivation, unless it wishes to contest the claims that people might consent to their being killed, and that actions which would otherwise violate rights no longer do so once affected parties consent. Thus an absolutist ethic need not suppose that every action which is absolutely wrong is a violation of a right.

Second, an absolutist ethic need not say that violating rights is absolutely wrong. Our ethic which holds that murder is absolutely wrong could also hold that burglary, while not absolutely wrong, nevertheless is wrong in all ordinary circumstances. It could then say that a particular burglary was wrong, since there were no extraordinary circumstances to justify it. Moreover, our ethic could say all this without maintaining that, besides murder, some other kind of action is absolutely wrong; our ethic need not run the fool's errand of finding some description which applies to just the same actions as 'burglary not justified by any extraordinary circumstances', and which, unlike that description, is fit to figure in a substantive moral principle of the form 'It is absolutely wrong to . . .'. Thus an absolutist ethic can concede that, in emergencies, property rights go by the board, and therefore that the wrongness of violating them is not absolute.

Third, an absolutist ethic need not hold that total abstention from absolutely wrong actions, or even from all wrong actions, is sufficient for acting well. You could live your entire life without once giving money to any deserving cause. Such a life would obviously be flawed. Yet such a life could be lived without performing a single action that would count as wrong by our ethic which holds that murder is absolutely wrong, and which adds that various things like burglary are wrong in ordinary circumstances. Moreover, it would be plainly silly to supplement our ethic by saying that 'not giving money to deserving causes' is a description like 'murder' or 'burglary'; for to say that actions which meet this description are wrong, either absolutely or in all save extraordinary circumstances, is to demand, not generosity, but utter fecklessness. Here then there is scope for supplementing our absolutist ethic with the thought that one should give generously to deserving causes. This supplement may not itself be absolutist; but it is entirely consistent with absolutism. For our absolutist ethic denies only that murder is a legitimate way of raising money for good causes; it does not deny that one should find ways other than murder in which to be generous. Similarly, our absolutism may accept that one should, when necessary, take steps to prevent the violation of rights; for it implies only that it is wrong to commit murder as one of those steps. And hence our absolutism is in a third respect distinguished from the constraint-based deontological view that violation of rights enters our moral calculations only as a wrong to be eschewed, and not as an evil to be prevented.[5]

## 3. CAUSING AND ALLOWING TO HAPPEN

In some circumstances, you cannot prevent someone's death unless you dismember a baby: one poignant example (rarer in medical practice than in philosophical theory) is where only the craniotomy of her baby will save a pregnant woman, and where, if she dies, the baby can subsequently be delivered by Caesarean section. The belief that dismembering babies is absolutely wrong entails that, in such circumstances, it would be wrong to prevent the mother's death; for any action that prevented her death would, in these circumstances, satisfy the description 'dismembering a baby'. This entailment is the basis of another objection to absolutism. The objection runs: whichever action the doctor does, whether he dismembers the baby or lets the mother die, someone will die who could otherwise have lived. Absolutism distinguishes strongly between these two deaths, the one that results from a dismembering and the other that results from a failure to save; for it forbids us to act with the one result, and requires us to act with the other. Yet between these two ways of resulting in death there is no difference strong enough to justify such a distinction. Hence absolutism is wrong.

Absolutists do indeed draw a significant distinction here. And of course they should rest that distinction on a correspondingly significant difference. What would such a difference be? It is sometimes suggested that absolutists need to invoke a difference between action and omission: performing the craniotomy takes some positive actions, whereas the mother can be allowed to die simply by omitting all positive actions, simply by staying still. This, however, cannot be the difference that absolutism needs. Suppose that I am in a boat from which you are diving. A rogue wave topples me onto the pipe through which you are breathing. Thus I find myself, for a moment at least, cutting off your air supply. I could of course take the positive action of moving away, in which case no harm would be done. But I am rather tickled by the thought that, as luck now has it, I can kill you without moving a muscle. So I stay still, until you suffocate. In this case, I fall directly within the scope of the absolutist prohibition of murder. The fact that I omit to move does not mean that my behaviour can be criticized only on some grounds other than its breach of that absolute prohibition. The difference that absolutism needs is therefore not one between action and omission.

What difference does absolutism need? The diving case helps answer this question too. In the diving case, by omitting to move, I deliberately cause your death. In the obstetric case, however, the doctor does not deliberately cause the mother's death by omitting to dismember her baby. He does not cause her death at all; he merely fails to prevent it. Here we have the difference needed by absolutism. It is the difference between causing and failing to prevent. Absolutists must say that since the doctor in the obstetric case merely fails to prevent the mother's death, he does not fall within the scope of the absolute prohibition which I violate in the diving case by causing your death.

There are three arguments purporting to show that the difference between causing and failing to prevent is too slight to bear the weight that absolutism puts on it. Let us review those arguments in turn.

The first maintains that 'causing' and 'failing to prevent' are simply alternative labels for exactly the same thing. Causation, it maintains, is to be analysed along these lines:

> we may define a cause to be *an object, followed by another, and where all the objects similar to the first are followed by objects similar to the second. Or in other words where, if the first object had not been, the second never had existed.*[6]

No doubt this analysis needs some fine tuning. But the basic idea is clear, and clearly right. Thus if, in our obstetric example, the doctor performs the craniotomy, then the craniotomy causes the death that ensues, since all similar operations are followed by similar outcomes for the person operated upon; or, in other words, if the craniotomy had not taken place, the baby would have survived. Exactly analogous things are true if the doctor does not perform the craniotomy and instead, as we say, 'allows' the mother to die. For any similar failure to perform a craniotomy is followed by a similar outcome for the mother; or, in other words, if there had been no failure to perform a craniotomy, the mother would have survived. Hence allowing events to happen differs only in name from causing them; and so, the argument concludes, there can be no moral difference between the two, let alone the strong moral difference that absolutists need to draw.

There is a simple flaw in this argument. If you cause the death of one person and you cause the death of another, then it follows that you cause the death of them both. In other words, deaths that you cause mount up. But the same is simply not true of deaths that you can prevent but do not. For you can be able to do each of two things separately which you cannot do together. Hence, if you can save one person and you can save another, it does not follow that you can save them both. Hence, even if you save neither, it does not follow that you could have prevented both deaths but did not. Therefore, in spite of suggestions to the contrary from Humean definitions of causation, letting things happen differs in more than just name from causing them. And so this first argument does nothing to undermine the absolutist contention that there is a moral difference between the two.

A second argument against the absolutists' moral distinction concedes that we can, at least in metaphysics, distinguish between causing and failing to prevent. This argument invites us to consider cases like that of the wicked bystander, who watches gleefully as a toddler drowns in a puddle: he could prevent the toddler's death, but does not; and he is plainly as wicked as someone who had caused it. Such cases, however, show only that some failures to prevent death are no less wrong than murders. And this is something that absolutists can accept. For in saying that it is absolutely wrong to kill innocent people deliberately, absolutism does not say that, so long as you avoid doing this, you are acting rightly. Absolutism can therefore well admit that the wicked bystander is indeed wicked, even though he does not cause the toddler's death. Absolutism need only deny that letting deaths happen is *always* the moral equivalent of causing them. Hence this second argument too is flawed; for it misunderstands the moral distinction that absolutists need to draw.

There is a third argument purporting to undermine the distinctions absolutists need to draw between causing and allowing to happen. This third argument concedes (unlike the first) that there is a metaphysical distinction between causing and allowing to happen. This third argument also appreciates (unlike the second) the character of the moral distinction that absolutists need to draw. It grants moreover (what sane argument does not?) that typical murders differ from typical failures to save life. This argument grants, for example, that it is one thing for you to spend on an evening out £20 that could otherwise have saved a life threatened by famine, and quite another thing for you to stab someone fatally. But, the argument continues, the moral difference between these two cases does not depend on the fact that in the former you merely allow a death that you could have prevented, while in the latter you cause one. It depends rather on the fact that killings are typically (but not universally) distinguished from failures to save by various further features and consequences. Here is a version of the argument from Tooley:[7]

> In the first place, the *motive* of a person who kills someone is generally more evil than the motive of a person who merely lets someone die. A person may let someone die out of laziness or apathy, and though I would insist that such inaction is seriously wrong, it is surely not as seriously wrong as the action of a person who kills someone else because he *wants* him dead. Secondly, the alternative to letting someone die – saving his life – may involve considerable risk to the agent, or a very large expenditure of society's resources. This will rarely be true of refraining from killing someone. Thirdly, if one performs an action that normally results in the death of a person, there is little likelihood that the person will survive. While if one merely refrains from saving someone's life, there is often a substantial chance that he will survive in another way. . . . It is these factors that make the difference, rather than the difference between killing and letting die.

This I find hard to believe. Imagine a mugger who knifes someone in order to steal £100 from her. He won't mind if she survives, for she couldn't identify him anyway. He knifes her simply to intimidate her into acquiescence. Of the £100 he steals, he spends £20 on an evening out. The remainder he contributes towards the local Citizens' Watch. This £80 prevents £100-worth of theft; in reducing future crime, it undoes any increase he might otherwise have caused in the public's fear of being mugged; and it even counteracts the tendency his action would otherwise have had to increase the amount of time spent in gaol for mugging. Meanwhile, his victim dies from the wound he inflicted. Which is really rather bad luck; for people have been knifed and lived to tell the tale.

Compare this mugger with the person who spends on an evening out £20 that could otherwise have saved a life threatened by famine. They are similar in two of the three respects that Tooley described: first, each goes ahead knowing that a death will then be liable to happen that would not happen otherwise, but neither 'wants' that death to happen; second, neither will be at 'considerable risk' if he does not go ahead, and not going ahead would not mean in either case any 'very large expenditure of society's resources', or even of the agent's own. In the third respect, the mugger may if anything be the superior: it may be that when he left his victim, she had a higher chance of surviving her wounds than the person to whom the £20 was not given had of surviving the famine. Moreover, the two cases are alike in other respects akin to those mentioned by Tooley: for example, in neither case does the agent increase the extent to which people fear crime, or suffer from it, or suffer as a result of committing it. It seems, in short, that if there is a moral difference between the two cases, then it is made by the difference between causing a death and failing to prevent one.

*If* there is a moral difference between the two cases. . . . When the debate reaches this stage, opponents of absolutism sometimes try to turn the tables. The two cases are indeed morally equivalent, they suggest, but not because murder shares the innocence that absolutists attach to not saving lives; rather, they are equivalent because not saving lives shares the wrongness that attaches to murder. Drawing the absolutist distinction is thus made to look like dodging duty; and eliding that distinction is thus made to look impressively austere.

This attempt to turn the tables cannot work. In any sane scheme of values, the goal of saving lives has to compete with other considerations. Any sane scheme of values allows us to divert some of our efforts and resources to having and rearing children; and no sane scheme demands that virtuoso medicine prolong a patient's life when that means only prolonging the patient's agony. Moreover, even if you do expend all your efforts and resources on saving life, deaths will still occur that you could have prevented. Allowing deaths to happen therefore cannot be anything like the wrong that murder is conventionally thought to be. Not only can it not be something that we should never do; it cannot even be something that we should do only rarely, or with reluctance. The equation of causing things with allowing them to happen cannot therefore require us to be punctilious about saving life; it can only require us to be lax about murder.

## 4. INTENDING AND FORESEEING

Absolutists need more than the difference between causing and allowing to happen. They need also a difference between two kinds of causing: the intentional and the unintentional. Such a difference is in some respects uncontroversial. If the reason why you are not causing something intentionally is that you are not aware of causing it, then all would agree that this could be morally quite different from intentionally causing such a thing: even if both cause death, nevertheless intentionally feeding people poisoned food may differ from feeding them poisoned food in the honest belief that it is wholesome. More controversial are cases where the effect is foreseen by the person who causes it. Absolutists say that there can be foresight without intent, and that sometimes it is not wrong to cause a thing knowingly, even though it would be absolutely wrong to cause that thing intentionally.

In saying this, absolutists have a double motive. On the one hand, absolutists wish to acknowledge that there is something you can rightly do, even when, for example, the plane you are piloting will crash somewhere in a city, and you know that if you steer your stricken plane away from a crowded stadium you will still cause the deaths of some innocent people. In order to avoid causing a larger number of deaths, you may rightly, absolutists wish to say, turn away from the stadium, even though you foresee that this turn will cause a number of deaths elsewhere. On the other hand, absolutists dare not allow that, just because it can sometimes be permissible to cause an innocent's death knowingly, it can sometimes be permissible to do such a thing intentionally. For this would mean allowing that, if people's ultimate ends are high-minded enough, and if they also feel a high-minded distaste for their chosen means, they can literally get away with murder. If absolutists are to have it both ways, then they need the distinction between intention and foresight: foreseen side-effects must differ from intended means.

The motive for the absolutist distinction may be clear. The distinction itself however is said to be thoroughly opaque. This objection has been pressed by Jonathan Glover:

> How do we draw the line in difficult cases between an intended means and a foreseen inevitable consequence? If, as a political protest, I throw a bomb into a football crowd, causing an explosion and killing several people, are their deaths intended means to my protest or inevitable consequences or it? On what principles do we decide whether the explosion alone is included in the means or whether we must count both explosion and deaths as part of the means? . . . The matter cannot hinge on whether or not the deaths are desired . . . [8]

The only difficulty with Glover's case is that it is underdescribed. Glover's description is compatible with the bomber's deliberating as follows:

'They'll continue to ignore us unless we show we really mean business. And the only sure way to do that, alas, is by a massacre too large and too public to be ignored. Unfortunately, they guard the Remembrance Day services quite closely these days. But with luck we should be able to smuggle a bomb into a football match...'. If this is how the bomber reasons, then he intends the deaths he causes; for the route he plans to his ultimate goal passes through those deaths. And to say that those deaths are not 'desired' is on a par with the ancient joke:

> EMPLOYEE: Can I have the afternoon off? I want to go to the dentist.
> EMPLOYER: That's the first time I've ever heard of anyone *wanting* to go to the dentist.

Glover's description is compatible also with the bomber's having some quite lunatic ideas about what causes what. It is compatible with the bomber's deliberating thus: 'The demon responsible for the government's evil policy lives in a football stadium. He won't be frightened by blood and corpses. In fact, nothing apart from a very loud noise can stop him. The only way to make a noise loud enough is to explode a bomb on the terrace above his lair. But they won't let me into the stadium except when there's a match on. And they search everyone who wants to go onto the terrace. So I'll have to throw the bomb from elsewhere in the stadium...'. If this is how the bomber reasons, then the deaths that he knowingly causes are reached only down a road that forks off from the route he plans towards his goal; and so the defect in his action is not that he intends those deaths.

In real life, or in imaginary cases that are fully described, the difficulties that Glover finds in his case are unlikely to trouble us much. For they are solved once we spell out the agent's practical reasoning. That may itself sometimes have difficulties of its own, for it is not always easy to tell how someone else is thinking. But absolutists can take those difficulties in their stride, if absolutism is primarily a guide to deliberating about one's own actions, and only secondarily a guide to judging the actions of others.

## 5. AGENT-RELATIVE CONSTRAINTS

Even if absolutists are conceded all the distinctions they wish to draw concerning causation and intention, there still remains another objection. How should you respond if someone threatens to dismember a dozen babies unless you dismember one? Suppose that dismembering babies is absolutely wrong. In that case, it would be wrong for you to dismember the one baby, even if the threat were entirely credible; you must refuse to breach the absolute prohibition, even if your refusal means in present circumstances that the prohibition will be breached a dozen times. A technical term has been devised for this feature of absolutism: an absolutist ethic is said to contain 'agent-relative constraints'. And the fact that absolutism contains agent-relative constraints is sometimes taken as a difficulty for it:

> For if the violation of agent-relative constraints is morally so objectionable, it seems extremely odd, on the surface at least, for morality to tell us that we *must not* act in such a way as to minimize their occurrence.[9]

Absolutism is not unique in containing agent-relative constraints. Utilitarianism does so too. This is because of what we might call the Dunkirk effect: people are normally rather lackadaisical about doing their best, but they show more zeal when desperate. Suppose I spend next weekend maximizing utility. This will, we may presume, mean leaving my close neighbours at large. They will potter round their gardens, each producing, let us say, ten kilobenthams of utility; and they will do this even though they could so arrange their affairs as to produce eleven kilobenthams apiece instead. In other words, if I myself maximize utility and leave them at large, the consequence will be a dozen failures on their part to maximize utility. Suppose now that instead of maximizing utility myself, I kidnap, bind and gag my dozen neighbours. In such a condition none of them will produce anything like ten kilobenthams; for it will be all they can do to keep breathing. But – and this is the important point – the dozen will under those circumstances do the best they can. For they will shun the less than maximally utile option of holding their breath; they will instead take the option of continuing to breathe, and none of them will have any third option more utile than that. Thus, if I kidnap my neighbours, there will be only one failure to maximize utility: my own. As a dutiful utilitarian, how do I spend my weekend? Do I maximize utility, and thus leave the neighbours free? Or do I kidnap the neighbours, and thus minimize failures to maximize utility? Obviously, a dutiful utilitarian chooses the former. In other words, utilitarians believe in an agent-relative constraint: they believe it wrong to fail to maximize utility, even though by committing one such wrong oneself, one can prevent a dozen such wrongs committed by others, and even though failing to maximize utility is a wrong so horrendous that, when faced with a choice between it and murder, one should commit the murder. Hence, if there is something objectionable about agent-relative constraints, the objection applies more widely than just to absolutism.

How could a moral code avoid endorsing agent-relative constraints? It seems that the only sure way to have a code without such constraints is to have a code which does not allow that people other than yourself can act wrongly. This would mean your regarding other people in the way that those of us with more commonplace codes regard animals. You might think you should not be cruel to other people; you might accept a certain responsibility to prevent other people harming one another; but you would not think of other people as having duties, any more than the rest of us think such things of wolves and sheep, even though we might shoot the former to protect the latter. You would be a sort of moral solipsist.

Not all forms of moral solipsism would provide a secure place at which to stop. For many of them endorse what one might call time-relative constraints, and time-relative constraints should seem as puzzling as the agent-relative constraints that moral solipsism is intended to avoid. This too can be seen by considering the Dunkirk effect.

Suppose, for example, that your moral solipsism takes the form of egoistic hedonism. You do not suppose that others should pursue either their own pleasure, or even yours. But you do believe that you should at all times pursue the greatest pleasure for yourself. You are on a luxurious cruise, and now find yourself standing by the taffrail. It would be the work of a moment to jump overboard. Once in the sea, you will be sure to do exactly what in those reduced circumstances will bring you most pleasure; for throughout your time in the sea (which might indeed be the rest of your life) you will be sure to try to avoid drowning, and you will have no pleasanter alternative. Hence, if you jump now, you will be sure hereafter to be doing what would be, by the standards of your egoistic hedonism, exactly the right thing. You acknowledge, however, that you tend to slack when things are going well: if the second best is sufficiently pleasant, then you tend to rest content with that, instead of going for the very best available. In particular, if you do not jump overboard, you will spend the evening on the liner, enjoying pleasures that, although far greater than any you would enjoy while trying to avoid drowning, are not the very greatest that the liner has to offer. Hence, if you do not jump now, you will be sure hereafter to be doing what would be, by the standards of your egoistic hedonism, wrong. How then do you choose between jumping and not jumping? Jumping means much less pleasure, but only a momentary lapse from the pursuit of the greatest pleasure; not jumping means much more pleasure, but whole hours in which you take less than the very pleasantest course available. Any ordinary egoistic hedonist would refuse to jump. But if you refuse to jump, you endorse a time-relative constraint: you refuse to commit one objectionable action at the present time, even to prevent yourself committing more such objectionable actions at other times. If you were impressed by the argument against agent-relative constraints, you should be equally impressed when it is deployed against constraints relative to time. For if there was any force to the argument 'How can it be wrong to minimize the occurrence of wrong actions?', then the argument still retains its force when wrong actions are failures to choose the most pleasant alternative available. And so you should jump overboard.

If you reject that conclusion, and still wish to reject agent- and time-relative constraints, then you will have to modify your egoistic hedonism. You can no longer think that you should at all times pursue the greatest pleasure for yourself. Instead, you will have to think simply that you should do so now, and you will have to lay down no standards for your behaviour at other times. You will have to think of times other than the present in more or less the way that, as a moral solipsist, you think of people other than yourself.

The moral code that results if we follow through the rejection of agent-relative constraints would thus be very weird: so weird that, according to one plausible criterion, it would not be a moral code at all. For a moral code, it is widely asserted, must be in some sense universal; and if you say 'It would be wrong for me now to...', while denying that the same might apply to other people, no matter how much they resembled you, and to yourself at other times, no matter how little you had changed, then your code could hardly be less universal. Moreover, the demand for universality is not here easily evaded by saying 'I don't see why my code of values should be, in this narrow sense, a *moral* code.' For the universality that leads to agent- and time-relative constraints is, unlike perhaps some of the things that have gone under that name, a demand of quite minimal rationality. Perhaps you can be rational enough without having any very robust sense of fairness; but there is a crazed egocentricity in believing that a general characteristic like wrongness could attach only to actions that are performed by you now. Absolutism's endorsement of agent-relative constraints is therefore no objection to it.

## 6. CONSEQUENTIALISM: THE RIVAL TO ABSOLUTISM

All views in disagreement with absolutism were once given the name 'consequentialist'.[10] Since then, the name has narrowed its application:

in current usage, it applies only to a rather special form of disagreement with absolutism. To count as a consequentialist these days, it is no longer sufficient merely to hold that no kind of action can be ruled out of consideration in advance as being absolutely wrong. For besides holding that whatever is within one's physical power is in principle at least something that one might rightly do, one must also hold some other views.

Consequentialism in the current sense means accepting as generally valid, for all decision-making, the correct account of decision-making in certain artificially limited circumstances, like gambling. Suppose you have allowed yourself £10 with which to lay a bet on a horse to win the Derby. You can easily say what your alternatives are (for each horse, you might put your tenner on that horse); you can easily measure the goodness of the various states that might result (the goodness of a state is measured by the amount of money you win in that state); you can calculate the goodness of each alternative (multiply the amount you might win by the likelihood of your winning it); and you should happily pick what these calculations show to be the best alternative (the circumstances have been so contrived that only this will do: it's your money at stake, and you quite reasonably wish to win all you can).

Consequentialism, when generalised from such artificially limited examples, consists in these four theses.

First, there is always a uniquely apt division of what is physically within one's power into a set of mutually exclusive and jointly exhaustive possibilities, or alternatives.

Second, there is a single scale whereby one can measure the goodness of each and every possible state of the universe.

Third, the goodness of each alternative can be calculated by summing the goodness of its consequences, that is, of those states of the universe that might ensue if one picks that alternative, discounting the goodness of each state in accordance with the probability that it will in fact ensue.

Fourth, one is always to pick an alternative whose goodness is at least as great as the goodness of any of the others; one must, in short, maximize.

The most celebrated version of consequentialism in this current and narrow sense is, of course, act utilitarianism, which is distinguished from other versions by its criteria (amounts of pleasant experience, satisfied desire, or the like) for measuring the goodness of states of the universe.

It is more than just a lexicographical quirk that the word 'consequentialist' has narrowed its application since it was first devised. For most people, if they start from consequentialism in the original sense of disagreement with absolutism, are liable to end at consequentialism in the current sense defined by the four theses we have listed.

Consider a man who is no absolutist, but who is still sufficiently tender of conscience to acknowledge that there is something wrong with buggering babies. Why would such a man think that buggering babies is, in spite of the acknowledged force in the demand that he do no such thing, nevertheless permissible for him under certain circumstances? How might he justify this thought? He will hardly feel it sufficient simply to indicate cases where he would, by buggering a baby, obtain some great good that was otherwise unobtainable: a huge payment, let us say, from a perverted billionaire. If buggering babies is to be rendered permissible by the goods that it enables him to obtain, then obtaining those goods would have to be, not merely desirable, but downright mandatory. Overriding the forceful demand that he not bugger babies would take a demand that is even more forceful; it would take a demand to which he must yield in all circumstances and at all costs, if he is going to have to yield to it even in circumstances where the cost of yielding is that he buggers a baby. But then, what would so forceful a demand be a demand for? It cannot be a demand for any of the things usually demanded by absolutists. It cannot, for instance, be the demand that he refrain from murder. For first, our high-minded objector to absolutism does not take such demands to be all that forceful; and second, such demands anyway do not conflict with the demand that he not bugger babies: one cannot, for example, imagine a case where buggering a baby is the only alternative to committing a murder. Our high-minded opponent of absolutism is liable therefore to believe in a particularly stringent demand of a quite unspecific nature; for instance, a demand that he must, in all circumstances and at all costs, minimize the evils of the world. This however means that our high-minded opponent of absolutism has more or less arrived at consequentialism in the narrow sense now current.

People might of course reject absolutism, because they simply see no objection to the things that absolutists think are absolutely wrong. Such people may well not become consequentialists in the current sense. They are however of more interest to the law than to philosophy; they need punishment, not refutation. They therefore do not count against the suggestion that philosophical doctrines which are consequentialist in the original sense are liable to be consequentialist in the current sense also.

## 7. FOUR ARGUMENTS FOR ABSOLUTISM

Hitherto we have been expounding absolutism, comparing it with its rivals and defending it against charges of incoherence. Something more positive can be done on absolutism's behalf if, as we just now argued, its only serious rival is consequentialism in the current sense; for if we were correct, then any argument against consequentialism in this sense is an argument for absolutism. To conclude, let us therefore present some arguments of this kind for absolutism, corresponding to the four consequentialist tenets that we expounded earlier.

First, what is within one's physical power cannot as a rule be partitioned into a uniquely obvious set of alternatives. We can take the alternatives all to be courses of action that will last for the next ten minutes; we can take them all to be courses of action that will last for the next five. We can slice what is possible for the next five minutes into one pair of alternatives (murder somebody/murder nobody); we can slice it into another (stay seated/don't stay seated); we can slice it into a trio (stay seated/murder somebody and don't stay seated/murder nobody and don't stay seated); and so on. Lars Bergström[11] has proved that what the best alternative is, and hence what action consequentialism requires, will depend on the partition chosen. Consequentialism will therefore remain useless until it finds some apt way of coming up with unique partitions.

Bergström's result is no problem for absolutists. If some kind of action is absolutely wrong, then any action of that kind will continue to be wrong, no matter what the alternatives are which constitute it, or which it constitutes, or with which it is being contrasted; and so the requirements of an absolutist ethic do not vary with different partitions into alternatives.

Second, if we cannot even rank states of the universe in an ordering of better and worse, then we cannot, as consequentialism requires, measure the goodness of a state. Yet no such ranking is possible. Given certain assumptions, Kenneth Arrow[12] has proved that there is no satisfactory procedure for combining several different orderings into a single ordering that takes due account of them all. Arrow's proof applies if we attempt to rank different states of the universe in terms of their relative goodness, all things considered. For the assumptions that Arrow's proof needs are all uncontentious here. They are assumptions as uncontentious as the following: there are at least three possible states of the universe; one state can be better than another in each of at least three respects (e.g. cheaper for me, more instructive for you, more entertaining for her); and if one state is better than another in some respects, and no worse in any of the others, then the one state is better than the other, all things considered.

Arrow's result too is no problem for absolutists. An absolutist ethic does not need to combine several different orderings into a single ordering, all things considered. At most, it has to combine several different absolutes ('Murder is absolutely wrong; so is buggering babies; and so is . . .') into a single judgment: 'This would be permissible, since it means neither murdering, nor buggering babies, nor . . .'. But the different moral absolutes are not, as it were, voters who each have an order of preference among the different possibilities, and whose preferences must be combined into a collective preference of the kind that Arrow shows there cannot be. The different moral absolutes are better thought of as exercising vetoes.

Third, the calculations to decide on the best alternative are, outside artificially simplified cases, quite beyond our power. This does not need proof; indeed, it is so evident a difficulty that consequentialists have often answered it. Their standard answer is that, instead of always doing the calculations, we may usually take our decisions as an absolutist would; for even if murder is not universally wrong by consequentialist standards, nevertheless murder is by consequentialist standards wrong often enough for us to be safe in usually eschewing it, even without making the calculations to confirm that murder is not the best alternative. There is, I dare say, some truth in this answer; at any rate, it is easy to believe that the typical murderer could find a better way to spend his time. It is easy to believe also that the typical television watcher could do something else with better consequences, and that watching television is therefore usually, though not of course universally, wrong by consequentialist standards. Yet it hardly seems right to treat watching television as the moral equivalent of murder.

Everyone agrees that absolutism does not put excessive demands on our capacity to calculate. For why else should consequentialists act like absolutists when consequentialist calculations are impossible?

Fourth, even in the special cases where the first three tenets of consequentialism apply, the requirement that one maximize may still be unreasonable. Suppose that for every alternative, there is a better: for instance, you can choose any amount of gold up to but not including one ounce; here you must forget maximizing, and just choose a biggish amount. Moreover, outside such special cases, there is even less reason to believe that maximizing will always make sense. How could one begin to choose the best alternative where the first three tenets of consequentialism do not apply? Why even think that there is such a thing to be chosen?

These objections to the superlative 'best alternative' do not apply to the positive 'good alternative'. We can say that someone has found a good area to live in, without indulging in the fantasies required to make sense of 'the best possible area to live in': the fantasies that there is a privileged partition of the world into areas, and that those areas can all be ranked according to how good each is to live in, all things considered. An absolutist ethic therefore has no need of maximizing. It can simply say that, within the bounds of the permissible, one should pick alternatives that are good. And so absolutism can escape this difficulty for consequentialism, just as it does all the others.[13]

## NOTES

1 Here is a sample of pagan, biblical, rabbinic, scholastic and Enlightenment endorsements of absolutism: Plato, *Republic* 442d–443a; Aristotle, *Nicomachean Ethics* 1107a 8–17; Romans 3:8; The Tosefta, Terumot 7:20; Thomas Aquinas, *Summa Theologiae* IIa IIae, Qu. 110, Art. 3, ad 4; Kant (1964), p. 97. Compare also Horace, *Odes* 3.3.1–8, the ultimate source of the saying 'fiat justitia et ruant caeli' ('let justice be done, although the heavens fall'), a saying that outrages those who think it their job to hold the sky up.
2 Smart and Williams (1973), p. 90; pp. 26–7 of the reprint; Williams's italics.
3 Sen (1982), p. 5; p. 189 of the reprint.
4 Sen (1982), pp. 7–12; pp. 191–6 of the reprint.
5 See Denyer (1982) and Denyer (1990) for more on how ethics which speak of absolute wrongness can be supplemented to acknowledge values of other kinds.
6 Hume (1902), p. 76.
7 Tooley (1980), p. 59.
8 Glover (1977), p. 88.
9 Scheffler (1988), p. 9.
10 Anscombe (1958), p. 12 (p. 36 of the reprint): '. . . *consequentialism*, as I name it . . .'. This use of 'consequentialism' predates all examples recorded in the *Oxford English Dictionary.*
11 Bergström (1971).
12 Arrow (1969).
13 Dorothy Denyer taught me much of what I know about ethics. I dedicate this paper to her.

## REFERENCES

Anscombe, G. E. M. (1958): 'Modern Moral Philosophy', *Philosophy* 33, pp. 1–19. Reprinted in Anscombe (1981), vol. III, pp. 26–42.
—— (1981): *Collected Philosophical Papers* (Oxford: Basil Blackwell).
Arrow, Kenneth J. (1969): 'Values and Collective Decision-making', in Laslett and Runciman (1969), pp. 215–232.

Bergström, Lars (1971): 'Utilitarianism and Future Actions', *Noûs* 5, pp. 237–252.

Denyer, Nicholas (1982): 'Chess and Life: The Structure of a Moral Code', *Proceedings of the Aristotelian Society* (New Series) 82, pp. 59–68.

——— (1990): 'Ease and Difficulty: A Modal Logic with Deontic Applications', *Theoria* 56, pp. 42–61.

Glover, Jonathan (1977): *Causing Death and Saving Lives* (Harmondsworth: Penguin).

Hume, David (1902): *An Enquiry Concerning Human Understanding*, edited by L. A. Selby-Bigge (Oxford: Clarendon Press).

Kant, Immanuel (1964): *Groundwork of the Metaphysic of Morals*, translated by H. J. Paton (New York: Harper and Row).

Laslett, Peter and Runciman, W. G. eds. (1969): *Philosophy, Politics and Society,* Third Series (Oxford: Basil Blackwell).

Scheffler, Samuel ed. (1988): *Consequentialism and its Critics* (Oxford: OUP).

Sen, Amartya (1982): 'Rights and Agency', *Philosophy and Public Affairs* 11, pp. 3–39. Reprinted in Scheffler (1988), pp. 187–223.

Smart, J. J. C. and Williams, Bernard (1973): *Utilitarianism: For and Against* (Cambridge: CUP). Partly reprinted in Scheffler (1988), pp. 20–50.

Steinbock, Bonnie ed. (1980): *Killing and Letting Die* (Englewood Cliffs, NJ: Prentice-Hall).

Tooley, Michael (1980): 'An Irrelevant Consideration: Killing versus Letting Die', in Steinbock (1980), pp. 56–62.

# 3 Natural Integrity And Biotechnology
### *Stephen R. L. Clark*

## 1. THE NEED FOR RULES

My aim is to show that even consequentialists must recognize that some acts are intrinsically wrong, and that there is therefore no good reason to reject other examples of intrinsic wrongness than those they, typically, acknowledge. So many ethicists assume the opposite that I must devote some time to showing the error of their ways, before pointing out some objections that can be seriously mounted against genetic engineering. First, I shall show that even consequentialists must be rule-consequentialists, and hence determine the rightness or wrongness of particular acts apart from the expected consequences of those acts themselves. Second, I shall make clear the unacceptable consequences for ordinary moral judgment of adopting even that rule-consequentialist outlook. An alternative approach is suggested by the example of genetic engineering: those who oppose such manipulation bear witness to 'natural integrity' or 'beauty' as vital factors in moral decency.

The question is: are modern biotechnological practices (AI, multiple conceptions, in vitro fertilization, and especially genetic engineering) objectionable in themselves, irrespective of any possible bad consequences (that might themselves be avoided with a little care)? And if they are thus bad, are they so bad that we should rule them out entirely?

It is unfortunately common practice amongst 'ethicists' to disregard the actual feelings and moral intuitions of those without a professional stake in the activity being described. Seamark, for example, claims that 'as *cogently argued* by Sandøe and Holtug . . ., most ethical worries concerning transgenic animals are probably baseless'.[1] But Sandøe and Holtug offer no such arguments, merely devoting a couple of sentences each to feeble rebuttals of seven arbitrarily selected slogans.[2] Häyry's conclusion,[3] that apparently 'categorical' (or intrinsic) objections to gene manipulation are either dissolved by closer scrutiny or revealed as 'conditional or pragmatic' (that is, extrinsic), is one for which he does offer arguments – but even he makes little attempt to understand the objections, and is scornful of any 'spontaneous human sentiments' that do not fit his theory. Committees, however, are the worst offenders, notably the House of Lords Select Committee.[4] Even animal welfare issues are mentioned only at paragraphs 5.21 and 5.22, and it does not seem to have occurred to the noble lords that there could be any serious objection even to onco-mice, once it was explained that there might be some advantages in their production (see 3.3: 'Transgenic animals [with near-exact versions of human diseases] have tremendous potential as research tools'). It is not obvious that this should settle the matter. For anyone who thinks animals count at all (and the Committee conceded that they count for something), it cannot possibly be enough to state the alleged advantages (to us) of inflicting injury (on them). This is not even consequentialism: it is merely dogma.

What lies behind the unexamined consequentialism with which public moralists profess to operate, and their insistence on judging actions only instrumentally? The argument would perhaps run as follows. All action is designed to make the world different from what it would otherwise have been. The action is identified by that actual or intended difference: what we do is (either) what difference we actually effect, or the difference we have it in mind to effect. After the event we can say what it was we brought about, and whether (all things considered) we can be glad we did. Before the event, while still deciding what to do, we must try to predict what differences we are in a position to make and how we should feel about them. An act is therefore judged to be 'right' if the total difference it makes turns out to be one that we welcome; 'justifiable' if there was sufficient reason at the time of decision to believe that it would make a welcome difference (even if in fact it does not). The agent who performs the act is reckoned 'justified' if she did have sufficient reason at that time, and acted like that because she did. Agents are 'virtuous' if they habitually act because they have good reasons to believe the differences they intend to make will be welcome ones (this is not to say anything much about their motives). Practices, both personal habits and social institutions, are justified if agents who engage in those practices do habitually do what is later judged to have been right. Since the practice of calculating the likely consequences of each individual act would probably often not result in right action (being difficult, costly, slow, liable to errors of thought and character), it is usually better to establish practices which reduce the need for particular calculation. In other words, 'rule-consequentialism' is a better policy than 'act-consequentialism', even if 'rule-consequentialists' sometimes act in ways that a well-informed and capable act-consequentialist, justifiably, would not.

The consequence is that, in practice, we do not judge particular acts simply by the difference they actually or expectably make: we prefer to consider the likely consequences of acting in accordance with such and such a rule over a reasonably long term. A particular lie may, actually or expectably, make a welcome difference: but the habit of lying when one thinks that such a difference will be made may itself have very unwelcome consequences – there will be many particular occasions when one's judgment was in error, and after a while, no one believes the liar. On some particular occasion, torturing a suspected terrorist (say, to discover where a bomb is) may make a welcome difference: but the chances of error are so high, and the likely consequences (in making enemies of people who might otherwise be on one's side) so disagreeable, that the practice of not torturing suspects should be preferred (whatever one's fallible expectation of making welcome differences by breaking the rules 'just this once'). In general, organizations where subordinates come to believe that 'the boss is only interested in results' (and does not care how they are achieved) are recognizably corrupt and dangerous – even to the boss.

So some acts, and some institutional and personal practices, should be identified as 'wrong' without regard to any actual or expectable consequences of the particular act. Instead of the act we assess the maxim. No one could reasonably expect to establish that one particular act (say, inflicting brain damage on a particular monkey) would have any welcome consequences. That particular act, even if some welcome information about brain damage eventually emerges from that laboratory's experimental work, is vanishingly unlikely to have been 'the crucial experiment that made the welcome difference'. It is various practices that are assessed, and not particular acts – though we may reasonably doubt that there has been any proper assessment of practice, and the differences such practices might make in this area. Once the judgment has been made that such-and-such a practice makes a welcome difference, particular acts are assessed only within the limits laid down by the practice itself.

So even those who emphasize the importance of consequences, or expectable consequences, for moral judgment, will agree that we must actually make our decision by reference to established rules which dictate, allow or forbid particular acts without regard to the expected consequences of those particular acts. We have the rules (so consequentialists say) because we know from experience that the practice of following one's own particular unregulated judgment is one that we could not reasonably recommend. So if we were eventually to decide that (say) genetic engineering would make very unwelcome differences we could establish rules that immediately outlawed all particular acts of genetic engineering, without any need to consider the apparent advantages of any one of them. If we decided that unregulated genetic engineering would be a practice with unwelcome consequences, our object would have to be to establish those regulations or rules under which genetic engineering could take place. Those rules would then determine what was 'right' or 'wrong' irrespective of particular expectable consequences. We may hope that the regulations will be ones that allow all acts of genetic engineering that will in fact make a welcome difference, and forbid all those that do not (or that make an unwelcome one), but this hope is probably unrealistic. We may have to choose between regulations that allow more 'wrong' acts, and ones that forbid more 'right' ones. The question will be: which error is worse? Just so, some jurisdictions are concerned to convict the guilty at the price of condemning some who are innocent; others prefer to absolve the innocent, even at the price of releasing some who are guilty. It is a fact of life that most jurisdictions probably do both, but the balance differs.

## 2. THE IMPOSSIBILITY OF NEUTRAL EVALUATION

So moral decision-making must include a 'deontological' element even if its basis is consequentialist (or 'teleological'): some acts are to be done because there is a law that says so, and not because they are themselves likely to make some welcome difference; some are not to be done because they are themselves forbidden, even if they would or might make some welcome difference. That is how the Home Office Inspectorate manages to oversee animal experimentation in the United Kingdom, in accordance with the decision model expounded in Smith and Boyd.[5] Some sorts of thing are not to be done at all; others only in the context of an 'important' research project. Consequentialists of various kinds would wish to assess, as well as we can, the effects of adopting one or another set of regulations. Once the rules are established particular acts are judged accordingly, without any need for further calculation. But calculation of the likely overall effect of adopting one set or another still requires a judgment of what effects are likely, and how welcome they may be. Unfortunately, it is not clear that this is possible. After all, the decision to adopt one set of rules rather than another is itself a decision whose effects we cannot certainly predict.

There is a further problem. The assumption behind consequentialist calculation is that we can assess the value of a difference without appeal to rules. The rules, after all, are established only by assessing the likely effects of adopting one set rather than another. To take a crude example: rape is to be judged wrong (alternatively: some acts are to be understood as rape) because the imagined world in which 'it' is allowed, or allowed under certain conditions, is less 'welcome' than one in which it is, however ineffectually, forbidden and punished. But it is of course less welcome (to us) largely because there would be a lot more cases of obviously criminal abuse in such a world. In a world where women or children are not assumed to have any will in the matter the very notion of 'forced intercourse' has no content. What we call rape would there be only 'marriage by capture' or the like, just as what we now call 'child abuse' was once a Spartan's duty. How would we go about comparing the utterly different social worlds (and the feelings of people brought up in them) to discover which, in the abstract, would be more welcome (more welcome, that is, to someone brought up in neither)? But of course there is something wrong, and even silly, about pretending to calculate the overall effect of forbidding sexual intercourse with minors, women who have not explicitly and publicly consented to the act, or women not in their right minds. The effects would, of course, include increased fear and frustration in the male population, tragi-comic misunderstandings, serious blackmail attempts and (possibly) an increased number of acts reasonably judged to be rapes. We do not even try to perform such a sociological survey once we have agreed that women and children have some will in the matter. People who have to be persuaded not to commit or countenance rape by talking about the overall advantages of *forbidding* 'rape' have not understood what is wrong with rape. It is not to be considered wrong because, all things considered, it would be better to have laws forbidding it: it is to be considered wrong (and necessary to have those laws) because sexual intercourse requires the real consent of all parties, a consent that is unobtainable unless there is a real equality of power and legal protection.

So strict consequentialists must somehow empty their minds of any prior commitment to particular moral judgments. Utilitarianism, in its clearest and most interesting form, is just that attempt. Rape is to be judged wrong if and only if there is more pure pleasure and less pure pain in a world where some acts are identified as rape and sometimes punished than one in which they are not. 'Pure' pleasure and 'pure' pain owe nothing to any prior moral judgment: we must not count 'the pain of being treated unjustly' nor yet 'the pleasure of seeing justice done against the offender' in our reckoning. A world in which people are 'naturally' sympathetic to the victims of sexual assault may be one where rape would, on balance, be judged wrong; one in which they are not might be a world where rape was not, on balance, wrong (or rather, there would be no concept of *rape* at all). In practice, even staunch utilitarians make no serious pretence to have carried out these calculations, and themselves take sides for other reasons. According to strict utilitarian principle, if pain is inevitable we should 'relax and enjoy it' (we should, that is, enjoy the pain of others, and thereby build a greater stock of pleasure in recompense for the pain), but very few utilitarians are pleased with this conclusion. Malice and cruelty, axiomatically, are wrong – but that is to admit that some things are evils, irrespective of any later gains.

To recapitulate: the reckoning-up of consequences is not a sensible way to make particular decisions; but neither is it a sensible or convincing way to choose between different practices. The consequences that matter to us are already deeply affected by our moral attitudes: considering only 'pure' or 'neutral' consequences gives us no answer or a foolish one. So rules are not simply the best way of achieving good consequences: they may dictate what is to be held good about the consequences. It follows that we must find a different way of specifying good rules.

## 3. SLAVERY AND DOMESTICATION

What might be said against the practice of genetic engineering, the attempt to introduce novel genetic material into the genome of existing species, either by literal infection or by altering existing genes to match some desired alternative? Unlike selective breeding, it enables us to produce creatures with some characteristics hitherto confined within a different gene-pool, a different species. 'Transgenic animals', in popular parlance, are therefore usually supposed to be animals with characters derived from another species. In fact, the term is used within the trade to signify any animal with a gene that has been altered from its ancestral type by human intervention. The alteration is not necessarily one that confounds species boundaries.

We can agree, for the moment, that the practice would be wrong if it imposed pain and suffering on the animals thus engineered, or on the animals from whom material was drawn. This could be true even if many affected animals were not thus hurt, so long as we could devise no regulations that prevented pain and suffering. It is already certain, of course, that the practice *has* caused considerable pain and suffering, and it is difficult to believe that we can forestall such suffering in the future. We can similarly agree that there might be serious social and environmental consequences to allowing the practice which would be so bad as to require outright prohibition or regulation designed to avoid all such consequences. Others may prefer to weigh up advantages and disadvantages (so allowing some pain in animals, some serious social effects in order to gain the benefits), but this 'weighing' will be purely subjective, a product of earlier, unexamined maxims about the value of animal life or the importance of progress. It will certainly not be more 'scientific' than the decision to outlaw some practices entirely, even if it is couched in spuriously quantitative terms.

One approach to this issue is to imagine as purely 'beneficial' a case as possible. Suppose that no pain or suffering has been involved in the production, say, of sheep which secrete Factor VIII in their milk. Suppose that such sheep live contented (not merely pain-free) lives, human haemophiliacs are helped, some commercial firms make a reasonable profit and there are no further unwelcome social consequences. What could be wrong with it? One immediate response might be to insist that cases cannot be thus abstracted from the real world. The production of such sheep is part of an agricultural and pharmaceutical industry that has undoubtedly caused pain and suffering to animals over many generations, and probably damaged the lives and welfare of human beings inside and outside the business too. Serious criticism of socio-economic structures is not well answered by abstracting particular cases from their historical setting. If we have good reason to think that capitalists (or state socialists) have presided over a system that regularly discounts the feelings and interests of those without sufficient economic (or political) clout, it is no answer to say that they have – in some selected cases – done no particular harm. It may still be true that, in those very cases, they are using the same powers, and displaying the same attitudes, as have elsewhere had far worse effects. Some slave-owners, some of the time, were relatively benign. Those opposed to slavery might still have thought they had no right to exercise 'benignity' like that. Sometimes the thing that victims most resent is that the oppressor did them some minor good, or used them, without causing any other injury, for a worthwhile end. It is bad enough that the oppressor is, all things considered, an oppressor: that we are sometimes expected to be grateful to him for occasional benignities is almost worse. There may be a real difference between self-styled 'stewards' and admitted 'despots', and many a decent officer of the British Raj (for example) may have served India well – but the world of nature needs our patronage even less than Indians needed the Empire. Who asked us to be 'stewards'?

In brief: one objection even to an admittedly harmless or benign piece of genetic engineering may be that we have no business exercising power like that. Why should we suppose that pain is the only intrinsic evil? The argument that it is an evil at all rests only on our dislike of it: if we also, when we come to think more clearly, dislike injustice as such, why should we not? The British (perhaps) should not have been in India at all, and therefore should not even have done good there. The objection is not that, by exercising imperial power even for immediately good ends, they also sapped native morale and fed their own self-conceit (an objection in terms of wider consequences which might have been avoided). It is simply that they 'had no business there', any more than I have any right to organize my neighbour's life – even if I would do it 'very well'. This objection, of course, is explicitly one that could be mounted against most or all farming practices for all recorded history. This is not (*pace* Sandøe and Holtug) an *answer* to the criticism. We ought not to manipulate the germ-line to produce creatures more to our taste (or to our medical need) for just the same reason that we ought not to have been domesticating, imprisoning, mutilating, breeding, killing them before. It is perfectly normal for people not to realize that they are doing wrong until their imagination is caught by some particular example of wrongdoing. It may well be that the wrong that awakens them is not really much more serious than many they have winked at or not seen. Brigadier-General Dyer probably did nothing very different, at Amritsar, than many worthy agents of the British Raj before him. His act nonetheless converted many because they were suddenly compelled to see what British rule implied. Until the eighteenth century every human society kept, and bred, (human) slaves: if we still did, I have no doubt that we would already be enforcing selective castration, AI and multiple conceptions. The next step on, to extra-uterine gestation and genetic engineering, is one that we may yet take (and reinvent slavery). Someone who objected to that step would not necessarily be much consoled to learn that we had already done almost as much. Should King David, on being told the story of the poor man's ewe, have decided that since he had himself (and most previous kings) behaved in much the same way, the rich man too was blameless?[8]

So the first objection to genetic engineering, even when there are no particular adverse effects to the animals involved (which of course there already have been), is that only someone unreasonably or immorally convinced that they had a right to interfere in the lives of others would even consider doing it. In the past we had some reason to believe that we did indeed have such a right over 'brutes', that God had given them into our hands (a view certainly not confined to Christianized Europe), and that they were of some radically different kind from ours. If those beliefs are false, it is difficult not to see 'domestication' as a cosy word for slavery.

Slavery may sometimes have been chosen by the slaves themselves, as an alternative to extermination. This is hardly a free contract, and does not obviously justify continued slavery for the first slaves'descendants.Those who campaigned (and still campaign) against human slavery may sometimes have been excited by particular abuses that were not really worse than others they neglected. Maybe it was the unfamiliarity or symbolic resonance of some abuse, far more than any ill effect upon the slave, that made them remember or re-imagine what slaves were. Similarly, genetic engineering may only be a novel manifestation of an attitude to brutes already displayed in earlier technocratic methods, and in 'traditional' farming practice. Its novelty may be enough to change our views of what we have already long accepted.

## 4. MAKING ARTEFACTS OUT OF ANIMALS

But *is* genetic engineering nothing more than a novel version of selective breeding? The fact that there is no one line between the two does not prove that they are the same (any more than twilight proves a real identity of dark and light). Ever since we 'domesticated' animals we have exerted pressure on them to conform to what we wish from them. But in earlier days that pressure was little more than we inflicted on our own species: all members of the early tribe or state were expected to conform, to do their duty even unto death, so that new lives might come to serve the gods, the ancestors, or what you will. Individual brutes might have as good a chance of living their lives as they preferred, within those constraints, as any individual humans. They could have 'normal' social relations with their conspecifics (sexual, parental, tribal) and with the humans who 'looked after' them (and maybe, in their fashion, even loved or worshipped them). But the balance has been shifting steadily: we human 'owners' have taken more and more away from what we call our 'property'.[9] In the beginning farm animals were herd animals, and there would usually be fewer males than females within the breeding stock. (The fate of young male mammals is almost always hard!) That suited our convenience, and we needed to do little more (at most) than help the males whose characters we preferred to win the mating game. We preyed upon the herd, but let it live. The progress of agricultural science, however, has taken more and more of this herd-life away. Our herds are no longer herds in the old sense: even if they are not 'intensively reared' they do not live in the polygynous groups they were first made for, nor do the breeding males have any other function than the stud. Genetic engineering is an obvious extension of the practices of keeping stud animals separate from the herd, artificial insemination, multiple ovulation, extra-uterine conception and the rest. We have tried to turn the brutes we once lived with into artefacts, and genetic engineering gives us, in prospect, the chance to design those artefacts just as we please. Holland[10] suggests that this objection to treating creatures as artefacts or instruments can be answered by proposing that we not treat them *only* as instruments. 'There is a distinction', he says, 'between using another creature's ends as your own – which is acceptable – and disregarding that other creature's ends entirely – which is not'. But when the creature's ends are only what the engineer has made them, this distinction seems to be vacuous. Old-style pastoralists identified the animals' ends, and worked out how to profit from them. New-style artificers work out where the profit lies, and mould the ends to suit them.

So it is not merely the novelty of the practice that awakens us to what we have been doing anyway: genetic engineering is a new thing, because we thereby achieve what some of us long wanted, but had not managed. The objection to it, irrespective of any particular adverse effect upon the animals concerned, is that the animals concerned are artefacts. That they are artefacts indeed may well subvert the welfare considerations that (we have agreed) must obviously carry weight. 'Shall the pot contend with the potter?' Insofar as we have made this or that transgenic animal, nothing that it suffers as a result of our genetic engineering can really be called an injury. As O'Donovan has pointed out, in a delicate and worrying enquiry into the application of these techniques to (putatively) *human* subjects, it would not be unreasonable to argue that 'no one can sue for injury who is dependent upon the alleged injury for his standing to sue'.[11] The transgenic brute is no 'worse off', however uncomfortable its life may be, because it would not be at all if the engineers had made it differently. If (for some reason) we did not want our artefacts to grumble (however irrationally!) we could engineer them otherwise – perhaps, at the extreme, as deaf, blind, legless, microcephalic lumps. This might cause less pain and suffering than any traditional practices (and to that extent appease welfarists) but would still be objectionable precisely in the failure to respect the real and independent existences even of present-day brutes.

This objection, to making living beings as artefacts, is not one that utilitarians could easily acknowledge. Oddly enough, it is not one that present-day 'rights theorists' would acknowledge either. Those microcephalic lumps are not the sort of creatures that have rights in Regan's theory, because they are designed not to be subjects-of-a-life at all.[12]

They are hardly more than tumours. The animals from whom they have been bred have rights in Regan's theory, but those rights, which do include the right not to be subjected to surgical invasion or enforced ejaculation, might be overridden to procure so great an improvement in the lives of 'natural' brutes (or such of them as we permitted to survive and resume their herd-life). Holland's position is more like the one I have sketched: 'I suggest that in general, and within the framework of a biotic community, there should be an objection to any practice which involves taking a form of life with a given level of capacity to exercise options and reducing that capacity significantly'.[13]

So genetic engineering may be wrong in itself because, first, it is one new instance of our wrongful oppression of our fellow creatures, and second because it completes the process whereby we have sought to deny all independent life to those we use. The first objection is to authoritarianism; the second to totalitarianism. Authoritarians allow their victims some life of their own, though they claim the right to discipline and direct them; totalitarians aim to obliterate all independent being.

## 5. THE INTEGRITY OF NATURAL LIFE

The mechanisms involved in the totalitarian enterprise may also be objectionable, precisely in that they divorce biological functions from the social nexus in which, at least for higher vertebrates, they have their natural being. The Vatican's somewhat stumbling argument that all sexual acts should take place within the marital relationship, and be open to the possibility of conception, may be unconvincing. It rests upon the widespread intuition that there is a natural order which, for us mammals, requires that functions not be dispersed. 'Taking the sex out of insemination' (a phrase used by veterinary students to describe a course in veterinary practice) is objectionable, to some, because natural living has its own integrity.

That notion of 'integrity' also occurs in objections to the copying of genetic material from one species to another. If there are real species, really different kinds, then their boundaries, it is said, should be respected. The ban on mixing kinds was derived, in Israel and Christendom, from *Leviticus* (19:19), and applies as well to the production of (infertile) hybrids by natural intercourse. Some people have even objected to 'miscegenation' within the human species – including a number of would-be politically correct social workers. Gene transference permits an even greater, and potentially more objectionable, erasure of boundaries. Creatures who can be induced to mate, or who willingly mate given the chance, cannot be so different in natural kind. Gene transference allows the possibility of radical miscegenation. Some of the objections here may turn upon an image of radical 'chimeras', creatures that do not fit within an existing species, which are not now feasible (which is not to say that they never could be). The characters that are currently being transferred are no more than minor, hardly visible alterations. The same alteration may be made by changing genes within the target organism to match a template from another species, but without even seeming to 'transfer an alien gene'. The kinds of alteration that are currently envisaged might even emerge by ordinary mutation. Even greater changes might emerge (and presumably did emerge, over many millenia) by such mutations. Are species (or any other biological taxa) really natural kinds?

Linzey[14] cites Vernon G. Pursel as saying, in response to criticism: 'I don't know what they mean when they talk about species integrity. . . . Much of the genetic material is the same, from worms to humans'. Why should we mind about allowing the transference or copying of genetic material across barriers that are largely fictitious? There are no sudden divisions in evolutionary history, and we here-now are of 'the same species' (except by arbitrary renaming) as creatures who have an equal claim to be 'of the same species' as chimpanzees or any other animal. Species are momentarily isolated groups of interbreeding populations, such that they may divide up into new species or even reform into a larger group (as lions and tigers, given the opportunity, just might.)[15] Nothing in current theory suggests that all members of a species have, or even ought to have, some morphological or behavioural or biochemical character in common that distinguishes them from members of another species. Genetic information probably already flows across the temporary boundaries (constituted by geographical or morphological or behavioural or biochemical barriers against successful interbreeding) through viral infection. Why worry about hurrying the process up, or even creating novel kinds more quickly than by traditional breeding practices?

It follows, of course, that 'human beings' do not constitute a natural kind, and that there is no distinctively 'human life'. Humanism, the proposal that all and only members of our species must be respected as creatures of a radically different kind even to other hominids, is dead. Even those of us who wish other animals to have something like the rights that have been assigned to humans need not be entirely glad of this. If 'human' no more names a real essence than does 'white' or 'European', then we may either seek to treat other animals with something like the respect we gave (or said we gave) to humans, or else (and perhaps more probably) begin to treat even our conspecifics with the same contempt we showed to 'brutes'. An ape-human hybrid might excite in us[16] a recognition of our brother or sister under the skin: he or she might as easily be hailed as having really 'tremendous potential as a research tool'. If 'human beings' do not constitute a kind all of whose members deserve a like, unique respect, what becomes of all the arguments in favour of using 'animals' for the sake of 'human beings'?

There are at least two available alternatives to humanism. The first, 'personism', accords a special moral status to creatures with a present capacity to communicate, reason, plan their lives, or share in 'normal' social life. A good many members of our species fall outside these different boundaries, and are accordingly often denied 'full human rights' (which are now attributed instead to 'persons', variously defined[17]). Personists do not object to invasive experiments on non-persons, so long as they are conducted 'humanely' (that is, without causing 'serious' pain or suffering). They probably have no serious objection to the deliberate production of such (biologically human) non-persons for experimental (or farming?) purposes. Any popular objection, they would be inclined to say, must rest upon irrational sentiment. Even 'human beings' that could develop into 'persons' have no special right to do so, and will not be injured by being reared to be non-persons if this happens to be convenient. There should, of course, be no public announcement of this policy until voters have been properly educated to accept it. Some personists are sufficiently alert to past corruption to recommend that we place 'fences around the law': all those born of woman should be given the benefit of any doubt. Even if newborns, imbeciles, lunatics, incorrigible criminals and the senile are not 'really' persons, we should pretend they are. We might also, and perhaps with better reason, pretend that great apes, dogs, cats and horses are.[18]

The second alternative to humanism has as yet no fully agreed form: 'animal liberation', 'radical zoophily', 'respect for the biotic community' have all been proposed as titles. Its essence is to demand respect for all the creatures with whom we share the world, and to propose for guidance that we live according to such laws as will give the best chance possible to all to live worthwhile lives according to their kinds.[19] 'Worthwhile lives according to their kinds': this is to assume that there are, after all, such kinds, and that different creatures will find fulfilment in different ways. Different animals have different natural *tele*.[20] Of the 'Five Freedoms' advocated by FAWC, the fourth ('freedom to express normal behaviour') is a diminished version of the radical demand. There is, after all, a difference between free living, in a habitat broadly adapted to one's interests, and being provided with 'sufficient space, proper facilities and the company of one's kind': the second might be available in gaol. Nonetheless, there is here some recognition that a 'normal life' is normative. The Home Office Inspectorate intends that GMOs (genetically modified organisms) will not be released from the protection of the Act of 1986 if they prove to be incapable of a normal life (without special human interventions): this also seems to rest on a perception that there is something 'normative' about the usual, free behaviour of creatures recognisably 'of the same kind'. This goes well beyond the mere avoidance of particular pains (even if mental pains, like boredom, loneliness or frustration, are taken into account).

Should zoophilists abandon talk of kinds entirely, and with that several apparent advances on the welfare front? If chickens (even unaltered chickens) can be induced to live and reproduce in battery conditions, is that any more oppressive than 'Nature's having induced emperor penguins to live in the Antarctic'? Everything that a particular gene-set can produce, within a given environment, is 'natural'. Some (perhaps all) genotypes are phenotypically variegated: what's wrong with that (as long as they don't 'suffer')?

It seems inevitable that those who urge respect for living organisms, and particularly animals, will suppose that there are more or less 'fulfilling' ways of life for them, that it would be possible at least to identify some failed phenotypes, some poor lives, even though there is no one 'perfect type' for any given species. In fact there need be no contradiction here. On the one hand, there are no rigid boundaries in nature; on the other, life realizes innumerable different forms of life. There are expectable natures, and natural norms of health and conduct. Species (that is, wholly or largely closed gene-pools) are created by the gradual adaptation of successive generations of an original species to different environments: that is, a new form of life emerges that is not well served by hybrids (who are therefore, along with parents inclined to hybridize, deselected). It will even, sometimes, be possible to say that most members of a given species are not living as their real natures would require. In one sense it may be 'natural enough' that they are living like that; in another, the life they are leading makes no real use of deeply significant capacities, or actively damages them. They are being asked to adapt to an environment so different from any that they or their ancestors have lived before that most of their capacities are unrealized or damaged. There is no need to suppose that there is only one environment, or even only one successful phenotype for creatures of that kind. Evolutionary theory itself suggests that species do divide, or are divided: but the new species do not step entirely outside the older way of life. Species are not fictions,[21] and neither are the natural kinds and families in which they fall.

So there is still some scope for concern about existing kinds, and maybe some good reason not to interfere too much. The variegated world of life is the product of a slow, exploratory process: a network of real forms, whose elegant beauty is often the real reason why researchers begin their work. With or without guidance, it seems to follow, the world of living nature offers us patterns that we should respect. At the very least, if we add to them, or fudge the boundaries, we should do so with a cautious love of what is actually there. It may seem tempting to suppose that we could remake our natures, and the natures of all other creatures here. There is undoubtedly a lot wrong with our natures: so why not remake them? But our recognition that we are imperfect beings itself rests on an acceptance of some given norms. One answer to disease is to prevent or cure it: another is not to mind. Which will be the easier condition to ensure, among domesticated brutes or 'lesser humans'?

## 6. BEAUTY AND THE BODY-SNATCHERS

Talk of natural *tele* apparently offends some biologists, who are inclined to detect mysticism or an obsolete Aristotelianism[22] in the term. There is no real need to be offended. The *telos* of a living being is simply that form of life for which it is fitted by evolutionary pressures, and by reference to which (as I have pointed out) we assess the positive well-being of the creature concerned. It is certainly *possible* that, by judicious interference, we could actually create a new form of life,[23] and associated organs and behaviour patterns: maybe there will one day be GMOs whose well-being will be by reference to a genuinely new *telos*. It is very unlikely, however, that, in the present state of knowledge, we will be doing anything but interfere in an existing form of life, and make it that much harder for the creatures concerned to live in the way that other aspects of their being would require.

Much of this objection rests on welfare considerations. But there is probably more to it than that. Pluhar[24] cites a paper by Stephen Jay Gould (*Discover*, January 1985) which is at once highly critical of Rifkin's book *Algeny* (presumably because Rifkin tried to enlist Gould himself in an attack on neo-Darwinian theory) and eloquent in its claim that scientists *love* the organisms they study. 'Scientists', he says, 'would not dissolve this handiwork of four billion years to satisfy the hubris of our species. *We respect the integrity of nature*' (my italics). It is not clear to me that Gould really speaks for scientists as a class upon this point, and I have some doubts about the meaning of the term 'love'. But I see no reason to doubt that he speaks for many. Some people doubtless enter their chosen profession only because it is there, or only to make money. Some scientists, like some picture salesmen, see nothing in the objects of their craft but instruments of their own profit. It is difficult for me to believe that this is the dominant view, or that such people are good craftsmen.

It may not be quite absurd to say that 'a species is not merely a hardbound volume in the library of nature. It is also a loose-leaf book, whose individual pages, the genes, might be available for selective transfer and modification of other species'.[25] The same is true of volumes in the local library: maybe a better book, in some sense, can be made by interweaving pages from existing books (maybe that is what most of us are doing much of the time!). But would a serious librarian happily do this? Existing beauties have their own claim on us. We are very unlikely to make *more* beautiful creatures, and even if we could we should continue to admire and love the old. Treating existing creatures merely as material is wrong, not simply because each such individual creature should be treated 'as an end, not merely as a means', but because, as living creatures, they display a beauty that good scientists admire.

It is this same beauty which perhaps explains some deeply felt reactions that too many established moralists despise. The suggestion that eggs might be taken from aborted foetuses, and fertilized, was greeted with disgust. Utilitarian moralists at once leapt in to say that such a reaction was 'irrational': why ever not allow new lives (or at least new experimental subjects) to be retrieved from what, by definition, was no use to anyone? For such moralists an aborted foetus is only 'a clump of cells', which might provide material. Even those women who have sought abortions do not usually regard the matter quite so lightly. Some respect, they usually believe, is owed the nascent being whom, for reasons that seemed good to them, they have evicted. Granted, the dead foetus has no opinion in the matter (and neither would the living one), and will not be hurt or harmed any more than she already has been by the removal of her eggs. Similarly, the dead bodies dug from their graves by nineteenth-century body-snatchers did not, then, care. Utilitarian moralists (at least of the cruder kind) did not care about the horror felt by the urban poor at the prospect that their dead, or they themselves once dead, would be dug up and dissected.

That horror may have been contaminated with some half-articulated thought that the dead would be affected by the act. It may also have fed upon the thought that people who would do this kind of thing must be so lacking in ordinary emotional affect that they could not be trusted not to do still worse to the living. But much of the horror rested in a wish to live, and die, 'in beauty'. Graveside ceremonial was mocked, and rendered meaningless, by body-snatchers. Removing eggs from aborted foetuses makes the ugliness of the act explicit, and affects our attitude to any possible human being born from those stolen eggs. 'The Frankenstein Thing' is a powerful association, as are ghouls: both lack the beauty that we will to see (and often do see) in nature.

We are horrified by what we see as ugly: we see as ugly what horrifies us. There is no point asking for any proof that these reactions are appropriate. Those who do not feel them will hardly understand them. It does not follow that we can, or should, dispense with them, or 'educate' ourselves out of them, even if there may be occasions when we come to see particular horrified reactions as misplaced. Of course, we sometimes change our mind, and learn to see a novel beauty: it does not follow that we are always wrong, but, on the contrary, that we are sometimes right. If nothing deserves an immediate response of love or horror, then neither does the Truth, or Rationality, or Human Welfare, or any other imagined ground of action. If something or other does, why not the very things to which most of us easily react? There is something wrong, ugly, horrifying about the sight of a living creature made so wretched that it can no longer even care; there is something wrong, ugly, horrifying about mammals transformed into milk machines, or microcephalic lumps. Or if there isn't, what becomes of rhetoric about how much biologists 'love' living creatures? If nothing at all could be done (say) to the Mona Lisa that would horrify a purported art-lover, what becomes of any claim that it is beautiful, or that the person in question loves it?

## 7. CONCLUSIONS

Even if genetic engineers had not already, and irrevocably, committed obvious wrongs, there are other categorical criticisms of the practice. We have no right to domesticate (enslave) our fellow creatures; we have no right to turn them into artefacts; we have no right to separate sexual and social functions; we have no right to ignore the pattern of kinds evolved through millions of years; we have no right to ignore the visceral response encapsulated in complaints about the use of foetal eggs. Overt and immediate consequences are not all that count. Some acts demonstrate a perverted judgment even if, by the grace of God, they do not bring direct disaster. It is at least worth wondering if modern biotechnological practices belong in that class.

## NOTES

1  Seamark (1993), p. 13; my italics.
2  Sandøe and Holtug (1993), p. 114ff.
3  Häyry (1994), p. 213.
4  House of Lords (1993).
5  Smith and Boyd (1991), p. 140.
6  Sandøe and Holtug (1993), p. 115.
7  Dyer compounded his apparent villainy by bragging of his behaviour in the presence of a young Indian lawyer named Jawaharlal Nehru, who was thereby converted to the Independence Movement: see Draper (1985), p. 178ff.
8  2 *Samuel* 12: 1–14.
9  On which history, see Ingold (1986).
10  Holland (1990), p. 170.
11  O'Donovan (1984), p. 84ff.
12  Regan (1983).
13  Holland (1990), p. 172.
14  Linzey (1990), p. 184.
15  Wilson (1992), p. 39 notes that lions and tigers did not interbreed even when their ranges overlapped: their habits are too different for 'adults of the two species to meet and bond long enough to produce offspring'. But their habits are not *essential*: times and types may change.
16  As Dawkins (1993) suggests; and see Clark (1993a).
17  See Teichman (1994).
18  See Singer and Cavalieri (1993).
19  See Clark (1989), pp. 135–58.
20  See Rollin (1981), (1986); Fox (1992), pp. 22–4.
21  See Wilson (1992), p. 43.
22  Aristotle himself, *pace* too many popular histories, did *not* believe in immutable and essentially different species.
23  See Pluhar (1986).
24  Pluhar (1986), p. 15.
25  Thomas Eisner, cited by Wilson (1992), p. 302.

## REFERENCES

Clark, S. R. L. (1988): 'Is Humanity a Natural Kind?', in T. Ingold (ed.), *What is an Animal?* (London: Unwin Hyman), pp. 17–34.
—— (1989): *Civil Peace and Sacred Order* (Oxford: Clarendon Press).
—— (1993a): 'Apes and the Idea of Kindred', in Singer and Cavalieri (1993), pp. 113–25.
—— (1993b): 'The Better Part', in A. Phillips Griffiths (ed.), *Ethics* (Cambridge: Cambridge University Press), pp. 29–49.
—— (1994): 'Modern Errors, Ancient Virtues', in Dyson and Harris (1994), pp. 13–32.
Dawkins, R. (1993): 'Gaps in the Mind', in Singer and Cavalieri (1993), pp. 80–7.
Draper, A. (1985): *The Amritsar Massacre: Twilight of the Raj* (London: Buchan and Enright).

76     *Human Lives*

Dyson, A. and Harris, J. (1994) (eds.): *Ethics and Biotechnology* (London: Routledge).
Fox, M. W. (1990): 'Why BST Must be Opposed', in Wheale and McNally (1990), pp. 87–92.
—— (1992): *Superpigs and Wondercorn* (New York: Lyons and Burford).
Häyry, M. (1994): 'Categorical Objections to Genetic Engineering', in Dyson and Harris (1994), pp. 202–15.
Holland, A. (1990): 'The Biotic Community', in Wheale and McNally (1990), pp. 161–74.
House of Lords (1993): *Regulation of the UK Biotechnology Industry and Global Competitiveness* (HMSO).
Ingold, T. (1986): *The Appropriation of Nature* (Manchester: Manchester University Press).
Linzey, A. (1990): 'Human and Animal Slavery', in Wheale and McNally (1990), pp. 175–88.
O'Donovan, O. (1984): *Begotten or Made?* (Oxford: Clarendon Press).
Pluhar, E. (1985): 'On the Genetic Manipulation of Animals', *Between the Species* 1, pp. 13–18.
Polkinghorne, J. (1993) (chair): *Report of the Committee on the Ethics of Genetic Modification and Food Use* (HMSO).
Regan, T. (1983): *The Case for Animal Rights* (London: Routledge and Kegan Paul).
Rifkin, J. (1984): *Algeny* (Harmondsworth: Penguin).
Rollin, B. (1981): *Animal Rights and Human Morality* (Buffalo: Prometheus Books).
—— (1986): 'On *Telos* and Genetic Manipulation', *Between the Species* 2, pp. 88–9.
Sandøe, P. and Holtug, N. (1993): 'Transgenic Animals – Which Worries are Ethically Significant?', *Livestock Production Science* 36, pp. 113–16.
Seamark, R. F. (1993): 'Recent Advances in Animal Biotechnology: Welfare and Ethical Implications', *Livestock Production Science* 36, pp. 5–15.
Singer, P. and Cavalieri, P. (1993) (eds.): *The Great Ape Project* (London: Fourth Estate).
Smith, J. A. and Boyd, K. M. (1991) (eds.): *Lives in the Balance* (Oxford: OUP).
Teichman, J. (1994): 'Freedom of Speech and the Public Platform', *Journal of Applied Philosophy* 11, pp. 99–105.
Thompson, P. B. (1993): 'Genetically Modified Animals: Ethical Issues', *Journal of Animal Science* 71 (Suppl. 3), pp. 51–6.
Wheale, P. and McNally, R. (1990) (eds.): *The Bio-Revolution: Cornucopia or Pandora's Box* (London: Pluto Press).
Wilson, E. O. (1992): *The Diversity of Life* (Cambridge, Mass.: Harvard University Press).

# 4 The Moral Uniqueness of the Human Animal

*Brian Scarlett*

Peter Singer crusades against what he sees as a deeply entrenched form of barbarism, the common human attitude towards non-human animals. (I will generally call them 'animals' for short.) His advocacy of animals explicitly relates their claims to those of humans, denying the possibility of a species-based difference in treatment. The closure of the customary gap between humans and animals could take the status of one of the pair as fixed and shift the other. But the way Singer does it leaves neither where it was: animals are promoted and humans are demoted. The latter caused Singer trouble in Germany in 1989, trouble which he and his associate Helga Kuhse attribute to a reaction to their advocacy of euthanasia 'for severely disabled newborn infants'.[1] Their opponents, they say, were misled by a defective translation, including a sentence which they repudiate and deny ever having uttered, *viz.* that it is 'possible and necessary to distinguish between life that is worth living and life that is not worth living, and to destroy that which is not'.[2] Allowing this disavowal, the fact remains that their book clearly sanctions the killing of infants whose lives are admitted to be worth living, and it does this, not in any possibly equivocal or inadvertent aside, but in a detailed argument over thirty pages long.[3] The claim of misinterpretation is disingenuous.

'All animals are equal', Singer proclaimed in 1973,[4] but the proclamation requires some care in interpretation. In the light of various qualifications outlined in his article, this is what it amounts to: *we should extend to other animal species the basic principle of equality of consideration, not necessarily of treatment and rights, that applies to all members of our own species.*

Equality of *consideration* is said to be required because there are many cases where you cannot grant equal rights to animals and people. People have a right to vote; animals cannot have a right to vote because voting is beyond them. But this, we are told, does not weaken the claim to equality of all creatures: biological differences produce differences in the rights of men and women, in the matter of medical treatment for example. Still, in some sense, men and women have equal rights.[5]

We are told that the argument for equality of consideration does not rely on factual equality: it is a statement of an ideal. People frequently

77

argue for equality or inequality on the basis of objective evidence, but Singer thinks that his approach 'goes more deeply into the question of equality'. The profound approach recognizes that factual differences between people constitute a problem: '[I]f the demand for equality were based on the actual equality of all human beings, we would have to stop demanding equality. It would be an unjustifiable demand'.[6] Nor is it any good to claim that individual differences are submerged in group similarities: this approach offers too many hostages to scientific progress, and even if it turned out to be true it would provide no defence against bias against individuals who were inferior in the relevant capacity.[7] The solution is that:

> the claim to equality does not depend on intelligence, moral capacity, physical strength, or similar matters of fact. Equality is a moral ideal, not a simple assertion of fact... The principle of the equality of human beings is *not a description of an alleged actual equality* among humans: it is *a prescription* of how we should treat humans.[8]

And again,

> if humans are to be regarded as equal to one another, we need some sense of 'equal' that does not require *any* actual, descriptive equality of capacities, talents, or other qualities.[9]

This is a departure from the tradition of struggle for equality. *A Supplement to The Oxford English Dictionary* locates the first use of the word 'speciesism' in 1975, in a book by R. D. Ryder:[10]

> I use the word 'speciesism' to describe the widespread discrimination that is practised by man against other species. Speciesism and racism both overlook or underestimate the similarities between the discriminator and those discriminated against.

Thus the first recorded use of the word defines it in terms of overlooking salient similarities. That is certainly the way racists and misogynists proceed, and it is in these terms that they are rebutted. Someone might argue that women should not be allowed to vote or to be fighter pilots or university professors – whatever the issue might be – because they are as unqualified to do so as dogs and cats. The straightforward reply is that this claim is *demonstrably factually wrong*. We know that women are capable of these activities, because we have witnessed them performing these or similar tasks. And we know that dogs and cats cannot do anything remotely like the tasks mentioned. One of the faults of the misogynist's position is that it is based on a nonsensical factual claim. As Hannah

Arendt said about anti-Semitism, it is 'an outrage to common sense'.[11] That this is the way the equality tradition has proceeded is evident from the following quick reminder of the sorts of claim it has involved:

> The American Declaration of Independence proclaimed, as *self-evident truths*, 'that all men *are created equal*, that *they are endowed* by their Creator with certain unalienable Rights'; the Declaration of 1789 echoed: '*Men are born* and live free and *equal in their rights*'; and that of 1948: '*All human beings are born free and equal in dignity and rights*'.[12]

The facts asserted here are salient in an account of human life and important consequences follow for the way we ought to treat each other. The claims are factual *and* prescriptive, though the prescriptive element is not explicit in the brief digest which we have before us. Such factual talk can be recast as pure prescriptions, not involving claims about fact, but why bother? If all we have to do is prescribe, animal liberation is no better placed than stuffed toy liberation or animal extermination.

In any case, there is no need for this draconian solution. The drafters of the declarations of rights would have been stupid indeed if they thought that people are equal in strength, beauty, wisdom, intelligence and so on. They thought that, inequalities aside, there is a basic human reality in which we are equal, so that racism and sexism are not acceptable. If they were wrong, there would be no basis for opposing racism and sexism. Just so, advocates of animal rights must show that there is a factual basis underpinning their prescriptions. Despite his preference for prescriptivism, Singer also frequently takes this line. A passage in his *Practical Ethics* suggests that he is interested in a factual basis, but holds that it will not serve to refute racism and sexism: we have to consider individuals individually.[13] I will refer to this atomistic individualism later. He says that he doubts that there are any natural qualities underpinning equality but then goes on to speak about the undesirability of pain *qua* pain, no matter who or what is suffering it.[14] He sounds Aristotelian when endorsing sociobiology which 'enables us to see ethics as a mode of human reasoning which develops in a group context, building on more limited, biologically based forms of altruism'.[15] He quotes with approval Bentham's claim that the crucial question about animals is, 'Can they suffer?'[16]

The capacity to suffer and enjoy is a *right-conferring characteristic*. If you are an enjoyer and sufferer, you qualify for consideration. To get to equality of consideration you need only to suppose with Bentham, first that there are no other right-conferring characteristics, and second, that 'quantity of pleasure being equal, push-pin is as good as poetry'.[17] That we have here a genuine basis for consideration is made clear by the opinion that animals are automata, a view illustrated in a story told about the Cartesian philosopher Malebranche:

> M. de Fontenelle told the story of a time he went to visit Father Malebranche at the Oratory on the Rue Saint-Honoré. They had a large dog in the house, a pregnant bitch. This dog came into the room where they were walking up and down and started rubbing itself affectionately against Father Malebranche and rolling over at his feet. After several ineffectual attempts to chase her away the philosopher gave her a vigorous kick. The dog yelped with pain and M. de Fontenelle cried out compassionately. 'What', said Father Malebranche coldly, 'surely you know that that thing doesn't feel anything at all?'[18]

If animals are automata, as Malebranche supposed, we cannot wrong them; if they have a capacity for pain, we can. Consider the story in chapter 5 of Dostoevsky's *Crime and Punishment*, where a man cruelly beats his small and overloaded mare, eventually being joined by his drunken friends in killing her. The horror of this story cannot survive the substitution of a car for the horse. Destroying the car may wrong someone, but it is not the car; the car does not know about it, has no preferences, has no interests either way. The horse suffers, and that is morally significant. I might, on Benthamite grounds, leave all my property to the lost dogs' home; I could not leave it in trust to have my car maintained in perpetuity by caring mechanics.

Among the views which Singer wants to attack there is the claim that humans have a right to inflict suffering on non-humans for trivial purposes. A reflection on Malebranche's dog and Nikola's mare shows that he is right to object. But there is nothing radical about this view. It enjoys such wide agreement that it would not be misleading to call it The Common View. I take that view to be approximately the following: non-human animals are inferior forms of life compared with us; it is permissible to kill animals for food and to use them for other human purposes; it is, however, wrong to treat them cruelly. There is debate and disagreement within The Common View – it is not a case of there being only attacks from outside. Still, there is agreement on the main lines indicated. That consensus provides at least a version of what Singer demands, equality of consideration without any inevitable equality of treatment. Since Singer's thesis is meant to overthrow the consensus, something appears to have gone wrong.

The issues involved can be made clearer by way of a political analogy. Suppose that to qualify as an elector you must pass a property qualification – let us say an income of $50,000 per annum. This level of wealth is a *threshold property.* Jack and Jill are equal in respect of being qualified as electors, even though she is ten times richer than him.[19] The arrangement, as described, is silent on whether there is provision for the wealthier getting more votes. Let us call the arrangement where no one gets more than one vote a *simple threshold constitution.* A different system, drawing on the model of the distribution of dividends to shareholders, provides that there is a correlation between wealth and votes: perhaps each $10,000 over the threshold provides one extra vote. Let us call this arrangement a *simple cumulative constitution.* This superimposes inequality on the equality involved in the *simple threshold constitution.* But further inequalities can be produced. Let us suppose that a certain high level of wealth qualifies the elector for public office, not merely for additional votes. We could call this a *simple hierarchical constitution.*

The point in calling all of these 'simple' is that they recognize only one source of rights and they deal with the distribution of a simple and restricted class of goods. *Complex constitutions*, in various permutations, are obviously possible – but even the simple constitutions provide models for thinking about equality and inequality. Ignoring this complication initially, I will refer simply to the threshold model, the cumulative model and the hierarchical model.

All of these arrangements, even the least egalitarian (the hierarchical) provide for equality of consideration. All the electors are equal in having their wealth recognized. They are equal in being included on the electoral roll, and in what follows from being enrolled. Similarly, equality of consideration for animals can be illustrated by that model. The welfare of each sentient creature is considered, just as each person who makes the income qualification is permitted to vote. Beyond that equality it is all inequality. The adherents of The Common View draw the line at cruelty, just as the oligarchs draw the line at disenfranchising those at the lower end of their scale of wealth. They thus both satisfy the demand for basic equality overlaid with inequality.

If any position on animal rights approximates to the threshold model, it would be Bentham's. The capacity to suffer and enjoy establishes the claim to consideration and 'quantity of pleasure being equal, push-pin is as good as poetry'. Mill could not accept this, holding that:

> It is better to be a human being dissatisfied than a pig satisfied; better to be Socrates dissatisfied than a fool satisfied. And if the fool, or the pig, is of a different opinion, it is because they only know their own side of the question. The other party to the comparison knows both sides.[20]

If Mill is right we ought not to be thinking in terms of threshold require-ments. Socrates should have his interests routinely and in principle preferred to the interests of any pig. In particular cases, e.g. provision of veterinary medicine and pigsties, Socrates misses out. But on Mill's eva-luative schema he generally and overwhelmingly prevails over the pig. Mill is endorsing not just the cumulative model, but the hierarchical model, elevating some creatures – humans – to an entirely different plane. His judgment is in accord with The Common View.

We can make some progress in resolving the Bentham-Mill dispute by seeing what falls within the Kingdom *Animalia*, the beneficiaries of the equality thesis. It includes us, and it includes the great apes, but it also in-cludes some rather unlikely candidates for equality: sponges, jellyfish, sea anemones and coral, flatworms, ectoparasitic and endoparasitic flukes, tapeworms, leeches, ticks and mites, fish lice, slaters and wood lice, milli-pedes and centipedes, insects, snails, sea cucumbers, and so on.[21]

How do these lower creatures rate on the capacity to suffer and enjoy? Many rely here on the Cartesian argument from analogy, accepting the ineluctable privacy of the mental but believing that behaviour analogous to our own pain-avoidance behaviour is similarly caused by similar pain.[22] There is also, not surprisingly, a good deal of scepticism about an-imal pain. J. S. Kennedy regards Descartes' bête-machine hypothesis as a rather splendid intellectual achievement in the face of vitalism and anthropomorphism.[23] Peter Carruthers suggests that we could under-stand animal consciousness along the lines of certain familiar human performances (like driving without being consciously aware of what we are doing), a phenomenon exploited by David Armstrong as a reduction-ist model of human consciousness.[24] P. D. F. Murray suggests that proto-zoan responses to stimuli are probably unconscious.[25] Some biologists tend towards agnosticism: '. . . we have no way of answering questions of the general type "do worms feel pain?" '[26]

Singer is plainly impatient with scepticism about animal minds, sug-gesting at one point that '[r]eaders whose common sense tells them that animals do suffer may prefer to skip the remainder of this section' . . . all six pages of it.[27] But this perfunctory treatment does not solve the pro-blem. Singer finds it necessary to move from the simple hypothesis, that animals feel, to a restriction to those with physiology similar to ours, and he cites without protest an authority who restricts it to higher mam-malian vertebrates.[28] But let us start at a low level.

It is well known that stimulus-response connections can be found not only in the lower animals but even in plants, not presently candidates for equality. Tropisms, such as are witnessed in the behaviour of bean shoots, have not yet been enough to engender sympathy. Amoebae, which do not qualify for membership in the Kingdom of *Animalia*, are capable of animal-like movements away from unfavourable environments. Pain gets a foothold here, as Wittgenstein said of the wriggling fly.[29] We cannot rule amoebae out of consideration merely because they are not animals: that would be kingdomism. Suppose, then, that we set aside our scepticism and adopt the view that amoebae are capable of pain. We believe that the amoeba has some measure of consciousness, and that some of the conscious episodes in its life are painful, i.e. that what we understand to be avoidance behaviour is accompanied by states of consciousness which are phenomenologically distressing and which function as causes of the avoidance behaviour.

If an amoeba can suffer pain, then we and the amoeba are alike in that respect. But we and the amoeba do not have an equal capacity for pain. Just so, Jack and Jill are alike in being wealthy but, since she has ten times as much money as he has, they cannot be said to be equally wealthy. If we wanted to maintain human-amoeba equality in the face of the known inequality, we would have to invoke the idea of threshold requirements. Then we might say that we and the amoeba are equal in suffering pain. But if we do, we must expect to be misunderstood as maintaining the false thesis that we and the amoeba have an equal capacity to suffer pain. Similarly, if we say that Jack and Jill are equal in being wealthy we can expect to be misunderstood as meaning that they are equally wealthy.

Such attenuated equality of humans and amoebae is not adequate to sustain equality of treatment, nor is it adequate to sustain anything beyond a threshold equality of consideration. That requires only that pain, no matter what suffers it, is a reason for not doing what causes the pain. In the amoeba case we would have a reason to condemn the gratuitous introduction of drops of acid into a bowl of water containing amoebae. But it does not follow that we have a weighty reason, nor does it commit us to regarding amoeba pain as seriously as, say, elephant pain. Unless we have succeeded in generating a thoroughgoing Walt Disney theory of amoebae, we are likely to think that amoeba pain would be dim and feeble. We are also very likely to regard it as episodic in a way which undermines its claim to be treated seriously: suppose that the amoeba has no psychological history, and its pain episodes, atomistically functional, are utterly disconnected from each other. Then an amoeba would not qualify as a sufferer in the way a creature with a memory of its past could be a sufferer. The simple threshold model, therefore, does not provide an equality thesis in any interesting sense. The consideration given to the creatures which merely satisfy the threshold requirement might not be significantly different from

the consideration given to inanimate systems recognized as being of value
– mountain ranges, for example. There is nothing in this to found a distinction between Singer's equality thesis and The Common View. With all
the anthropomorphizing goodwill in the world we would find ourselves
adopting the cumulative model at least, if not the hierarchical model.

You might say that I am being unfair to Singer, that he has no intention
of extending equal rights to amoebae, tapeworms, and the like. But there
is a question of how seriously we are to treat his endorsement of
Bentham's idea that the key question is, 'Can they suffer?' He can restrict
equality of consideration to higher animals – dogs and cats, the apes, ele-
phants, sheep and cattle, and so on, but at a cost. For the restriction is a
form of speciesism. If it is speciesism to make a cut between humans
and apes, why is it not speciesist to make a cut within the animalia? Why
do we make the cut, and why do we make it just where we do? Is it simply
a recognition of the inescapable deficiencies of the threshold model,
or are there higher forms of life after all? If Singer's arguments work
against The Common View, they work also against this revised version
of speciesism.

The argument so far has proceeded on the assumption that a simple
model is adequate for the case, that is to say that there is only one right-
conferring characteristic. This assumption is favourable to the equality
thesis, since it tends to submerge the characteristic capacities of humans.
But it is a bizarre way of looking at life, since there are many specifically
human capacities which are relevant to moral status. Beliefs, according
to Frank Ramsey and D. M. Armstrong, are maps by which we steer.[30]
This is a fruitful analogy in this respect: some maps are very schematic,
featuring food, drink, sex, danger, pain. Others are much more detailed,
adding to these features efficiency of tactics and policies, suitability for
our nature, the rights of others, nobility and baseness. Such maps are
more interesting but harder to read – and we can get into trouble trying
to read them. We can be overcome by existentialist *angst* or become
addicts of discourse, as Gilbert Ryle once said of Hamlet. We wear ourselves out poring over our maps instead of acting quickly and cleanly like
a cat. We can, in short, become victims of information overload. A
simple form of this is neatly expressed in the last verse of Robert Burns's
poem 'To a Mouse':

> Still thou art blest, compar'd wi' me !
> The present only toucheth thee:
> But och! I backward cast my e'e,
>       On prospects drear!

An' forward, tho' I canna see,
     I guess an' fear!

The difference noted by Burns affords special opportunities for pleasure and pain, frustration and satisfaction, and they make the threshold model useless for an equality thesis. The stakes are being raised, but we are nowhere near the limit. A further step takes us to moral and legal responsibility.

Animals are not guilty, whatever the offence might be. They sometimes do undesirable things, and sometimes we apply punishment to train them not to repeat the damage. And sometimes we kill them to make sure, as in the case of man-eaters and savage dogs. But we do not hold that they are to blame. We may be speciesists, but we do not accuse the lion and the leopard of speciesism, or of murder, when they kill and eat antelopes, nor even when they kill and eat people. At least, we do not usually – though Singer once seriously considered the possibility of eliminating the carnivores, rejecting the proposal because of a lack of confidence in our capacity for ecological management.[31]

Legal proceedings against animals have a long history. Plato provides for them.[32] A standard work on the subject lists cases of the prosecution and legally imposed punishment of animals as late as 1906, the year of the book's publication.[33] The thinking behind this fascinating anthropomorphism is beside the point here. For my purposes it is enough to recognize that if these proceedings are to be taken at face value they involve a colossal misclassification. But in identifying this animal-human difference we have still not yet reached the limit of what persons are capable of. To jump ahead a suitable distance, we can invoke Charles Taylor's notion of strong evaluation. Taylor discusses two fundamentally different levels of self-criticism, occasioned in this case by the habit of over-eating. One is in terms of qualitative contrasts, the other merely in terms of outcomes for one's health and the enjoyment of other goods. The distinction is neatly summed up in a speculation about a gluttony pill:

> Someone might even invent some drug which would allow me to go on eating rich desserts and also enjoy all those other goods, whereas no drug would allow me to eat my cake and attain the dignity of an autonomous, self-disciplined agent which I pined after on my first reading of the issue.[34]

We have come to a very high-level capacity. People have lives and projects in a way that is far beyond the capacities of animals. Indeed, it is not just the higher of these two forms of appraisal which is beyond the capacity of animals. We can see, then, that self-consciousness varies greatly in scope, kind and degree. It varies in scope as it spreads from the present and immediate future backwards and forwards over a whole life: it is whole lives which are, or can be, the subject of human strong evaluation. It varies in kind as it moves from pleasure and pain through efficiency, variously construed, to meditations about what is suitable for our nature. It varies in depth as it moves from weak to strong evaluation. Since we have this wide variation, no appeal to sub-personifying characteristics will close the gap.

Now Singer is certainly aware of differences of at least this general type, and finds no difficulty in them. Snails do not have plans for the future; fish are less conscious of themselves as continuing beings than we are; animals are not as subject as we are to anticipatory dread.[35] Moreover, he has no objection to a hierarchical ordering of forms of life on the basis of consciousness, self-awareness and rationality;[36] he says that the possession or lack of self-consciousness makes the difference between a creature's being replaceable or not.[37] Yet again Singer's views align themselves with The Common View. How is his purported novelty or radicalism to be salvaged? Only, I think, by a revision of the extension of the concept of a rational, self-aware being, including some animals and excluding some people.

On The Common View, claims of animal equality are unjustified because they apply to animals a level of psychological and moral sophistication which they do not have. In the matter of criminal prosecution of animals, for example, defence counsel would have no problem in showing that the accused animals did not satisfy the test for sanity embodied in the McNaghten Rules. Animals are not autonomous in the required way. Their incapacity is partly linguistic. If the animals are to be *guilty* they must have concepts of intention, of right and wrong, of temptation and of resistance, of virtue and vice. If we were to believe they had these concepts we would need *behavioural evidence*. Conceptual schemes are ways of making distinctions about the world. If the life of an individual or group does not reveal discriminations based on these distinctions, this counts as evidence either that they do not have those concepts or that, if they do, they are not operative in their lives.

In the case of the animals, we can rule out one of those possibilities over a wide range of cases. They may have the primitive ancestors of some of the moral concepts, but they plainly lack others. There is a *Punch* cartoon in which two hippopotamuses in a lake on a treeless plain are conversing. One says to the other: 'I keep thinking it's Tuesday.' What is Tuesday to a hippopotamus? Nothing. But it is not clear that Singer would agree that this is anything but a contingent disability.

In 1661 Samuel Pepys wrote in his diary a comment on the intellectual powers of the great apes:

> At the office in the morning and did business. By and by we are called to Sir W. Battens to see the strange creature that Captain Holmes hath brought with him from Guiny; it is a great baboone, but so much like a man in most things, that (though they say there is a Species of them) yet I cannot believe but that it is a monster got of a man and she-baboone. I do believe it already understands much english; and I am of the mind it might be tought to speak or make signs.[38]

At around the same time his countryman, the philosopher John Locke, in a section of his *Essay Concerning Human Understanding* headed 'Brutes abstract not', said:

> this, I think, I may be positive in, that the power of *abstracting* is not at all in them; and that the having of general *ideas* is that which puts a perfect distinction betwixt man and brutes, and is an excellency which the faculties of brutes do by no means attain to. For it is evident we observe no footsteps in them of making use of general signs for universal *ideas*...[39]

Was Pepys absurdly credulous? Was Locke absurdly sceptical? Locke required behavioural evidence and found none. Did he look hard enough? Singer would think not. He suggests that there is behavioural evidence that apes, dolphins and even dogs can think.[40] Elsewhere he and Kuhse report the evidence that some apes can be taught sign language and exhibit other symptoms of thought.

Certainly chimpanzees and gorillas show some degree of self-awareness. Washoe, the first chimpanzee to be taught sign language, was asked, as she was looking into a mirror, 'Who is that?' She made the signs for: 'Me, Washoe'. There is also good evidence that chimpanzees plan for the future. Jane Goodall, observing wild chimpanzees in Uganda, has given an account of how a lower-ranking chimpanzee who noticed a banana in a tree did not move directly towards the fruit, but instead went elsewhere until a higher-ranking chimpanzee had left the area; only then, some fifteen minutes later, did the first chimpanzee return and take the fruit.[41]

The case which springs to mind here is that of Clever Hans, the supposedly telepathic horse which was eventually discovered to be responding to cues from a human attendant. Rationality requires caution in these cases; a sound rule is the psychological corollary to Occam's razor articulated by Lloyd Morgan:

In no case may we interpret an action as the outcome of a higher psychical faculty, if it can be interpreted as the outcome of one which stands lower in the psychological scale.[42]

Even an informal application of this principle of intellectual hygiene casts doubt on the veracity of the claims. Jane Goodall, rightly cited above as an authority on chimpanzee behaviour, does not share the enthusiasm of Singer and Kuhse. After quoting the story about 'Me, Washoe', and making it clear that she regards the sign language learning as of considerable significance, she says:

> Man is aware of himself in a very different way from the dawning awareness of the chimpanzee. He is not just conscious that the body he sees in a mirror is 'I', that his hair and his eyes belong to *him*, that if a certain event occurs *he* will be afraid, or pleased, or sad. Man's awareness of Self supersedes the primitive awareness of a fleshly body. Man demands an explanation of the mystery of his being and the wonder of the world around him and the cosmos above him . . . . It should not be surprising that a chimpanzee can recognize himself in a mirror. But what if a chimpanzee wept tears when he heard Bach thundering from a cathedral organ?[43]

Perhaps explanations of the Clever Hans type can be excluded. But that would be far from enough because the 'intellectual' performance claimed is too feeble to cause blurring of the boundaries. Many people have drawn attention to these problems. A current school textbook of psychology, a very superficial work confessedly aimed at providing a quick survey of the field, finds it necessary to report difficulties for the Washoe story (and, incidentally, for Piaget's doctrines about the capacities of human infants.)[44] Readily accessible surveys of the field tell the same story. Richard Gregory, in discussing these claims, notes that symbols preceded humans; he lists sexual recognition, warning for danger, the location of nectar, threat, enticement and play as animal activities with a symbolic component.[45] The nectar location case involves the transmission of information of great complexity. Why then do the bees not qualify for equality? Well, for one thing they do nothing but transmit information: they do not question, argue, make jokes, wonder whether it all matters. Their performance, impressive as it is, is by contrast singularly restricted.

Washoe's case is similar: a repertoire of 132 signs and the capacity to conjoin up to five of them. She asks for things but does not ask questions.[46] But even this presupposes that the Clever Hans model can be ruled out. A critic of the Gardners' work with Washoe complains that their reports do not exclude the possibility that the appropriate answer was indicated by the experimenter's pointing to it.[47] Indeed there is a substantial body of critical material which has severely diminished the original enthusiasm for the ape language hypothesis.[48]

The other side of the attempt to close the human-animal gap is the denigration of the capacities of human infants. The two tendencies come together in the following passage in which Singer and Kuhse endorse Michael Tooley's suggestion,

> that we reserve the term 'person' for those beings who are capable of understanding that they are continuing selves. In this he follows the seventeenth-century British philosopher John Locke, who defined a 'person' as
>> A thinking intelligent being that has reason and reflection and can consider itself as itself, the same thinking thing, in different times and places.
> ... Neither human foetuses, nor human infants, nor humans with very severe retardation or brain damage would be persons. On the other hand chimpanzees might be, and so might some other non-human animals as well. Thus the notion of a person ... reflects no arbitrary, species-based boundary, but characteristics of obvious relevance to the wrongness of killing.[49]

Elsewhere Singer quotes and endorses Bentham's claim that 'a full-grown horse or dog is beyond comparison a more rational, as well as a more conversable animal than an infant of a day or a week or even a month.'[50]

Just as the promotion of the animals has been subject to scientific criticism, so has the demotion of infants. Much of our thinking about the capacities of children derives from the work of Piaget, but that has been criticized on the grounds that the young subjects of his 'decentration' experiments of 1956 did not understand the instructions.[51] Psychology provides systematic accounts of what virtually any parent of an infant knows, that they are much more capable than has been supposed:

> babies no more than a few minutes old may adapt their orientations and states of alertness to fit the motions of objects that are remote from their bodies ... they rapidly acquire rules for making perceptual distinctions, and they record the timing and location of recent happe-

nings... Events caused by human movements hold the greatest interest for them.
Conditioning tests, in which new-born infants have to react to and anticipate repeated events, show that they may generate predictive strategies... Expressions of concentrated puzzlement, surprise, pleasure, and displeasure are clearly delineated... Evidently babies are ready to show a variety of feelings to others.[52]

Signs of infant sociability, so striking a feature of ordinary life, are also vindicated in a convergence of psychology and common experience. Trevarthen notes that paediatricians and mothers subliminally pick up behavioural signs of an infant's condition and needs which have only recently been studied with precision by developmental psychologists. He catalogues various signs of interpersonal relations from the infant point of view and, referring to the denial that infants can imitate others, says: 'Denial of this ability to imitate reflects a strange, culturally induced belief that a new-born cannot have awareness of persons as such.'[53]

Now even if all of this domestic and scientific criticism were to be shown to be baseless, the Singer thesis is philosophically seriously incomplete. Consider the following premises to be used in a case for the prosecution on the charge of speciesism:

1. The actual performance of any infant is well below the actual performance of some animals.
2. We nonetheless discriminate in favour of infants.

Even if (1) were true, the case is not complete for at least two reasons, the first of which is that it does not consider the moral relevance of potential. To argue that infants may be killed for utilitarian reasons because they are not persons presupposes that their vastly higher potential does not make a difference — that if they are not now producers and consumers of units of hedonic or rational value, they have no current claim on the status of persons. The case therefore needs a further premise, say

3. Differences in potential do not justify any difference in treatment.

It is hard to see how this premise is compatible with an interest in the utilitarian accumulation of units of pleasure. More seriously, it is hard to see how we might impugn our regular use of potential to justify preferential treatment, both positive and negative. For example, we sometimes give jobs on the basis of potential, preferring the promise of brilliance to solid established performance. Again, moving to a case where life and death are the outcomes, if we found that the children's playground contained a large number of young tiger snakes, only potentially venomous, we would certainly not rule out killing them to protect the children from the actually venomous adult snakes that they were on the way to becoming.

The above cases satisfy the desideratum of a well-developed categorical basis for potential.[54] Certainly actual possession of a capacity provides a stronger entitlement than mere potential: I may boil an egg, the repository of avian potential, but I may not boil a living bird, the actual possessor of avian capacities. Even so, a telling case can be provided of life and death preference for potential where there is only a remote categorical base. Suppose that I have in my charge a single fertilized egg of the rare whooping crane and fifty adult Rhode Island Red hens. The economy of the situation is that I cannot both foster the egg and treat the hens which are suffering from a curable but fatal disease. I choose the welfare of the egg, reasoning that an uncertain contribution to the survival of an endangered species is more valuable than saving fifty boringly commonplace birds. Here potential is preferred to actuality, even though the value which the potential has (to develop as a member of an endangered species) is a purely extrinsic one, not at all as important as the difference between humans and animals.

The relevance of potential aside, there remains a final philosophical obstacle, namely an ambiguity in the concept of a person. Aquinas cites and endorses the definition of person offered by Boethius: a person is an individual substance of a rational kind. He also says that a person is what is most perfect in the whole of nature.[55] The former observation, Boethius's definition, is capable of two interpretations:

1. The individual is a member of a class which is characterised by rationality.
2. The individual is itself actually rational.

Singer would no doubt say that a condition of the acceptability of Aquinas's perfection thesis is that the definition of person be understood in the second sense. But if we consider the species label *homo sapiens, rational* man, it is clear that we understand that label in the first of these senses. Again, we could describe our species as the *laughing* species, and you could say that we are characteristically *makers and builders* of things, and characteristically *sexual* beings. All of that is true even if some of us are relentlessly gloomy, never make anything, and utterly unmoved by sex: in these cases it is the capacity rather than its exercise that is criterial. Jenny Teichman supports this approach:

The idea that a creature can have a rational nature without being rational... does not appear to me to be any more intrinsically problematic
than the idea that all cattle are mammals – even the bulls.[56]

In one sense this is blindingly obvious. A ship, essentially a machine
for floating on water, is still a ship when in dry dock; a three-legged ca-
nine is a dog, even though dogs are essentially quadrupeds. Just so, presumably, the very young and the very old should qualify as persons, even
if they were as defective with respect to rationality. The dead, of course,
would not: death is a substantial change; a corpse is not a member of the
human species nor an individual of a rational kind.

Membership of the class of persons is not the only area in which the
young and the old have been marginalized in philosophical thought, excluded from the range of a stern and parochial myopic focus on the mid-
dle years of life. Consider Descartes's search for infallible knowledge of
our inner states. Here we have a fixation on the judicious adult trained
observer with advanced linguistic skills. Anyone who has ever heard a
child declare 'I am NOT tired' will see what is wrong with this idea. It is
false about the dotty also. Yet in this fundamental area philosophers are
blinded by their preoccupation with young and middle-aged adults (and
not even all of these). And then conclusions which may be plausible for
that population are applied to people as such without restriction.

Suppose that we accept this use of 'person', yet insist that only currently rational and sentient persons have rights. The trouble with this is
that no one could afford an unguarded sleep; no one could suffer mild to
moderate intellectual deterioration without fear that their lives would be
snuffed out. Anaesthesia would be a hazardous medical option. For what
guarantee of support or sympathy could be provided? If the basis of my
rights is that I am currently a reasoner and an enjoyer, I have no reason
to hope for sympathy. It might be given, but the theory says it should not.
Any amelioration of this moral Thatcherism is to be welcomed, but on
what theoretical basis could it rest? I am not suggesting that Singer would
approve the utilitarian killing of a sleeping or anaesthetized person, but
how is he to avoid such an approval? If he says that a sleeping person is
to count as currently rational and sentient, that relaxation of 'current'
will prove hard to control. If it covers normal sleep, is it to be extended to
cover the abnormally long sleep of the exhausted? Then what about co-
mas of short, intermediate and long duration? And what about the defective rationality of the Alzheimer's sufferer? No principled barrier this
side of death will be possible, and Singer's tendency to converge on The
Common View on animal rights will be matched by a tendency to con-

verge on common human sympathy for fellow human beings, giving them a higher status than that accorded to the lower animals. He will, in short, be governed by pretty much the normal limits of human sympathy. These limits are striking and frequently need criticism, but they are much broader than those permitted by the atomistic current-state view.

Granted that I cannot sympathize with an insensate person on the basis of his current pain, since he has none, I can still sympathize with him as a sufferer of one of the disabilities to which we are all subject, and which frustrate complex human purposes and disturb human relationships beyond the capacity of our lower fellow creatures. It is here that equality of consideration finds its natural place. In fact, as Aristotle taught us, it is first actuality that matters.[57]

## NOTES

1  Peter Singer and Helga Kuhse, 'Bioethics and the Limits of Tolerance', *The Journal of Medicine and Philosophy* 19 (1994), p. 130.
2  Ibid., p. 133.
3  Helga Kuhse and Peter Singer, *Should the Baby Live?* (Oxford: OUP, 1985), pp. 160–92. The case is introduced as involving an infant 'born handicapped, but with reasonable prospects of a life sufficiently free from suffering to be worth living...' (p. 161). The verdict is: 'we think that a community might properly decide that its resources are more urgently spent on other tasks than caring for handicapped new-born infants whose parents are not prepared to care for them' (p. 192).
4  Peter Singer, 'All Animals Are Equal', *New York Review of Books*, 5th April 1973. A later version of the paper appears in his edited collection *Applied Ethics* (Oxford: OUP, 1986), pp. 215–28. It is the later version which I am using.
5  Ibid., p. 217.
6  Ibid., pp. 217–8.
7  Ibid., p. 218.
8  Ibid., p. 220 (my emphasis).
9  Ibid., p. 226 (my emphasis). The stress on prescription is also to be found in chapter 1 of his *Animal Liberation* (London: Jonathan Cape, 1990, 2nd. ed.).
10  R. D. Ryder, *Victims of Science* (London: Davis-Poynter, 1975), p. 16.
11  Hannah Arendt, *The Origins of Totalitarianism* (N.Y.: Meridian Books, 1958, 2nd. ed.), chapter 1.
12  S. I. Benn and R. S. Peters, *Social Principles and the Democratic State* (London: George Allen and Unwin, 1959), p. 107 (my emphasis).
13  Peter Singer, *Practical Ethics* (Cambridge: CUP, 1993, 2nd. ed.), pp. 19–20.
14  Ibid., pp. 21–2.
15  Peter Singer, *The Expanding Circle: Ethics and Sociobiology* (Oxford: OUP, 1981), p. 149.

16 Peter Singer, 'All Animals Are Equal', p. 221.
17 John Stuart Mill, 'Bentham', in *Collected Works of John Stuart Mill, Volume 10: Essays on Ethics, Religion and Society*, ed. J. M. Robson (Toronto: University of Toronto Press, 1969), p. 113.
18 M. l'Abbé Trublet, *Mémoires pour servir à l'histoire de la vie et des ouvrages de M. de Fontenelle* (Amsterdam, 1761), p. 115. The translation is my own.
19 Threshold requirements are similar to Rawls's 'range properties', rejected in *Practical Ethics*, pp. 18–19.
20 John Stuart Mill, *Utilitarianism* (Indianapolis: The Library of Liberal Arts, 1957), chapter 2, p. 14.
21 Bruce Knox, Pauline Ladiges, Barbara Evans (eds.), *Biology* (Roseville, N.S.W.: McGraw-Hill, 1994), pp. 1023–4.
22 See, for example, Marian Stamp Dawkins, *Animal Suffering: The Science of Animal Welfare* (London: Chapman and Hall, 1980), chapter 2, and her 'The Scientific Basis for Assessing Suffering in Animals', in Peter Singer (ed.), *In Defence of Animals* (Oxford: Blackwell, 1985), pp. 27–9.
23 J. S. Kennedy, *The New Anthropomorphism* (Cambridge: CUP, 1992), pp. 1–3.
24 Peter Carruthers, *The Animals Issue* (Cambridge: CUP, 1992), pp. 170ff.; David Armstrong, *The Nature of Mind and Other Essays* (St. Lucia: University of Queensland Press, 1980), pp. 59ff.
25 P. D. F. Murray, *Biology* (London: Macmillan, 1960, 2nd. ed.), p. 6.
26 Knox, Ladiges and Evans, *Biology*, p. 588.
27 Peter Singer, *Animal Liberation*, p. 10.
28 Ibid., pp. 12–13.
29 Ludwig Wittgenstein, *Philosophical Investigations* (Oxford: Blackwell, 1963), s.284.
30 Frank Ramsey, 'General Propositions and Causality', in his *The Foundations of Mathematics* (London: Routledge and Kegan Paul, 1931); D. M. Armstrong, *Belief, Truth and Knowledge* (Cambridge: CUP., 1973).
31 Peter Singer, *Animal Liberation*, pp. 225–6.
32 Plato, *Laws* IX, 873c–874a.
33 E. P. Evans, *The Criminal Prosecution and Capital Punishment of Animals* (London: Faber and Faber, 1987, 2nd. ed. (orig. pub. 1906)), p. 286.
34 Charles Taylor, 'What is Human Agency?', in Theodore Mischel (ed.), *The Self* (Oxford: Blackwell, 1977), p. 110.
35 Singer, *Practical Ethics*, pp. 90–1; *In Defence of Animals*, pp. 7 and 9.
36 Singer, *Practical Ethics*, p. 107.
37 Ibid., pp. 126–31. See also 1st ed. (Cambridge: CUP., 1979), pp. 102–3.
38 The extract is from Samuel Pepys' diary for 24 August 1661. I have taken it from *A Pepys Anthology*, edited by Robert and Linnet Latham (London: Unwin Hyman, 1987), p. 167.
39 John Locke, *An Essay Concerning Human Understanding*, Book 2, chapter 11.
40 Singer, 'All animals Are Equal', pp. 226–7.
41 Kuhse and Singer, *Should the Baby Live?*, p. 122.
42 Derek Davis, entry on 'Morgan, Conwy Lloyd (1852–1936)', in Richard L. Gregory (ed.), *The Oxford Companion to the Mind* (Oxford: OUP, 1987), p. 496.
43 Jane van Lawick-Goodall, *In the Shadow of Man* (Boston: Houghton Mifflin, 1971), p. 251.

44 Dennis Coon, *Introduction to Psychology: Exploration and Application* (St Paul: West Publishing Co., 1992, 6th. ed.), pp. 240, 281, 400.
45 Richard L. Gregory, *Mind in Science* (Harmondsworth: Penguin, 1984), p. 417.
46 loc. cit.
47 E. M. Macphail, *Brain and Intelligence in Vertebrates* (Oxford: Clarendon Press, 1982), p. 296. Macphail reports the Gardners' own suggestion, in 1971, that such sign order as Washoe can manage is a matter of imitation of humans (p. 298).
48 See, for example, J. S. Kennedy, *The New Anthropomorphism*, p. 40ff., and T. A. Sebeok and J. Umiker-Sebeok (eds), *Speaking of Apes: A Critical Anthology of Two-Way Communication With Man* (New York: Plenum Press, 1980).
49 Kuhse and Singer, *Should The Baby Live?*, p. 132.
50 Peter Singer, 'Prologue: Ethics and the New Animal Liberation Movement', in Singer (ed.), *In Defence of Animals*, p. 6.
51 Gregory, *Mind in Science*, p. 36.
52 Colin Trevarthen, 'Infancy, Mind In', in Gregory (ed.), *The Oxford Companion to the Mind*, p. 363.
53 Ibid., pp. 364–5.
54 For a discussion of this point, see John Bigelow and Robert Pargetter, 'Morality, Potential Persons and Abortion', *American Philosophical Quarterly* 25 (1988) 173–81, especially p. 178.
55 St Thomas Aquinas, *Summa Theologiae* I.29.1, objection 1; I.29.3, *responsio*.
56 Jenny Teichman, 'The Definition of *Person*', *Philosophy* 60 (1985) 175–85; see pp. 180–1.
57 Aristotle, *De Anima*, Book 2, chapter 1, 412a, 23–8.

# 5 In Defence of Speciesism

## Tim Chappell

[T]he taking into account of the interests of the being, whatever those interests may be – must, according to the principle of equality, be extended to all beings, black or white, masculine or feminine, human or nonhuman... It is on this basis that the case against racism and the case against sexism must both ultimately rest; and it is in accordance with this principle that the attitude that we may call 'speciesism', by analogy with racism, must also be condemned. Speciesism... is a prejudice or attitude of bias in favour of the interests of members of one's own species and against those of members of other species... If possessing a higher degree of intelligence does not entitle one human to use another for his or her own ends, how can it entitle humans to exploit nonhumans for the same purpose?.... As long as we remember that we should give the same respect to the lives of animals as we give to the lives of those humans at a similar mental level, we shall not go far wrong.

(Peter Singer, *Animal Liberation*)[1]

1. I want to defend a position which I think deserves the name speciesism. So I had better start by defining it. Speciesism, as I shall use the word, is the belief that differences of species can, do and should provide sufficient reason, in themselves, to ground major differences in moral significance, in a way in which (for example) differences of gender, race, intelligence or sensitivity to pain do not and cannot ground such differences.

2. Whether speciesism in this sense is quite the same thing as Peter Singer has in his sights in his book *Animal Liberation*, I am not sure. For Singer defines what he calls speciesism as 'a *prejudice or attitude of bias* in favour of the interests of members of one's own species and against those of members of other species.' But since prejudices and biases are bad by definition, this simply entails that speciesism is a bad thing; and there seems little point in trying to defend what is indefensible by definition.

The interesting question is what *counts* as a prejudice or bias in moral comparisons between species. Does *any* discrimination between species, purely on the basis that they are different species, count as prejudice or bias? Or are some such discriminations reasonable, while others are not?

I want to argue that the answers to these questions are 'no' and 'yes' respectively. So if it is speciesism to think that, sometimes, moral discriminations can and should be made purely on the basis that the objects of the discrimination are of different species, then I am happy to defend speciesism.

3. Of course, one might wonder whether speciesism in this sense is not too easy a thesis to prove. Indeed, one might wonder whether even Singer himself is not a speciesist in this sense. Certainly Singer alleges that there is an analogy between discrimination purely on the grounds of race or gender, and discrimination purely on the grounds of species: an analogy which seems to suggest that he thinks that *any* discrimination of the latter sort is just as wrong as any discrimination of the former sorts. However, we should not let Singer's surface polemics confuse us, for he also writes as follows:

> There are obviously important differences between humans and other animals, and these differences must give rise to some differences in the rights that each have... The extension of the basic principle of equality from one group to another does not imply that we must treat both groups in exactly the same way, or grant exactly the same rights to both groups. Whether we should do so will depend on the nature of the members of the two groups. The basic principle of equality does not require equal or identical *treatment*: it requires equal consideration.[2]

4. Here Singer seems perfectly happy to accept the idea that differences of species can entail differences in rights. That seems to make him a speciesist too, on my definition of the term. So what is my dispute with Singer?

5. The answer is implicit in the following remarks:

> If a being suffers there can be no moral justification for refusing to take that suffering into consideration. No matter what the nature of the being, the principle of equality requires that its suffering be counted equally with the like suffering... of any other being. If a being is not capable of suffering, or of experiencing enjoyment or happiness, there is nothing to be taken into account. So the limit of sentience... is the only defensible boundary of concern for the interests of others.[3]

What this passage shows is that Singer accepts the famous criterion of moral importance proposed by Bentham: 'The question is not, Can they reason? nor, Can they talk? but, Can they suffer?'.[4] That is, Singer holds the following two beliefs:

(i) Something has moral significance if and only if it has a capacity to feel pain and pleasure;

(ii) pain and pleasure are the same thing, and can be measured in the same way, for all creatures that feel them at all.

(This in spite of some evidence that Singer thinks that what makes creatures morally important is their intelligence: 'As long as we remember that we should give the same respect to the lives of animals as we give to the lives of those humans *at a similar mental level* [my emphasis], we shall not go far wrong.' It should be clear from his remarks about pain and pleasure, and from his own attack on speciesism, that Singer cannot consistently make mental capacity the criterion of moral significance (unless Singer mistakenly thinks that mental capacity is analytically connected in some way with capacity for pleasure and pain). If it is *speciesism* to use species membership as the criterion of moral significance, presumably it must be *I. Q. ism* (or whatever) to use intelligence in this way. As Singer himself asks: 'If possessing a higher degree of intelligence does not entitle one human to use another for his or her own ends, how can it entitle humans to exploit nonhumans for the same purpose?')

**6.** The statement of beliefs (i) and (ii) suffices to locate my disagreement with Singer, which is over the truth of (i), and the importance of (ii) in any sense in which it is true.

(i) is false. The capacity to feel pain and pleasure is not a necessary and sufficient condition, but (at most) only a sufficient condition, of moral significance. Certainly, if X has a capacity to feel pleasure and pain, then X is morally significant. But it does not follow, and it is not true, that if X is morally significant, then X has a capacity to feel pleasure and pain. Two examples will suffice to prove this.

First consider A. A is a normal human being except that he has no C-fibres in his body at all (for simplicity's sake I shall assume that C-fibres are the physiological basis of our experiences of pain); nor has he anything in his makeup which would make it possible for him to experience pleasure. A, then, cannot experience pain or pleasure. Does it follow that A is morally insignificant? No. Or (to make a favourite utilitarian move) is A only of *indirect* moral significance – morally significant only because he is so much like normal human beings, who *do* feel pain and pleasure, that there is significant disutility in not lumping A together with other humans? Once again, the answer to this ought to be 'No'. A is not merely indirectly morally significant because A lacks all capacity for pain and pleasure. He is, I suggest, directly morally significant *simply because he is a human being*.

Second consider B, a beech tree. B, naturally enough for a beech tree, has no way of experiencing anything. *A fortiori*, B has no way of experiencing anything like pain or pleasure. Does it follow that B is morally insignificant? It does not. Beech trees could be morally significant – they could have rights, and we could have duties to them, if you wish to use that vocabulary – *just in virtue of the kind of things they are*, and irrespective of any subjective capacities which they might have (but presumably do not). (Note that I am not asserting that beech trees do have moral significance in their own right; merely registering that it is possible that they do.)

7. Singer and Bentham are, then, committed to an arbitrarily narrow account of what makes something morally significant. It has an attractive air of moral urgency to focus on the vivid and readily comprehensible notions of pain and pleasure as criterial for moral significance; but to take these (undoubtedly very important) cases as the *only* ones that matter, or could possibly matter, in defining our criterion is to succumb to a case of ethical tunnel vision disturbingly like that which Singer so accurately diagnoses in the case of the apologists for cruelty to animals.

8. The cases of A and B show two very simple and obvious ways in which living things (or systems of living things) could have moral significance without there being any prospect of their experiencing pleasure or pain. So why might A and B have moral significance though they cannot feel pain or pleasure? The answer I have suggested already is, simply, because of the kinds of thing A and B are. Let me put the same point another way: A and B can have moral significance because we have a conception of what it is for A or B to *flourish*; and because we take it that it is a good thing that A or B should flourish.

9. I submit that it is this notion, of a capacity for well-being or flourishing and its opposite, not the Benthamite notion of a capacity for pleasure or enjoyment and its opposite, which is what in general furnishes us with our criterion of moral significance. As the examples of A and B show, this criterion is more widely applicable than the Benthamite criterion could hope to be; for it captures cases which presumably ought to be captured, but which Bentham and Singer's criterion cannot possibly capture.

10. Moreover, the criterion of flourishing is not just more widely applicable than the criterion of pain and pleasure. It is also naturally taken to be more important than the Benthamite criterion of moral significance in cases where both apply. Pain is, typically, an obstacle to well-

being, and pleasure, typcally, alleviates an unflourishing condition; nevertheless it is better to be flourishing *though* in pain than to lack well-being *despite* experiencing pleasure. In fact, pain and pleasure only matter insofar as they are *components* of well-being or its opposite. The criterion of flourishing or its opposite *supersedes* the criterion of pleasure or its opposite because it *subsumes* it.

(This is why I said, above, that the capacity to feel pain and pleasure is *at most* only a sufficient condition of moral significance: for it is only that *per accidens*, and if there is nothing else but a capacity for pain or pleasure on which to judge a creature's capacity for well-being.)

11. Let us return to the beliefs (i) and (ii) which I ascribed to Singer in section 5. The line of thought pursued in sections 6–10 leads us to replace Singer's

(i) Something has moral significance if and only if it has a capacity to feel pain and pleasure

with

(i*a*) Something has moral significance if and only if it has a capacity to flourish or not flourish.

But once that is done, what is to become of Singer's (ii)?

(ii) Pain and pleasure are the same thing, and can be measured in the same way, for all creatures that feel them at all.

(ii) is, I think, true; but, in the light of the replacement of (i) by (i*a*), it is no longer clear that (ii) has the central importance we thought it had. It is natural to think that, if (i) is to be replaced by (i*a*), then (ii) also ought to be replaced, perhaps by (ii*a*):

(ii*a*) Flourishing and its opposite are the same thing, and can be measured in the same way, for all creatures that experience them at all.

But the trouble with (ii*a*) is that it is plainly false. Human flourishing is *not* the same thing as feline flourishing, even if (as seems probable) human pain is pretty much the same thing as feline pain; and rain forest flourishing, racoon flourishing, lugworm flourishing or cetacean flourishing are different things again.

12. Now this fact is a vital one when we are considering the moral status of various sorts of animals: perhaps we should call it *the* vital fact regarding the moral status of different animals. For I am presupposing the view that what determines how we morally ought to treat any (sort of) being is (roughly) our respect for what is good for that (sort of) being; and that

what determines what is good for it, is what counts as flourishing or well-being for that sort of being. Now since different sorts of state count as flourishing for different sorts of being, it follows that different sorts of treatment are morally appropriate to different sorts of creature *just in virtue of the fact that they are of different sorts*, i.e. different species. This is speciesism, in the sense of that word which I think worth defending.

**13.** Now consider three further moves. First, as we have already seen, what counts as flourishing for a given species is dependent upon what that species is *like*. This can be expanded. By 'what a species is like' I mean, more or less, what its characteristic lifestyle is; as a zoologist would say, what its ecological niche is; or as Aristotle would say, what its function is. Flourishing for a species means flourishing in its ecological niche; in another vocabulary, flourishing for a species means performing its function well. A flourishing tiger is, *inter alia*, a fierce one; a flourishing gazelle is, *inter alia*, a fast one; and so on.

Secondly, the well-being of different species can and often does conflict. Well-being for tigers and well-being for gazelles are obviously not completely compatible; the realization of either to the greatest degree is incompatible with the realization of both to the greatest possible degree: and the latter is a matter of natural balance. This is why I say that what determines how we morally ought to treat any (sort of) being is only *roughly* what is good for that (sort of) being; for there may (and usually will) be the interests of other sorts of being to balance against the interests of this sort of being.

And thirdly, there is only one species on earth which is in a position to do this balancing, and that species is us – *homo sapiens*.

**14.** If you put these three claims together you get the conclusion that the position of the human species relative to the whole of the rest of nature is a unique one: it is that of a (reverent) regulator, as and when a regulator is needed (which is certainly not everywhere). The ecological niche of a tiger naturally involves it (*inter alia*) in reproducing and eating gazelles. The ecological niche of a gazelle naturally involves it (*inter alia*) in reproducing, eating grass, and avoiding being eaten by tigers. In the current state of things – and whatever may have been the case in past stages of our evolution – the ecological niche of *homo sapiens* now involves us (*inter alia*) in being prepared, if necessary, to regulate the relations between the occupants of other ecological niches, e.g. to prevent the tiger from eating the gazelle into extinction, and to prevent the gazelle from eating itself *and* the tiger into extinction by overgrazing.

In virtue of their unique position in nature – or perhaps one should say, *outside* nature – human beings have a unique ecological niche or Aristotelian function. That consideration, *not* alone but together with other considerations about what humans are like, yields an account of human flourishing; it also yields the conclusion that what flourishing is for humans is quite different from what flourishing is for any other creature. This in turn yields the conclusion that humans, just in virtue of the species that they are, have a different moral status, right, and role from every other species, and this is the application of the speciesism which I think worth defending to the case of the human species.

15. What gives us this role? What gives us this right? What gives us the right is the plain fact that we do have the role. Thanks to science, human beings just *are* in a position to regulate nature, in a way that is quite unlike the position of any other animal or species. It is not hubris to observe this; it is merely a statement of what we all in practice take for granted. Whales and gorillas, bats and orang-utans are marvellous species, and in some respects they all surpass humanity. But we do not see them measuring their own or other species' effects on the environment, or running projections of their own or other species' population growth, or analysing gene pools. Man is the only scientific animal: that is one of the differences that gives us our special role among, and our special duties towards, the other animals.

'And' – no doubt one might wish to retort – 'a fine mess we've made of it, too.' We certainly have, unfortunately. But we could not have succeeded or failed in this role unless we *had* the role. Nor can we give it up. At this stage of development, the human species can no more choose not to be distinct from the rest of nature in the way I am describing than we can now choose not to be linguistic creatures.

16. Humans, uniquely, have the right to do what they consider necessary to bring about as much flourishing as possible, for as many of the existing species and individual animals as possible, within the context of the flourishing of the whole earth. Indeed not only is that their *right*; it is their *duty.*

17. More specifically, then: what does this right or duty, this moral task, consist in? It consists in one positive duty (a duty to act in certain ways) and one negative duty (a duty to abstain from acting in certain ways). The positive duty is to act to promote and defend the flourishing of the natural world. The negative duty is not to act so as to harm or damage the flourishing of the natural world.

Notice the very generalized nature of these duties, which apply directly to the whole of the natural world, and only indirectly, and in consequence of that application, to individual species (let alone individual animals). This move from talk of our duties towards an individual animal or species to talk of our duties towards the whole of nature is one which we are bound to make in the light of the two facts considered above: first, that the flourishing of different species or individual animals can conflict; and secondly, that only humans are in a position to arbitrate when they do. For what humans have to consider when engaged in such arbitration is, as has already been suggested, not primarily the flourishing of any given species or individual animal taken in isolation, but the flourishing of the whole of the system of which that species or animal is a part.

**18.** Possible examples of the practical consequences of applying these two principles are, like possible applications of any moral principle, indefinitely numerous. But, I suggest, on any plausible reckoning they will certainly include something like the following:

(i) The negative duty of not acting so as to harm or damage the flourishing of the natural world rules out all human activities which threaten the existence of species or which affect the natural world in a way which it cannot readily sustain or assimilate. One example is whaling for rare species of whales, or more generally the hunting (whether for pleasure or for profit) of any rare species. Another example is the development of nuclear and biological weapons. (There are, of course, other sufficient reasons why we should not develop such weapons; but it is worth noting that consideration for other species and the rest of the natural world would alone give us sufficient reason not to, even if those other reasons did not exist.) A third example is the indiscriminate use of the motor car.

(ii) The positive duty of promoting and defending the flourishing of the natural world could plausibly be said to include taking such actions as are necessary to prevent one species from driving another species to extinction, or from destroying some habitat or part of the natural world which has value in its own right. For example, ring-fencing Caledonian pine forests is plainly justified to prevent red deer from destroying those forests, even if a side-effect is that more deer die. Again, if there is no other way of preventing a wild ungulate species (deer or sheep or goats or whatever) from overgrazing an area of sensitive grassland, it is legitimate to cull the numbers of ungulates by shooting them. Or, third, if human ivory poachers can only be prevented from driving the wild African elephant to extinction by lethal force, then so be it.

In all such cases the rule will be that one should defend whatever form of natural flourishing it is that has been identified as worth defending by the least destructive and least cruel available means. As to the question

of what forms of natural flourishing ought to be so identified as worth defending, and at what price: that difficult question is to be answered by reflection on what *localized* forms of natural flourishing can most
plausibly be seen as contributing distinctively and valuably to the *overall*
flourishing of the natural world.

It is a corollary of all this, of course, that it is inconsistent with a general
commitment to promote and defend the flourishing of the natural world
that one should permit or condone arbitrary and avoidable cruelty in individual cases. This obviously means no fox-hunting or badger-baiting,
which is arbitrary cruelty – that is, arbitrary interference with the well-
being of the creatures in question. But it also means no animal experimentation and no meat-eating, since both necessarily involve a great deal of
avoidable cruelty (and a great deal of arbitrary cruelty, too). Take such activities as breeding and rearing animals with the intention of slaughtering
them for food, or practising our dissection techniques on living frogs, or
implanting electrodes in cats' brains to monitor their neural activity. The
only possible defence for such activities would be to claim that we are un-
avoidably led to them by our general commitment to the overall flourishing of the natural world, or of those animals as part of it. But no sane
person could possibly claim that he was so led. Therefore such activities
are morally inexcusable. (So, to come back to whale-hunting: there are
two sufficient reasons why we should not hunt *rare* whales; and there is
one sufficient reason why we should not hunt *any* whales.)

19. My account is bound to raise at least the following three questions:
(i) If it is wrong to eat animals because this adversely affects their
well-being, why isn't it *pari passu* wrong to eat vegetables?

The obvious reason is that the way in which the well-being of vegetables is affected by their being eaten is not morally significant to the same
degree as the way in which the well-being of animals is affected by their
being eaten. In particular, being in pain or distress are important ways
in which a sheep or a hen can lack well-being, and a carrot cannot. It is
possible for a sane person to sympathize with a veal calf; it is not possible
to sympathize with a King Edward potato. These are just the sorts of fact
about differences between species which, as claimed above, are fit to
ground differences in the way we ought to treat different species.

Notice that I do not claim that we owe carrots or King Edward pota-
toes *no* moral duties. It seems to me plausible to suggest that we might.
Nonetheless, it seems certain that there is nothing about what well-being
consists in for vegetables which makes it true that we are required not to
eat them.

(ii) If we may cull deer, why may we not cull humans?

The answer is the same as that given to (i): because the way in which the well-being of deer is affected by their being culled is not morally significant to the same degree as the way in which the well-being of humans is affected by their being culled. It is part of humans' flourishing to be responsive in a rational way to the need to exercise self-control and self-regulation over the question of how much we may reproduce. This is not part of the way in which deer live well. Consequently it is no insult to deer to treat them as incapable of participating in that sort of self-control, e.g. by culling them (if that is the only way of preventing them from overbreeding). It is no insult so to treat them, because they *are* incapable of that sort of restraint. The same is not true of humans, however badly they may in practice fail in self-restraint. Given what human nature is, it would be an insult to human nature not to begin (at any rate) by trying reasonable persuasion; or to end by forgetting that that capacity to be persuaded is there, and demands particular sorts of respect from us, even when it is abused by its owner. Once again, the moral difference here is grounded in a difference in way of life and in what counts as flourishing for the species in question.

(iii) The question of culling raises the question of killing. In what circumstances may we kill humans or other animals? What are the differences between the rules about killing which apply to different species?

All I shall say on this difficult question here is that I suspect the rules about killing are less different between species than one might at first expect. There seems to be a legitimate overall principle to which we may appeal in the case of any species at all: this is the principle that you need a special reason to kill anything.

This, of course, is not much practical help until we know how special a reason has to be before it is good enough to be a reason to kill. To start with, we can say that wanton, playful, routine or casual killing is always wrong, whatever one kills. (That rules out blood sports.) So is any killing which is done as a means to any end, but which is not a necessary means to that end. (That rules out meat-eating, which is a means to human nutrition, but not a necessary means, seeing that we can get adequate nourishment from other sources.) So is any killing which is done as a necessary means to an end which is not of the right sort to warrant that killing. (This is what rules out experiments on animals, when they are not ruled out by the ban on casual killing.)

Does one need a more special reason to kill members of some species than of others? In the responses to questions (i) and (ii) above I have already, in effect, argued that you do, and that once again the differentiating criterion is to do with what counts as flourishing for the species in question. (Notice, incidentally, that on the principles defended here the same rules about what makes killing members of a species licit apply to *any* member of that species; including, for example, those members of that species in the womb.)

**20.** Even at the price of making my own cause seem, in some eyes, guilty by association, it may be illuminating to compare the form of argument which I have been using with a notorious argument advanced by Aristotle:

> Consider therefore all men who are as different in their natures from proper men as the body is from the soul, or humans from animals [N.B.]. It is those whose specific function is the use of the body, those for whom this is the best for which they are fitted, who are in this condition. Such men are slaves by nature; it is better for them to be ruled by a master... He is a slave by nature who has the capacity to belong to another and therefore *does* belong to another, and who partakes of reason so far as to recognize it, but not to possess it.[5]

If I am right, this Aristotelian defence of slavery is a perfectly valid argument. There is nothing wrong with its *reasoning*; it is the *truth* of the argument's premises that we should question. Specifically, it is just false that there is one specific account of flourishing for free men (namely, what in other circumstances we would call the *human* account of flourishing), and another specific account for slaves (namely 'the use of the body,' 'being ruled by a master,' '[realizing] the capacity to belong to another,' 'partaking of reason so far as to recognize it, but not to possess it'). There are *no* such natural differences as these between different types in the human species. But there would have to be if it were to be possible to ground Aristotle's claim that different accounts of well-being apply to different human types.

However, though Aristotle has got the answer badly wrong, he has asked the right question. For if there *were*, as a matter of fact, such differences as his bad faith in the matter encourages him to imagine between natural free men and natural slaves, then these two types of humans would (in effect) be different species with different final goods; in which case it *would* be justifiable to treat free men and slaves as having significantly different moral statuses. Here a familiar point emerges: the dependence of moral arguments – whether about slavery or speciesism – upon *biological matters of fact* about what kind of state of affairs constitutes human (or a free man's, or a slave's, or animal) flourishing, the good living of life which is characteristic of the species. If these facts were different from what they are, then the moral discriminations which we make would differ too. No one but a philosopher could fail to see the relevance of *these* sorts of 'ises' to 'oughts'. But then no one but a philosopher could fail to understand why it *mattered*, for example, to refute the phoney science whereby Hitler's servants showed that 'non-Aryans' were less intelligent, less sensitive to pain, etc., than 'Aryans'.

**21.** My position as outlined in this paper has had two salient emphases. On the one hand I have insisted, in sections 17–18, that we may *not* do whatever we like to the natural world. Our attitude toward it should be one of benevolence and an unselfish concern for *its* flourishing (which, of course, has *our* flourishing as a part of it). It should not merely be one of concern for nature's efficient provision for us of what we want; still less should it be the indiscriminate and unfeeling consumerism which is the effective policy of our society as presently constituted. Specifically this commits us, among other things, to vegetarianism, unilateral disarmament, opposition to animal experimentation, and (in many cases) getting rid of our cars.

On the other hand, against Singer and others, I have tried to show that if we want to argue for radical conclusions like these about animal welfare, it is not necessary to start from the hysterically extreme principles which they have sometimes insisted upon. In particular, I have defended the following three relatively moderate claims:

(i) It is a creature's capacity for flourishing or its opposite which is the necessary and sufficient condition of its being, in its own way, morally significant. It is not the case, as Singer thinks, that a creature's capacity for pain or pleasure is the necessary and sufficient condition of its being morally significant in the same way as anything else.

(ii) Since different accounts of flourishing apply to different species, and since it is the account of flourishing relevant to any species which ultimately grounds the moral rights of that species, it follows that we can, do and should make moral discriminations between species purely and simply on the basis that they are different species – including, crucially, moral discriminations between humans and other species which often, though not always, will be in favour of humans.

(iii) When we consider animal welfare, it is the flourishing of the natural world overall which should be paramount in our thinking. The flourishing of individual species or animals is necessarily subsidiary to that.

**22.** I began with a quotation from Singer with which I largely disagreed. I close with a quotation from Williams which I think is more or less exactly right:

> A concern for nonhuman animals is indeed a proper part of human life, but we can acquire it, cultivate it, and teach it only in terms of our understanding of ourselves... Before one gets to the question of how animals should be treated, there is the fundamental point that this is the only question there can be: how they should be treated. The choice can only be whether animals benefit from our practices or are harmed by them. This is why speciesism is falsely modelled on racism and sexism, which really are prejudices. To suppose that there is an ineliminable white or male understanding of the world, and to think that the only choice is whether blacks or women should benefit from 'our' (white, male) practices or be harmed by them: this is already to be prejudiced. But in the case of human relations to animals, the analogues to such thoughts are simply correct.[6]

# NOTES

1 Peter Singer, *Animal Liberation* (London: Jonathan Cape, 1990, 2nd. ed.), pp. 5–6, 21.
2 Ibid., p. 2.
3 Ibid., pp. 8–9.
4 Bentham, *Introduction to the Principles of Morals and Legislation*, edited by Burns and Hart (London: Methuen, 1970), XVII.i, p. 283.
5 Aristotle, *Politics*, 1254b16ff.; the translation is my own, from the Loeb text.
6 B. Williams, *Ethics and the Limits of Philosophy* (London: Fontana, 1985), pp. 118–19.

# 6 Young Human Beings: Metaphysics and Ethics

*Grant Gillett*

## 1. INTRODUCTION

Human infants are beings who are obviously vulnerable to the vicissitudes of life in general and who tend to invoke in us special concern and care. One might therefore expect that our moral thinking would show why this special regard somehow cohered with basic moral features of the human condition. It is somewhat surprising that one of the major theories of moral value should not only devalue the intuitions that surround human infants but actually suggest that such intuitions are radically mistaken.[1] I shall use this counterintuitive conclusion about young human beings to explore the basic claims and commitments of consequentialism as a metaethical theory.

A metaethical theory aims to reveal the basis of moral judgment and thereby to make explicit the grounds on which reasoned moral discussion can take place between those whose moral judgments differ. Consequentialism is committed to the basic claim that the moral value of an action is determined by its consequences. What is more, consequentialists are undaunted by the fact that some of their conclusions are counterintuitive and insist that theirs is the only rational strategy for determining moral value. Thus, if this theory is to prove adequate as a metaethical theory, it should be able to articulate how the reasoning should go in determining moral value and also offer us some way of assessing the relative value of different possible consequences of a given action. At this point, the usual consequentialist move is to invoke a utilitarian calculus of some type to yield the value assessments of the relevant outcomes. This way of doing things is subject to a great deal of criticism, much of which focuses on the incalculability and even incommensurability of different types of outcome.[2] Glover tries to relieve utilitarianism of this burden by asking that we not require a precise method of assigning relative values and urging us to accept that utilitarianism is 'an approximate guide to conduct'.[3] However, we are surely entitled to a little more than this. In fact, I think we are entitled to hope that the relevant value assignments be somewhat tractable, so that one might at least begin an approximate

109

weighting of different outcomes. But for there to be some way of comparing relative outcomes, certain simplifications need to be put into place.

One important simplification is that each human life should count as equal to every other. This egalitarian assumption removes from the task of comparing lives and the moral values of outcomes which differentially affect different lives any essentially individual factors that could complicate decisions. Thus an outcome in which we produce five good quality years of life for individual A should roughly equate to an outcome which produces five good quality years of life for B (other things being equal). There still remains the basic problem of performing relative calculations of moral value for the alternative consequences of an action where those consequences can be thought of as members of different general types, such as a year of pain-free life for A versus restoring the sight of B. Let us say, however, that we opt for a commonly accepted way of assessing consequences and relate them to the satisfactions made available as a result of the actions to be evaluated. We have already noted that these quality assessments of different general satisfaction types should not be complicated by particularizing their values to the individuals concerned and therefore we need a conception of the satisfaction-values which is indifferent between the individuals to which they accrue; call this *the indifference claim*. This implies that it is incompatible with a principled approach to moral reasoning that anything essentially individual, such as, for instance, the death of a particular person, should form part of the moral assessment of a given situation (apart, that is, from its contribution to the sum of generalizable value that is brought about).

If we now combine a consequentialist thesis about moral value with the generalizations about value implicit in the indifference claim, we can derive two important implications.

*First*, there is no direct wrongness in killing. This follows from the fact that all that is to be counted are the value weightings of the consequences of the killing. Thus, provided that side-effects such as the effect on other people and the loss of future positively valued states can be taken into account, the actual killing itself is not to be negatively assessed.[4] This becomes important when we consider the institution of infanticide or the replacement of one child by another.

*Secondly*, animal lives must be considered to be essentially equivalent to human lives which realize the same general types of satisfaction.

These two implications are particularly important in making plausible some widespread consequentialist views on young human lives.

Before we move in to a focused discussion of infants and other young human beings, we need to consider one further complicating factor that will have to be admitted into any tolerable consequentialist reasoning. In addition to the bare comparisons of satisfaction sums across different lives, there are certain practices which are going to engender widespread disaffection. Thus, for instance, it might be considered counterproductive to regard individual preferences as of merely quantitative importance, because it is plausible that a universal feature of human societies is the security of knowing that in general one's own preferences should be regarded as inviolate unless some compelling justification can be given for overriding them. This would provide a consequential basis for social rights sufficient to stabilize a community against the disruptive effect of 'warre where every man is Enemy to every man'.[5] In discussing this issue, Glover describes an hypothetical policy in which we regularly kill off members of the population whose lives are substandard in their value content to make space for other more promising lives to replace them. Glover remarks:

> [T]he side-effects of such a policy would obviously be calamitous. The remaining population would feel grief, resentment and insecurity on an extreme scale.[6]

He concludes that these consequences 'do not show how terrible utilitarianism is, but rather show that it is not a policy a utilitarian would favour'.[7] In fact, a preference utilitarian such as Singer or Tooley has an even stronger case. The basic claim here is that 'an action contrary to the preference of any being is, unless this preference is outweighed by contrary preferences, wrong',[8] call this the *preference utility claim*. We can assume that most of the population do want to go on living, even if their cups are not brimming over with highly valued experiences, and we can therefore conclude that the 'kill and replace' policy for melancholics would be wrong. However, this underpinning provided by a consequentially-based institution which protects individual rights does not extend to anybody whom one need not consider as having any well-enunciated preferences. This is especially so if victimizing those people would not have a significant impact on the pursuit of one's own satisfactions.

There is a further problem for this kind of utilitarianism as stated. The basic claim[9] implies that the preferences to be weighed should be held by the same person. However, contra this implication, if we combine the basic (preference utility) claim with the indifference claim we are left devoid of an obvious way to import an individual-linked specification of the preferences that count into the thesis. Thus if my preferences to go on living were outweighed by a body of preferences that I should die, even where the second set of preferences are not mine, then presumably my preferences are outweighed and the right thing to do is kill me. There is, however, a way to fix this up (at some cost in philosophical purity).

We could suggest that the only way to reconcile potentially conflicting preferences in a way that avoids widespread social disruption and the disutility consequent upon that is to invoke some kind of social contract whereby the preferences of each are, within certain limits, to be respected. Such a social contract, by freely negotiating participants all of whom should be heard, does however, as a corollary, remove consequence from its role as the direct arbiter of moral value and impose accordance with the social contract as a practical guide to action. One might argue, after the spirit of certain criticisms of rule utilitarianism, that this poses the consequentialist with a dilemma. If consequences are to have the all-encompassing role they are supposed to have according to the base theory, then in any actual conflict a weighing of consequences ought to be the final arbiter and so the social contract becomes indefinitely and diversely subject to exceptions – perhaps even worthless. However, if the social contract is going, for practical purposes, to settle any moral debates that arise, we no longer have consequentialism except as an impotent and rather abstract Olympian ideal. I will not attempt to suggest how a consequentialist might avoid both Scylla and Charybdis in this philosophical guise but merely note that it is a difficult problem which should make us wary of any easy assurances that the difficulties facing the base theory can be ignored.[10]

The problem I wish particularly to explore is the problem of those who cannot have a role in the utilitarian-based social contract of mutual respect and a right to life.

## 2. CHILDREN

Children are one group who would be especially vulnerable to a consequentially-grounded social contract as a rationale for the recognition of individual rights. This is because 'no one capable of understanding what is happening when a newborn baby is killed could feel threatened by a policy which gave less protection to the newborn than to adults'.[11] It is, in fact, a prominent feature of consequentialist writing about infants and foetuses that the inviolacy of the individual human life does not carry over to these groups. For instance, consider two children each aged three weeks old, both of whom required access to a scarce health care intervention such as a neonatal intensive care bed. A consequentialist could consistently argue that the relative merit of competing claims on behalf of each should be resolved in favour of the one who had the best chance of achieving higher net satisfaction in life. On this view we might regard a child suffering from any kind of defect as being displaceable or replaceable in favour of a child not so affected. We might even go further and regard a particular attachment to any individual infant rather than their potential competitor (for instance, a possible future child) as irrational or emotional and therefore to reflect a kind of *psychologism* about ethical reasoning. Singer claims that we are particularly prone to this kind of thing when children are being discussed.[12]

Psychologism is generally regarded as unacceptable in philosophy, because it substitutes a statement about human psychology for a clear analysis of the concepts being discussed and a critical evaluation of the conceptual claims made on the basis of that analysis. In logic or epistemology this substitutes the judgment that many people are persuaded by a certain line of thought for the demonstration that the line of thought is valid. In moral theory, psychologism is a more difficult position to define, because it is plausible that there is an intrinsic connection between the psychology and responses of normal human beings and what is in fact good and bad. However we should be able to defend some principled difference between what we *happen to* feel about a given claim and what we *should* think about that claim, where the latter has some sense of arguability or corrigibility beyond a statement of personal or contingently shared dispositions. Consequentialism claims that we ought not base our dispositions on emotive intuitions about particular acts or intentions but rather we should tune our moral judgments to an impartial assessment of the outcomes of actions. The judgments might themselves be based on intuitions – such as the intuition that suffering is bad, or that pleasure is typically good – but a statement of intuitive responses could not be the stuff of argument and therefore the consistent consequentialist has to supplement this in some way. The obvious way is to allow the relevant (intuitively assigned) values to be reduced to some common rationally endorsable type so that like can be compared with like. This adds to our intuitions (about basic things like preferences and suffering) a structure which quantifies and therefore makes contestable the moral dimensions of a problem. We can illustrate this by returning to the problem of young human beings.

We have noticed that in the search for a plausible and universal dimension to apply to assessments of the moral significance of different lives, the idea of preference satisfaction is a plausible candidate. An important set of such preferences concerns the desire to go on living, sometimes called 'future-directed interests', or the sense of continuing identity.

Tooley argues that these cannot plausibly be ascribed to newborn and young infants and therefore that there is no rationally defensible reason why supposed or attributed future-directed interests should influence decisions we make about such infants.[13] Tooley seeks a grounded argument to justify the attribution to any being of a right to life. He finds it by making the right to life co-extensive with a desire to go on living. Commenting on Tooley's view, Singer remarks:

> But only a being who is capable of conceiving herself as a distinct entity existing over time – that is, only a person – could have this desire [to go on living]. Therefore only a person could have a right to life.[14]

It is a small step from here to the denial of any such right to an infant, neonate, or foetus.

> There are many beings who are sentient and capable of experiencing pleasure and pain, but are not rational and self-conscious and so not persons... Many non-human animals almost certainly fall into this category; so must newborn infants and some intellectually disabled humans.[15]

The conclusion that obviously follows is: 'No infant – disabled or not – has as strong a claim to life as beings capable of seeing themselves as distinct entities, existing over time'.[16] This conclusion would also apply, a fortiori, to the life of a foetus where the pregnancy is ended by an early termination. Singer is quite explicit about the application of this view to embryos and 'defective infants':

> We can now look at the foetus for what it is – the actual characteristics it possesses – and can value its life on the same scale as the lives of beings with similar characteristics who are not members of our species.[17]
> Infants are sentient beings who are neither rational nor self-conscious. So if we turn to consider the infants in themselves, independently of the attitudes of their parents, since their species is not relevant to their moral status, the principles that govern the wrongness of killing non-human animals who are sentient but not rational or self-conscious must apply here too.[18]

The fact that there is no defensible right to life for young human beings and the fact that the essentially general quantum of (preference) satisfaction is the sole determinant of the worth of a life, taken together, yield the conclusion that any individual young human life $A$ is disposable and replaceable by another $B$ if certain conditions are met. One relevant condition is that life $B$ is likely to exhibit more good experiences than life $A$.

A further side-issue which we ought to clear out of the way at this point is the contention that the child does have a preference to go on living. This is usually based on the fact that the child has a number of survival-enhancing dispositions. But here Glover is quite clear that the existence of such dispositions does not mean that the child has a conscious preference to avoid death or go on living:

> [A] baby cannot want to escape from death any more than he can want to escape the fate of being a chartered accountant when he grows up. He has no idea of either.[19]

Glover goes on to remark that 'the objection to infanticide is *at most* no stronger than the objection to frustrating a baby's current set of desires, say by leaving him to cry unattended for a longish period'.[20]

To this significant devaluation of the instinctive regard we tend to show for young human lives, we can add a further consideration which diminishes the moral significance of such lives. Given that children are seen as being of less moral worth because they have less self-regarding interests, their worth is largely going to be determined by the way that other significant moral agents value them; thus, according to Singer, some cases of infanticide are wrong because parents and others find the death distressing – but this indicates nothing about the intrinsic moral value of the infant life concerned.[21] This complication, which Glover calls the 'side effects' on others, does not allow us to attach any except derivative value to the life of the infant. For this reason, the consequentialist view has an unattractive and radically counterintuitive implication in the case of child abuse.

Consider the problem of child abuse. The theory tells us that no special regard attaches to the lives of small infants, although they might derive moral value from the preferences of their parents. If those closest to it value its life then an infant, for that reason, becomes a valued object. But this is very bad news indeed for children whose parents abuse them. If the child is resented and abused so that its life is marked by suffering and mortal danger then we must conclude that the life of the infant has minimal or even negative value to the parent. Thus the judgment of strong consequentialism must be that we should be morally indifferent in such a situation between killing the abused child and censuring or punishing the parents. If this already seems an obnoxious conclusion, then there is worse to come. Given that we will override the preferences of the abusive parents by punishing them and that there are no intrinsic moral goods to be preserved in the life of the infant, then the morally right thing to do is to kill the child. According to Glover and Singer, we should not shrink from the intuitive abhorrence of this conclusion merely on the basis of an intuitive response: either '[t]he general principle must be abandoned or modified or else the unpalatable consequence must be accepted'.[22] It is clear which choice is recommended by the consequentialists in question.

The four essential tenets of what I will refer to as a strong utilitarian consequentialism concerning the moral worth of children are as follows:

(1)  A life is of value because of features which are essentially generalizable across life types rather than particular to any individual life;

(2)  A life is morally assessable in its own terms (allowing that ancillary factors such as parental preferences or social consequences must be factored into some decisions);

(3)  There is a core of morally relevant facts determinable impartially in moral situations, so that certain natural feelings should take no part in our principled moral judgments about infants;

(4)  Any act such as killing an infant is assessable in terms of predictable consequences and our assessment should have nothing to do with other aspects of it.

## 3.  METAPHYSICAL REDUCTIONS

There is a famous passage in moral philosophy in which Hume attempts to illustrate the fact that moral judgments involve passion and not merely an appreciation of the facts. He claims that there is no factual difference between patricide and the situation in which an acorn falls from an oak tree and, as it takes root and grows, eventually causes the death of its progenitor.[23] Hume argues that the facts in these two cases are the same and therefore that our moral response to patricide draws on passion and not on reason. I will call his move *the Humean reduction*. A moment's reflection suffices to reveal, contra the Humean reduction, that there are some very important differences between the two cases. The son has had a relationship with the father involving interpersonal conversation (in its broadest sense), nurture, training and modelling of certain behaviour, mutual understanding to some extent, and the many inarticulate things that pass between person and person over the course of lives in close proximity with each other. Thus the whole character of the father–son relationship goes beyond anything that could be found in the plant kingdom. Moreover, when one recognizes that all these facts are plausibly central to moral judgments, it becomes obvious that there can only be the remotest resemblance between the two cases that Hume claims are factually equivalent. For this reason an informed moral judge cannot view with indifference a case of patricide, whereas she might justifiably take that attitude toward natural events such as those involving the trees or, to take an even closer case, that of an alligator eating its offspring.

If natural events, even where they involve the death of sentient creatures, do not suggest clear moral judgments, then they are significantly different in nature from the patricide case. We can concede that any moral judge, for instance in the case of Oedipus, might not be able to come to a clear-cut moral judgment of the son, and might even endorse what he does – but there will always be important considerations here, and indifference would be a sign of ignorance rather than rationality. There are, therefore, metaphysical facts that will influence our assessment of the moral content of our decisions. Take a different case: were we to decide that an incommunicative individual deformed in ways reminiscent of vegetative human beings actually had experiences that mattered to him – that caused a sufficiency of mental acts and attitudes such as feelings of distress, gratification, rejection, preferences, regret, anger and so on – then it would be almost impossible to neglect the implicit moral claims of his existence. In this case a particular metaphysical belief, about his mental life, influences a range of actions. So far we have no disagreement with the consequentialist. However, having said this, the relationship between his moral properties and our metaphysical beliefs about him may be quite complex and not go through an explicit syllogism of the following type:

a. A person has preferences.
b. These preferences concern his life and liberty.
c. In general his preferences should be respected.
d. This is a person.
e. Therefore he is, prima facie, entitled to have his preferences respected especially when they concern his life and liberty.

The premises may, in fact, be only a crude selection from the metaphysical facts that apply to the situation of any person. It is plausible that the nature of human life is inextricably interwoven with an interconnected raft of ideas such as those that combine to yield Strawson's 'reactive attitudes'.[24]

Strawson argues that our beliefs in such things as the freedom of the individual and his responsibility for his own actions are inseparable from a range of reactive (including moral) attitudes such as resentment, indignation, praise, blame, entitlement, compassion, and so on. He argues that these attitudes are part of a rationally consistent conceptual scheme which is an integral part of our everyday life as human beings who live out our lives in relation to one another. This scheme is, however, quite distinct from a scheme in which we regard human beings as bits of biological stuff caused by impersonal forces to behave in this or that way on the basis of internal mechanisms (although that might also be a true description of us in terms of a certain kind of discourse). What is more, he argues that the reactive attitudes scheme – which includes concepts like *belief, intention, respect, freedom,* and *resentment* – is not only permissible for us to employ in the sense that it informs our normal dealings with other human beings, but is unassailably rational. It is rational to hold fast to the descriptions and conclusions that emerge within this scheme, because as a scheme it is indispensible to those dealings with each other in which such things as justification, meaning, intention, action, assertion, and so on are employed. By contrast, the 'objective or reductive scheme' in which we consider purely physical descriptions of objects, mechanisms, and impersonal forces as the only facts holding sway in the world would, if uncritically applied to human behaviour, undermine the interpersonal attributes that structure our discursive and moral universe. For Strawson, it is not rational for us to allow any theory to preempt ways of acting and relating that are intrinsic to our nature as rational social beings.

When we search around for similar patterns of thought in relation to very young human lives, it is evident that we are torn between wanting to regard them as human beings and acknowledging the fact that they are not the kind of human beings with whom we are in reciprocal moral discourse. If we then extend our reflection to things such as human embryos, we find ourselves in a domain of thought in relation to which our moral judgments no longer have clear implications. It should, therefore, be no surprise to us that we commonly experience moral conflict in relation to life-and-death decisions about embryos and foetuses.

However, when we try to understand this conflict, firmly based in our (essentially reactive) ways of relating to human beings, we find that consequentialist interpretations are unhelpful. For instance, many of us would appeal to something like potentiality to defend the intrinsic value of young human lives. But here the consequentialists are quite severe. Singer says we must look at the very young human life for what it is, that is, in terms of 'the actual characteristics it possesses'.[25] What are these actual characteristics, and what does it mean to say that a young human being is a potential person? That is not at all obvious. Consider the following analogy. I hold a ticket to the FA Cup Final (or NBA finals if you prefer). My wife casually announces one evening, 'I was so sick of you not getting your trousers cleaned I emptied the pockets and sent them to the dry cleaners.' My heart sinks because that was where I kept my ticket. I ask about the ticket and learn that she threw it in the rubbish (or garbage if you prefer). I am upset (to put it mildly). She says, 'What are you upset about, it was only a little piece of paper.' Now my wife is right: it was only a little piece of paper, in terms of the actual characteristics it possessed – but she is producing a paradigmatic Humean reduction. I would contend that a similar move is going on in the consequentialist view of potentiality.

Basing our attitudes to things on the consequences of a certain course of events going in a particular way leaves us perplexed about what it is that concerns us in the case of human embryos and foetuses. By treating each individual human embryo as the mere focus of a set of events that might result in a person if not interfered with by ourselves or other influences, we lose a number of conceptual connections which relate what we think of that thing to what we think of other things which have a certain place in our universe of discourse. In particular, this view completely obscures what is important about an object whose future is destined to be destroyed before it is a person. The reading of potential as projectible future (depending on the consequences of intervening events) yields the conclusion that a to-be-ended young human life is of no moral consequence. But the intrinsic nature of the young human life is not so easily disconnected from the person-to-be. My ticket carried the significance it did because of a complex place in human discourse and a number of things that mean a great deal to anybody who understands the values inherent in being a soccer (or basketball) fan. In the case of embryos, the relevant discourse involves us all because it is the discourse of human origins. In this discourse, things like embryos have a unique place not captured by an austere description of their physical characteristics. For this reason there is merit in the view that a human embryo has potential as an intrinsic feature of its nature and its moral status must include that of a person-to-be. If we shut out such a basic meaning or significance as this, then our view of the being in question loses the kind of links with our moral attitudes that are, in general, basic to our ethical thinking about any of the beings whom we encounter.

This counter to the consequentialist focus on a fairly narrow conception of the 'actual characteristics' of young human lives allows us to connect our moral reasoning to the range of judgments, perceptions, and reflective techniques that inform us about the world in general. Things are subject to many descriptions or significations and various of these are more or less adequate to various tasks. We ought to command and be able to work with a range of these, conscious of the things that they differentially make visible and invisible. The problem with the Humean reduction is that it deprives us of the descriptions that are most apt to the kinds of reasoning proper to ethics. But it now begins to look as if, at least in relation to young human lives, consequentialism has the same tendency to obscure relevant thoughts as does the Humean reduction of patricide. Further reflection will, I hope, make that conclusion even more compelling.

## 4. ANTI-CONSEQUENTIALIST THOUGHTS ABOUT YOUNG HUMAN LIVES

The central tenets of strong consequentialism[26] suggest a number of points at which we could attack this general framework of argument about children. My counter to the consequentialist programme, although presented as a series of separate questions, is in fact an interwoven set of moral theses whose connection to each other and overall anti-consequentialist thrust will, I hope, become apparent. One could almost say it embodies a substantive alternative moral theory to consequentialism.

(1) Does the moral worth of a human life depend on the quantity of essentially general satisfaction quanta that that life currently realizes or is likely to realize? I will argue that the case of children suggests that this is not true to our moral thinking and that therefore this tenet, basic to most types of consequentialism about the value of human lives, should be rejected. It is only tenable if a selective Humean reduction is allowed to colour the metaphysics of young human lives and the assessment of their moral value which are, in fact, inextricably tied to one another.

(2) Is each life separable from every other and individually assessable for its intrinsic moral value? We could see this as questioning a kind of reductive methodological individualism about human lives and their value. I will suggest that such individualism is not sustainable and therefore the utility intuitions based on it are also flawed.

(3) Which characteristics are legitimately excluded from moral judgments and which can only be excluded if we run the risk of ignoring important features of moral situations? In particular, can we justify the exclusion of significant particular emotional attachments and commitments from rational moral deliberation? I will say that we cannot and that a false conception of the dichotomy between fact and value falsely

exposes us to rationalistic bullying (of which consequentialism is the most obvious type) in the area of moral reasoning.

(4) Are act types properly evaluated according to consequential assessments of them so that, for instance, contraception = abortion = infanticide? I will suggest that the currently favoured consequentialist analyses of the issues surrounding young human lives are quite untrue to our reflectively endorsed intuitions and should be abandoned.

*(1) In what does the worth of a young human life consist?*

Why do the lives of persons matter morally? A utilitarian would say that they matter because each person's life has the consequence of adding to the (indeterminate) sum of preferences and satisfactions abroad in the universe. We have noted that this gives us no basis for claiming that any particular individual matters, all things being equal. However, we can say that the early death of someone like Mozart matters because of three factors: (i) he is deprived of a future life which he would prefer to have; (ii) those near to him are deprived of his company in which they find pleasure; and (iii) he might have significantly added to the pleasures of many others through the extra music he would have composed had he gone on living. Even for lesser mortals the first two of these apply. For *young* lesser mortals, however, only (ii) applies.

Thus, when asked why children matter and why, in particular, it should matter to a parent that a particular child should die from cot death, we find ourselves rendered relatively silent by the strong consequentialist. Given that the child might be replaced by another,[27] and that we might find equal satisfactions in raising that other child, and given that the alternative child will, by and large, be in the same state of well-being, then it seems irrational to regard the loss of the particular child as anything special. Therefore, for a consequentialist, our moves to devote health care resources to saving particular infant lives – through, for instance, a cot death prevention programme – would be a moral mistake. The fly in this ointment is the irrational attachment that seems to form between parents and particular children and so the consequentially endorsable moral conclusion only goes through if the population at large can be converted to 'right-thinking', i.e. consequentialist, convictions.

However, most of us believe that each individual child does matter and that the way in which they matter is quite independent of any attitudes towards them that are taken by their parents. In fact, rather than making parental attitudes definitive of the moral worth of children, we would look askance at parents who did not form a caring and individually directed attachment to each of their children. Who is right here?

To decide what a genuinely informed rational attitude might be, we will need to avoid any Humean reduction in our 'factual' characterization of the nature of a child. It is not clear that a consequentialist characterization which portrays the child as a relatively undifferentiated locus of certain occurrent states of satisfaction or inchoate preference manages to avoid this mistake.

A child, from birth at least (and, some would claim, from conception) can truly be perceived to have a unique relational and discursive place among us. I am reminded of a little boy, whose infant brother subsequently died when a few weeks old, and who said, when holding his brother on his knee, 'I am your older brother'. This boy had already identified that infant, as had the whole family, as being a unique human being with his own name, and history, and time of coming into the world, and any number of other features which subtly but unambiguously made that infant both one of us and different from any other individual one of us.

This metaphysics of individuation is however inextricably embedded in the system of what Strawson has called 'reactive attitudes' – the stuff of our rationally articulated interpersonal and moral lives. Thus we cannot merely focus on a set of purely physical descriptions of objective characteristics when we try to describe the nature of and defend the importance of an individual infant. Reactive attitudes, with their intrinsic moral implications, are part of the recognition and essence of the intentional characteristics that were illegitimately excluded in Hume's reductive move. These same reactive attitudes and their conceptual progeny allow us to notice and nurture the characteristics which individuate infants. Judging according to the reactive schema also yields the factual basis on which we assess moral significance (because intentional properties include things like like preference formation and so on). Thus our basic moral responses to infants are, in part, formed amidst reactive attitudes and the attributions inextricably tied to them. For this reason, the individuality and indeed irreplaceability of each infant is a basic feature of our thinking about them. On the account of metaphysics that I have sketched the sparse view of 'actual characteristics' does not capture the metaphysics of young human beings and therefore fails to reveal the things that are directly relevant to value assessments in relation to them.

We could even say that a being is intrinsically of value if, even potentially, it is a being who is one of us, in a morally reciprocal sense. It has this value in that the only basis on which we can understand and relate to an infant as a metaphysical type takes origin in our complex of reactive and interpersonal attitudes which cause us to respect and value each other as individuals and the infant as one who belongs among us.

## (2) *Is methodological individualism sustainable in ethics?*

I have sketched a relational basis for the the metaphysical properties which are basic in the evaluative judgments underpinning utilitarian consequentialism. These properties, such as preference formation and other intentional phenomena, are however treated in isolation from the essentially reactive milieu in which the metaphysics of infant lives is located and makes sense. The reality is that in this milieu an infant is a being who has engaged me and offered me an opportuniy to show care towards him or her as an individual. These properties do not show up in the metaphysics of consequentialism, because they are essentially relational and they do not allow us to prise the individual loose from his or her discursive location so as to define his or her actual characteristics. Therefore it is only if the consequentialist bestiary of metaphysical properties is uncritically accepted that we can regard young human lives as replaceable. When we consider the uniquely instantiated set of relations I or we have with this particular named being who is among us, related to us, and is vulnerable to each of us in terms of its very survival, then this individual cannot be replaced. Of course, another individual child who will make the same kind of demand for my nurture and care might come to be in the same type of relation to me or us should the existing one be somehow disrupted – but this is a specialized sense of 'replacement' that carries its own moral and psychological hazards. It seems plausible that the morally relevant metaphysical characterisation of an infant or other young human life is that this life is that of a being who belongs among us and inspires nurture in the rest of us. The intrinsic relationality and particularity of each infant when this characterization is applied argues that a replaceability thesis is not sustainable.

There is a further fact that is relevant to our moral judgments in relation to young human lives. Such beings, as I have noted, are subject to non-contractual attitudes in that they cannot form reciprocal contracts of consideration and respect. Therefore the kind of moral response we adopt toward them is a reflection of the value we place on human life in general, as distinct from the value we place on the lives of those whom we have self-directed interests to respect. It follows that the way in which we answer the questions about young human lives reflects the extent to which we are committed to a basic stance in which we identify with one another and include in conceptions of what is good attitudes toward the values of being-with in contrast to attitudes based on individualistic conceptions of good. These latter can ultimately be differentially indexed to one's own good and therefore have different moral properties. Some of us would like to argue that attitudes of the communal or being-with sort are inherently more virtuous than any attitudes built on the individualist framework. We might go so far as to say that a moral system truly counts as such only in so far as it is built on attitudes of the former sort and as a result pays special regard to the vulnerable and powerless.

### (3) Making visible the sources of moral judgment

The speculations about what counts as a moral attitude lead naturally to reflection on the sources of moral judgment. We might ask of a consequentialist theory whether it illuminates those sources in any way which is at all satisfying or whether it relies on a declaration of the nature of moral primitives supported by quasi-rational prescriptions about what counts as moral reasoning. It seems that consequentialism is committed to methodological individualism, allied with a set of some preferred subset of properties surviving metaphysical reduction as the approved basis on which the relative values proper to different states of affairs are supposed to be assessed. I have tried to suggest that the fundamental bases of moral reasoning arise within relationships and include relational facts such as dependence and attachment. On this richer basis we might be able to locate intuitions that lie deep in our ethical reasoning. These deeper intuitions focus on the inherently intersubjective nature of human understanding and intentionality in general and the links that are forged between them. The central relatedness is not incidental but itself formative in human identity and issues in certain implicit demands and commitments that arise between human individuals. Consider the child who is held by his father and who therefore becomes *this little child whom I have held, who needs me, and in whose life I can play a nurturing role*. From that point, the father cannot regard this being with indifference just because it does not have the richness of conceptual content that he has. If I, as a father, could do so I would not be rational but rather evince an impaired personality. A psychopath could act in this way, but not a person whose moral judgment might claim any credence. The kind of moral sensitivity involved here does, of course, make me keenly aware of any consequence of my actions on this little child but that feature of my attitudes to what I do to the child is not at all like the detached, individual-independent considerations that figure in consequentialist writing about such situations.

### (4) Actions, consequences, and moral value

I have attacked a strong consequentialist position and yet, on the basis of the obvious role of consequences in our assessments of competing intentions, we might wonder whether a weaker kind of consequentialism would fare better in the face of the attack. But we have to ask whether the weaker consequentialism envisaged is a theory of the type that can have any interesting consequentialist implications. If it can, then some kind of consequentialism as a basis for moral judgment might still be sound.

We have already noted that certain kinds of social contract utilitarianism abandon some central consequentialist intuitions, unless the social contract is held to be vulnerable in any situation where the agent justifiably believes that the consequential calculus would recommend the opposite course of action to that which has been contracted. We might also challenge any attempt to use a consequentialist justification structure which includes such things as the general undesirability of having a society in which people are disposed to act in certain ways. This latter view comes so close to virtue ethics that the distinctive consequentialist conclusions die the death of a thousand qualifications.

We could go on along this path for some time but in the end I think that we ought to conclude that any variant which abandons significant tenets of the strong view is no longer clearly something we ought to call consequentialist rather than deontological, narrative, or virtue ethics or even an ethic of care.[28] Thus a view which allows that we ought to do certain things just because we are essentially beings-in-relation with certain types of dispositions arising as part of that metaphysic should be grouped with virtue theories rather than classified as a kind of consequentialism. And any view according to which we ought to treat certain beings in certain ways just because they are beings of a given ontological type should be grouped with deontological theories. Similarly, the theory that we ought to act in certain situations as guided by the caring relationships in which we find ourselves should be grouped with theories in the ethics of care. On any or all of these approaches we might consider the consequences of our actions and ask how consistent they are with the base on which moral value is built, according to the theory; but this does not mark those theories in any interesting way as consequentialist. The fact that all these styles of theory do make visible morally relevant but nonconsequential features of situations suggest that consequences are not an adequate way to ground our judgments of the moral value of actions.

## 5. CONCLUSION

I have defined a significant consequentialist theory which is widely recognized to have interesting implications for the treatment of human infants and our attitudes to the moral properties of young human lives. I have argued that the theory, as an exemplar of certain basic tenets of consequentialism, is subject to some serious problems such as that posed by justifying our respect for individual human preferences and furthermore, that even if we turn that trick, we have difficulty justifying a plausible response to the moral problem of child abuse.

I have tried to diagnose the underlying problem in terms of a range of related and highly suspect commitments of the theory. I have questioned the metaphysical reductions commonly used to set up the moral conclusions in consequentialist analyses of problem situations. I have then questioned the methodological individualism common in consequentialist arguments and argued that morally relevant properties are intrinsically relational and reflect our engagements with and attachments to one another. I have extended this point to argue that consequentialism actually obscures the habits of the heart or interpersonal perceptions and dispositions that fuel moral judgment, and illustrated this phenomenon by appeal to our intuitions about children. Lastly, I have questioned the idea that the consequences of action are the only morally relevant features and noted other features which can only be included in an ethical analysis at the expense of that analysis losing any seriously consequentialist character. For these reasons I believe that the moral problems posed by young human lives demonstrate the inadequacy of consequentialism as an ethical theory. What is more, consequentialism may lead us in a dangerous direction because it systematically devalues certain deep intuitions, such as those involved in the care and nurture of children, which some of us regard as of fundamental significance in the constitution of a moral agent.[29]

## NOTES

1  P. Singer, *Practical Ethics* (Cambridge: CUP, 1993, 2nd. ed.) (hereafter referred to as 'Singer'); M. Tooley, 'Abortion and Infanticide', *Philosophy and Public Affairs* 2 (1972) 37–65, reprinted in J. Feinberg (ed.), *The Problem of Abortion* (Belmont: Wadsworth, 1984, 2nd. ed.).

2  R. Crisp, 'Quality of Life and Health Care', in K. Fulford, G. Gillett, and J. Martin Soskice (eds.), *Medicine and Moral Reasoning* (Cambridge; CUP, 1994).

3  J. Glover, *Causing Death and Saving Lives* (Harmondsworth: Penguin, 1977), pp. 62–3 (hereafter referred to as 'Glover').

4  Glover, p. 71.

5  Hobbes, *Leviathan* (Oxford: Clarendon Press, 1909), p. 96.

6  Glover, p. 72.

7  Glover, pp. 72–3.

8  Singer, p. 94.
9  Singer, pp. 94–5.
10  Glover, p. 62.
11  Singer, p. 171.
12  Singer, p. 170.
13  Tooley, 'Abortion and Infanticide'.
14  Singer, p. 97.
15  Singer, p. 101; 'intellectually disabled humans' are referred to as 'mental defectives' in the first edition of *Practical Ethics* (Cambridge: CUP, 1979), p. 84.
16  Singer, p. 182; the first edition, p. 131, has 'defective' instead of 'disabled'.
17  Singer, p. 150.
18  Singer, p. 183. Compare the first edition, p. 132: 'Taking the infant in itself, what we have is a sentient being that is neither rational nor self-conscious. Since its species is not relevant to its moral status, the principles that govern the wrongness of killing nonhuman animals who are sentient but not rational or self-conscious must apply here too. These principles are utilitarian. Hence the quality of life that the infant can be expected to have is important.'
19  Glover, p. 158.
20  Loc. cit.
21  Singer, p. 173.
22  Glover, p. 26.
23  D. Hume, *A Treatise of Human Nature*, ed. Selby-Bigge (Oxford: Clarendon Press, 1960), Book III, Part I, sec. i, p. 467.
24  P. F. Strawson, 'Freedom and Resentment', in *Freedom and Resentment and other Essays* (London: Methuen, 1974).
25  Singer, p. 150.
26  I have outlined the four central claims above in Section 2.
27  The consequentialist doctrine of replaceability has been extensively criticised elsewhere: see S. Uniacke and H. McCloskey, 'Peter Singer and Non-Voluntary "Euthanasia": Tripping down the Slippery Slope', *Journal of Applied Philosophy* 9 (1992) 203–19.
28  N. Noddings, *Caring: a Feminine Approach to Ethics and Moral Education* (Berkeley: University of California Press, 1984).
29  G. Gillett, 'Women and Children First', in *Medicine and Moral Reasoning*.

# 7 Medicine, Virtues and Consequences
*John Cottingham*

## 1. PRELIMINARIES: TELEOLOGY, FUNCTION AND PURPOSE

In an interview for a serious medical journal, a famous doctor is asked what his main career goals are. 'To double my salary before I retire,' he replies; 'and to spend more time at the exclusive golf club to which I've just been elected.' There is perhaps nothing terribly wrong with either of these aims, but we can well imagine the interviewer being taken aback. What he wanted to know about was the doctor's aims *as a doctor.* The answers he got related to something else – personal goals, or 'off-duty goals' we might say, or even goals of the subject qua salary earner; but not his goals qua doctor.

The distinction is an old one. Socrates, in his debate with Thrasymachus, distinguished what the shepherd does qua shepherd, and what he does qua wage earner.[1] This may at first seem an artificial distinction: for most people, earning money (and all that this involves) is connected in a fairly integral way with career activities. But the Socratic distinction is still perfectly sound. It reminds us of the essential difference between that which is logically or analytically connected with a certain pursuit, career or profession, and that which is only contingently so connected. A shepherd would still be a shepherd if he worked for nothing; but if his activities are not directed towards things like looking after the flock (taking them out to pasture, protecting them from wolves, helping the ewes to give birth safely, and so on) he cannot, logically, be a shepherd.

One interesting result follows from these simple observations, namely that it is not up to the individual (or indeed society, or anyone else) to set the activities and goals that are characteristic of a given profession. Some philosophers have been very confused about this. Many seem to believe that because these are human activities, it is open to human beings to set the rules from scratch, as it were – to prescribe the goals appropriate for each profession or activity. In a well-known article on reverse discrimination, Ronald Dworkin suggests that having black skin could be a relevant *merit* possessed by certain applicants for law school. For the notion of 'merit' (he argues) is relative to the goals set by society;

and if society decides things would be better (fairer, more 'equal') if there were more black lawyers, then there is nothing to stop admissions officers ruling that being black is a 'merit' which entitles applicants of a given race to favourable consideration.[2] Yet whatever we feel about the rights or wrongs of reverse discrimination, or quotas for 'disadvantaged' applicants, this particular argument cannot be sound. The characteristic activities of the lawyer, like those of the shepherd, are logically determined by the nature of the profession; and this in turn places severe constraints on what can count as the qualifications needed to pursue those activities. Black skin just cannot (logically) be a 'merit', or a relevant qualification for a lawyer qua lawyer.[3]

It could be objected that to say the goals and activities of a profession are fixed by its nature presupposes the outmoded notion that human activities fit into an unalterable teleological framework that is somehow 'given'. 'Every action and pursuit aims at some good', says Aristotle: 'the end of medical science is health, of military science victory.' And he goes on to observe that these goals form a natural hierarchy (the skill of bridle-making, for example, is subordinate to that of horsemanship).[4] The Aristotelian notion of a *telos* or goal, and the associated concept of an *ergon* (job or function) is a broad one, embracing a wide variety of organized systems, and indeed (perhaps confusingly) applied to organs as well as organisms: the eye has an *ergon* and a *telos*, as does a plant and a cobbler.[5] This gives rise to the criticism that the Aristotelian framework confuses the kind of teleology that may be appropriate for explaining the functional properties of organs with the quite different concept of conscious purposive activity. Rick Momeyer, in a recent paper defending 'physician-assisted suicide', insists that although the domain of medicine is the body, with its various natural functions, medicine itself 'as an activity of human devising serving human purposes is just what we make it to be, not what nature decrees it must be.'[6] But there is a non sequitur here. Because a given activity is a purposive job, role or skill of 'human devising', it does not follow that it is 'just what we make it to be'. Bridlemaking is admittedly a human invention, devised for a human purpose, but we clearly do not have *carte blanche* to make it whatever sort of thing we choose. The natural, predetermined properties of horses, of leather and brass (or other appropriate materials), and indeed the natural features of human anatomy, place severe constraints on how the skill of bridle-making can be exercised. What counts as a good piece of bridle-making, of course, involves reference to human evaluations and conscious human purposes; but it also depends on naturally given features of the world that were in place long before we came on the scene.

Since I shall be making considerable use of the Aristotelian concept of a *telos*, it is worth taking a moment to see why some modern philosophers have come to see it as something to be wary of. Teleology first became suspect in the early modern period when the 'new' philosophers began to wean themselves off the traditional medieval worldview, broadly based on Platonic and Aristotelian elements incorporated within a Judaeo-Christian metaphysic.[7] The old picture was of a benign and intelligible cosmos, with the earth at its centre – a universe made up of substances whose nature could be understood in terms of readily graspable forms and essences (what Aristotle had called 'formal causes'),[8] and whose behaviour could be understood teleologically, in terms of a progression towards a series of specifically ordered goals or end-states. This last notion (corresponding to the Aristotelian idea of 'final causation') implied that we can understand natural phenomena by reference to the functions and purposes of things: plants have roots for the sake of taking up nutrients from the soil; cats have sharp claws for the sake of catching their prey. Construed in purely functional terms, such accounts seem unexceptionable (indeed, it is arguable that teleological explanations in this sense still have a central, perhaps ineliminable, place in the modern biological sciences);[9] but as developed in medieval and scholastic philosophy the idea of teleology became inextricably linked with belief in the plans and purposes of a benevolent creator specially concerned for the welfare of mankind: 'It is God's will', as Paracelsus put it in the sixteenth century, 'that nothing remain unknown to man as he walks in the light of nature, for all things belonging to nature exist for the sake of man'.[10]

The eventual result of the Cartesian, and then Darwinian, revolutions was that this picture was discarded and replaced with a view of man as confronting an essentially alien physical universe of purposeless particle interactions. No intrinsic purpose or meaning imbues this new universe; and any direction or goal it may appear to possess is either a function of the inscrutable and incomprehensible will of the creator (Descartes),[11] or else simply an illusion, masking the blind and directionless process of random physical mutations (Darwin). And the ethical corollary, which was swiftly articulated by the 'father' of the modern age, was that the determination of goals is left entirely to mankind: instead of seeing our fulfilment in terms of submission to, or attunement with, an harmonious and ordered cosmos, we are set over against the physical world as manipulators and controllers. Instead of 'speculative philosophy', the way is open for a new scientific philosophy which will make us 'masters and possessors of nature'.[12] Technological power replaces harmonious attunement as the key to the successful conduct of human life.

To explore the implications of this momentous shift in outlook would take us far beyond the scope of this paper. For the present purpose, the relevant point is quite simple. It is a confusion to suppose that abandoning the old picture of a naturally ordered and benign cosmos necessarily reduces all human evaluation to the domain of autonomous and arbitrary prescription. It is doubtful if it even makes sense to suppose that our lives are a *tabula rasa* on which we can sketch out whatever plans we choose. For the context of our human existence is, in very large measure, already determined by pre-existing structures which we did not, and cannot, create *de novo*. And it follows that in understanding the world we necessarily come armed with categories, classifications and concepts which themselves provide constraints on what we can coherently suppose to be of value. To bring this nearer to the case in hand, we cannot understand the workings of the human body without having some conception of the difference between a healthy and a diseased organism. And we cannot form a coherent picture of how human life could be valuable without supposing (what is already implied in the very notion of health) that it is better to be healthy than diseased. And, finally, we cannot have a coherent concept of medicine (the aim of which, as Aristotle notes, is health) while at the same time maintaining that medicine is 'just what we make it to be'. Humans are free to do many things, but they are not free to design from scratch the natural context within which their projects and evaluations must necessarily operate. 'It is he who hath made us, and not we ourselves': the ancient words of the Psalmist[13] are expressed in the language of creationism, but there is a profound sense in which the underlying message, that of our necessary dependence on processes and structures we did not create, remains true irrespective of where we came from.

## 2. MEDICAL VIRTUE

The notions explored in the previous section have important implications for the concept of a virtue or excellence. There is an analytic connection between the concept of an excellence (*arete*) and the concept of the good.[14] But 'the good' here cannot be construed in an arbitrary or purely prescriptive way, as a creature of human devising. To be a good marine navigator, to have the relevant virtues or excellences, is to adopt a role or profession of which the conditions for satisfactory execution are already in large part fixed by the constraints imposed by geology and meteorology (the wind, the tides, the shoals and sandbanks) and the demands of safe transport from port to port. It is not up to me, or anyone else, to decide what can go into the specification of 'good navigator', or what are the relevant excellences that have to be acquired. This is not, of course, to say that everything is eternally fixed with total rigidity: there are no doubt different ways of being a good navigator, different strategies and techniques available, different methods of training, and different technological resources from generation to generation, all of which allow for debate and discussion about the best way to go about things. But these instrumental differences only make sense against a relatively stable background of logical interconnections between the specification of the job (*ergon*), its overarching aim or goal (*telos*), and the kinds of excellence which are relevant to its achievement. Ἐν τῳ ἐργῳ ἡ ἀρετη ἐν τῃ ἀρετῃ το ἐυ ἐργαζεσθαι, as Plato had it, underlining an analytic but important truth: 'in the job lies the excellence, and in the excellence the good performance'.[15]

The moral I wish to draw from this is that there is a certain tension between the constraints logically imposed by the nature of a profession, role or job and the use of certain consequentialist modes of reasoning in ethics. During 1994–5, a documentary entitled 'Death on Request' was widely shown on television networks all over the planet. Made by the Dutch company *Ikon*, it filmed the killing of a patient, Cees, suffering from amyotrophic lateral sclerosis, an incurable wasting degeneration of the muscles. Cees was confined to a wheelchair, and unable to speak except with great difficulty, but entirely *compos mentis* and articulate (he communicated via the written alphabet), and with the full range of unimpaired cognitive and emotional capacities and responses. The doctor, Wilfred van Coyjen, explained to the patient's wife that 'you could give him drugs, but in the end it's only a stopgap. He's going to die and he knows it.' Told of his prospects, the patient himself repeatedly requested to be put out of his misery. The film showed the final visit to the patient's home. After asking the patient if he was ready, and receiving the laborious reply (spelt out on a alphabet chart) 'let's postpone it . . . no longer', the doctor administered first a sleeping injection and then a lethal dose of paralysing poison (a curare derivative). After a time breathing ceased, but the heart continued to beat strongly until it too gave out. Within the terms of the 'grey area' afforded by Dutch law (euthanasia has not formally been legalized in the Netherlands, but is not normally prosecuted provided certain conditions are met), the doctor had then to report the killing to the coroner, who in turn informed the prosecution service, which decided to take no further action. Explaining his decision to perform euthanasia, Dr. van Coyjen commented: 'I am giving people the possibility to make choices: what kind of quality of life, and death, do they want? I have seen a lot of people dying. Death is not always awful. With a good doctor, death can be faithful, like a good friend.'[16]

It would be a grotesque trivialization of the complexities inherent in this type of case, and the genuine human anguish involved, to try to pass a snap judgment on van Coyjen's course of action. Certainly, as far as could be ascertained from the film, his motives were those of a deeply caring and compassionate person. But the proposition I want to focus on for the purpose of the present discussion is his claim that he was acting as a 'good doctor'. I have already argued that it is not, and cannot be, up to us to define the goals of a given profession or activity from scratch. Medicine, qua medicine, is and must be aimed at the health of the patient: that is its *telos*, just as the goal of the bridle-maker is the making of tackle that conduces to the goal of efficient horse-riding. Suppose a bridlemaker, for political reasons (say to assassinate a tyrant), is induced to make a harness that will kill the horse, or cause the rider to break his neck. The question here is not whether such an action could be justified, but whether it could fall within the ambit of the good bridle-maker. And the answer is surely negative. It may be that the technical expertise which is acquired by the bridle-maker will help when it comes to the deliberate manufacture of defective and dangerous tackle, but in undertaking such a plan the bridle-maker is not longer acting *qua talis*; he is acting in a way which by definition debars him (on this occasion) from instantiating the excellences of his profession. Suppose, again, a doctor is prevailed upon to administer a lethal injection to a convicted murderer. If capital punishment can be justified, his action may be justifiable, but in doing it he is not, and cannot be, acting as a good doctor. For his action has nothing to do with furthering the health of the patient; if he acts as executioner he is stepping outside the role of doctor, and adopting a different role, that of state executioner. Even though he may keep his white coat and stethoscope on, and even though he may perform the task as decently and humanely as he can, this does not make his action that of a doctor, nor, a fortiori, of a good doctor.[17]

Though it is not the purpose of this paper to examine the ethics of euthanasia, a complication, which may lead some readers to resist our conclusions so far, needs briefly to be dealt with here. It may seem that talk of the 'health of the patient' as the *telos* of medicine obscures an important fact: that there may be cases (e.g. of terminal illness) when that goal is unachievable, and so the well-being of the patient is best served by killing him. But there is a crucial distinction to be made. 'Health' is a broad concept which certainly includes the palliative measures designed to keep the patient comfortable when he is sick and/or in pain: a patient is better off, from the point of view of his overall health, when he has the benefit of the doctor's knowledge of pharmacology which enables him to live free from the fear of prolonged agony or distress. But in this type of case the administration of narcotics, even when it is known this may shorten life, is still done with the intention of promoting (as far as possible, given the morbid condition) the overall (psycho-physical) health of the patient. And that is quite different from administering a poison precisely in order to kill the patient – an action which is not compatible with the *telos* of medicine.[18] The much maligned doctrine of 'double effect' still has something to teach us here. That doctrine is rightly criticized in so far as it suggests that an impermissible action becomes mysteriously permitted by glibly redescribing it – for example by characterizing a deliberate killing as merely the bringing about of a foreseen (but unintended) death.[19] But there is, nonetheless, a crucial moral difference between intention and foresight (or between 'direct' and 'oblique' intention, in Bentham's awkward and misleading parlance).[20] To give a student a bad exam result knowing it will cause them distress is compatible with the *ergon* of a good teacher and the *telos* of education; to give them the result precisely in order to cause them distress is not. And the same holds good, mutatis mutandis, for the doctor asking herself what she is trying to achieve (death or pain relief) in administering a heavy dose of narcotic drugs. Of course, things may reach the stage (this is an empirical question) where there is *nothing* the doctor has left in her medical repertoire which will achieve anything whatever for the health of the patient. But if killing or 'assisted suicide' is then decided on as the most humane option, we have now moved outside the ambit of medical virtue. Such actions may or may not be justified (that is not addressed here), but they are not logically within the ambit of what a doctor, and a fortiori a good doctor, can do. We may perhaps need death-technicians who kill people humanely when medicine has exhausted its resources, just as we may need demolition experts to destroy cars when they cannot be repaired; but the virtues needed for such jobs cannot logically be exhibited as virtues of the good motor repair man, or the good doctor.

One final complication. With the rise of modern hospital technology, coupled with the way the law of negligence operates in some countries, many legitimately fear they will be subjected to frantic and (miscalled) 'heroic' measures to prolong their lives when they are terminally ill. But the insistence that the goal of medical virtue is the promotion of the health of the patient does not at all imply unconditional support for such measures. It is a traditional and important part of virtue theory that each

virtue has its vice of excess as well as its vice of deficiency. The comman-
der who 'heroically' leads his men forward to charge a machine-gun post
when there is no prospect whatever of doing anything but sacrificing the
lives of the entire platoon is not manifesting the virtue of military valour;
on the contrary, he is manifesting the vice of foolhardiness, as much (or
nearly as much)[21] to be condemned as the vice of cowardice. And similarly, the doctor who frantically hooks up a patient with irreversible
brain-stem damage to a heart-lung machine is manifesting the kind of
misplaced zeal that is rightly characterized as excessive – as much (or
nearly as much) to be condemned as the vice of deficiency, of not doing
enough for the patient's health. To develop a virtue, an ingrained set of
habits of feeling and behaviour which will tend to make us act 'at the right
times, on the right grounds, towards the right people, for the right motive
and in the right way'[22] is no doubt extraordinarily difficult. But there is
nothing in virtue theory that entails that once a goal is set, the virtue analytically connected with that goal is a matter of pursuing an objective at
all costs or irrespective of circumstances; indeed, quite the reverse.

## 3. VIRTUES AND CONSEQUENCES

In the final section of this paper, I want to draw out some general implications of what has been said so far for the relationship between virtue
theory and consequentialism. To cultivate virtue (and this applies to both
professional and private virtues) is to enter into a network of commitments and goals which are structured by a certain *internal logic* – a logic
having to do with the adoption of certain roles in life. And that logic operates (as has already partly been indicated) in such a way as to preclude
certain kinds of consequentialist approach to decision making. This talk
of 'precluding' may seem to risk the danger of bad faith.[23] Suppose I say
'I am a solicitor [or a chartered accountant, or whatever], so I have *no
choice* but to report your dubious conduct to the authorities.' This kind
of remark may rightly incur a charge of pomposity or self-deception. For
human beings, the stage is never finally and irrevocably 'set': we always
have the option of stepping outside our chosen roles and exercising the
freedom to act in ways which the rules of a professional or personal role
formally prohibit. In that sense, we cannot use our roles to evade ultimate
responsibility for our actions. But this Sartrean point, important though
it is as a reminder of the inescapable anguish of human freedom, can lead
to a certain distortion – a misleading picture of the way in which humans
actually lead their lives. For the cultivation of virtues is not something

that we just do 'straight off', like buying a train ticket. Rather it is (as Aristotle saw) a matter of embarking on a long journey of systematically modifying and retraining our desires and responses over a long period of time. The initial choice to embark may have been 'free',[24] but once the dispositions are entrenched in our personal makeup, certain powerful ethical and psychological constraints will be in place which cannot lightly be shrugged off. Once you have thrown a stone, you cannot now call it back, even though you were free not to hurl it in the first place.[25] The Aristotelian analogy is not exact: even those of the firmest virtue can (perhaps) behave in ways which are inconsistent with their ingrained ethical dispositions to feel and act in certain ways; but to do so would require the overcoming of formidable inertial forces that have been set in train long before the problem calling for such a counter-inertial decision arises.

The point here is not just a psychological one. It is not just that the virtuous person *experiences difficulty* in setting aside the constraints associated with his or her possession of a given virtue. Rather, or in addition, the possession of a virtue involves the systematic cultivation and adoption of an *ethical mindset* which profoundly affects not just how we feel, but how we interpret the world. To be a good parent is to be committed, uncompromisingly and beyond what might seem to an outsider to be the rational calculation of costs and benefits, to the health and flourishing of one's children. In ways which would have been inconceivable for many people before they came to be parents, one's own child takes precedence not just over equally deserving others, but also over oneself. I do not mean obsessively or fanatically, for there are parents who become too preoccupied with their children's lives, manifesting a vice of excess as potentially damaging as the vice of not caring enough. What I mean is that the virtue of the good father or the good mother carries with it a logic of commitment which cannot be understood from an impartial, purely consequentialist perspective. For a parent to start weighing up the consequences of this or that act of love or affection from the global standpoint of an impartial spectator of all mankind would be to abandon the ethical mindset which is constitutive of parental virtue. As William Godwin failed to see, when he could not understand how it was right to save a relative from a burning building when there was a chance to save a worthier candidate (worthier from the point of view of their value to global utility),[26] family loyalty is a virtue which leads us not just to have certain funny irrational feelings about those related to us, but to interpret the ethical landscape in fundamentally different ways from those who lack this virtue.

The logic of the virtues thus involves constraints which are inherently contra-utilitarian: the ethical mindset of the virtuous agent is structured in a way which is incompatible with the bald application of consequentialist reasoning to the problems and decisions which arise in the context where the relevant virtue operates. I say 'bald application' to avoid the misleading impression that possessing an ethical virtue involves having a mind closed to all considerations of global welfare. As already partly indicated, an ethical excellence like courage does not involve a fanatical commitment to certain fixed objectives no matter what the cost. The virtuous person has habits that are carefully guided by reason, not brute propensities that operate in a way that is insulated from rational deliberation. And since reason cannot pick and choose among the factors which impinge on a given decision, it is never possible for the *phronimos* (Aristotle's name for the rationally virtuous agent)[27] to put on blinkers and exclude from consideration what the actual outcome of a piece of practical reasoning is likely to be. But nevertheless, the context in which those deliberations take place is the context of a continuing journey towards a destination specified by a certain 'internal logic'. If I am to remain a good parent, I have to take my decisions (about whom to rescue, about how to allocate my resources) *qua parent*. To start to think in wholly impartialist terms is not an option compatible with the journey on which I have embarked, the journey whose goal defines my life as a parent.

Some consequentialists may object here that talk of the 'contra-utilitarian' structure of the virtues ignores a crucial fact: that the virtues are cultivated in the first place because they are supposed to contribute to human flourishing. So why cannot an institutional or 'rule' version of consequentialism simply take on board all the constraints just referred to? Why cannot the cultivation and operation of the virtues, with all the internal logic relating to the relevant goals of each, simply be characterized as a signally effective way for humans to realize maximum utility, globally defined? Why cannot utility, or impartially defined good, still be the sole sun that shines, the sole ultimate source of value, albeit (in Brad Hooker's suggestive metaphor) *refracted through the prism* of human institutions,[28] including the professional and private virtues?

This is a formidable challenge which cannot be answered fully here. But I will conclude by suggesting one principal way in which it seems to me to fail. Let us return to our central case, the question of what belongs to the virtue of a doctor qua doctor. To embark on a life devoted to medicine is to embark on a life structured by a host of commitments logically connected with the goal of promoting and preserving health. Once those commitments are made, and once the relevant emotional and behavioural dispositions have been cultivated, the ethical landscape is profoundly altered. What might have been seen as an opportunity for making money, or for solving problems of population growth, or for social engineering, or for deciding which lives are more or less useful for society, is now seen, by the doctor, as first and foremost a consultation with a *patient* who is in need of *health care*. This is what his life as a doctor is *about*: the goal of promoting the health of the patient is what gives meaning to his profession, what defines his job or function, and what provides the materials for the exercise of that professional excellence to which he aspires (that which makes a doctor a *good* doctor).

What is more, the patient is not just someone whom the doctor happens to encounter; nor indeed is she merely *a* patient, but *his* patient. I have already indicated one virtue, that of good parenting, which is inherently partialistic, and I have argued elsewhere that it is characteristic of the great majority of the virtues that by their very nature they involve a certain kind of partialism.[29] Rather than repeating the arguments for that thesis here, I will simply suggest that it begins to look highly plausible once we start to look in detail at the traditional list of the personal virtues (friendship, filiality, neighbourliness, fidelity, loyalty) and the professional virtues (those of the priest, the teacher, the counsellor, the sea-captain, the soldier). But even if the thesis is not universally valid,[30] its truth 'for the most part', or even in some instances, is enough to support the anti-consequentialist case I am putting forward. At any rate a large number of what we think of as important virtues involve close commitments to individuals or groups who are defined as *special* in terms of the very goals which are analytically connected to the concept of the relevant excellence (what it is to be a good neighbour, a good teacher, or whatever).

It is this specialness that the consequentialist cannot ultimately accommodate. In practising medical virtue, the doctor is, and must be, committed to giving priority to her patients just because they are *hers*. To be a good doctor is not just to go around doing good things, not even to go around doing good things connected to the goal of heath, but to enter into close relations of trust and care with particular individuals who need medical help. It is essential to the fostering of those special relationships that all concerned know in advance that the actions performed by the practitioner will not be directly subject to global utility calculations. A doctor could not exercise her calling if it were known, or even suspected, that her medical decisions were not intimately structured by this kind of special, preferential commitment; this would be just as impossible as it would be for the institution of promising to function if promisees believed the execution of promises would depend on global utility calculations by the promisers.[31]

Yet this still leaves a loophole for the consequentialist: why should it not be the case that the doctor's medical decisions are *indirectly* subject to global utility calculations: that is, the doctor cultivates the preferential commitments logically linked to the exercise of medical virtue while nonetheless acknowledging that what gives the virtue its ultimate value is its role in the global promotion of the good?

Reflection reveals that this solution is unstable. The consequentialist genie, once let out of the bottle, cannot be stuffed back in. If, at the back of his mind, the doctor knows that what valorizes the practice of medical virtue is its role in the promotion of global utility, then this knowledge will sooner or later exert a corrupting influence on every aspect of his practice of virtue. His special commitments will come to be seen by him for what they are, as ultimately only instruments within a complex apparatus of institutions designed to maximise the good. So whenever those instruments seem blunt in comparison to other tools ready to hand, he will have no sound reason to persist in using them. How will he doggedly persist in fighting for his patient's health, aware that by killing the patient he could release resources for greater overall health care (or even greater general utility quite unconnected with health)? Perhaps we could 'inculcate' (a word much beloved of consequentialists) such a firm commitment to traditional Hippocratic values that our doctors are psychologically blocked from allowing wider utilitarian concerns to percolate through to their consciousness.[32] But, of course, that is a desperate last resort for the consequentialist, presupposing a grotesquely artificial separation between 'us' the inculcators and 'them' the practitioners of virtue; it is a separation which is incompatible with the most basic democratic ideals of open debate and respect for individual autonomy.[33]

The theory and practice of virtue involves renouncing the chimerical allure of some overarching value system that is supposed to encompass all aspects of human life. Human lives are valuable not in virtue of how far they contribute, individually or collectively, to some giant amalgam called 'the good', but in so far as they are lived in ways which make the short journey each of us has to undergo meaningful and precious. Such meaning and preciousness reside in those 'minute particular' relationships whose cultivation is the business of private and professional virtue.[34] Goodness grows from the inside outwards. It is not that there is some external, impartially defined good which irradiates, either directly or though a prism, our individual lives; rather, it is the light within each of us, fostered and strengthened by the long hard disciplines of virtue, that enables us to achieve the limited excellence of which we are capable, and so to irradiate the lives of our fellow human beings.[35]

## NOTES

1 Plato, *Republic*, 345–6.
2 R. M. Dworkin, *Taking Rights Seriously* (London: Duckworth, 1977), ch. 9, pp. 223–39. For more on this, see J. Cottingham, 'Race and Individual Merit', *Philosophy* 55 (1980) 525–31.
3 Though this is not to settle one way or the other the question of whether society might justifiably make it a policy to recruit less meritorious, or less well qualified candidates for certain professions. (It is sometimes argued, incidentally, that skin colour could be a relevant qualification, since it might help lawyers to 'relate' better to people of their own race. But allowing this argument would seem to open the door to all sorts of blatant racism – for example the white restaurant owner insisting that white waiters 'relate' better to the customers.)
4 *Nicomachean Ethics*, Book I, ch. 1.
5 Ibid., Book I, ch. 7.
6 Richard Momeyer, 'Does Physician Assisted Suicide Violate the Integrity of Medicine?', *The Journal of Medicial and Philosophy* 20 (1995) 13–24, p. 17.
7 For an illuminating exposition of some of the basic ingredients of this traditional picture, see Charles Taylor, *Sources of the Self* (Cambridge: CUP, 1989), Parts I and II.
8 In the well-known Aristotelian schema, there are four types of cause or explanation: formal, material, efficient and final. To provide the *formal* cause is to specify something's essential nature – 'what it is to be something'. The *material* cause specifies something's constituents or ingredients; the *efficient* cause is the motive or productive agency that brings something about ('that from which the first origin of change proceeds'); and the *final* cause is what something is for, or 'that for the sake of which' something comes about. See Aristotle, *Physics*, Book II, ch. 3; *Posterior Analytics*, Book II, ch. 11; *Metaphysics*, Book Delta, 1013a29. For more information on these notions as used in the seventeenth century, see J. Cottingham, *A Descartes Dictionary* (Oxford: Blackwell, 1993), s.v. 'cause'.
9 For a discussion of the philosophical issues involved here, see A. Woodfield, *Teleology* (CUP, 1976), and C. Price, 'Functional Explanations and Natural Norms', *Ratio* 8 (1995) 143–60.
10 *Sämtliche Werke*, ed. K. Sudhoff and W. Matthiessen (Munich: Barth, 1922–5) I, 12, p. 148ff.; in *Selected Writings*, ed. J. Jacobi (London: Routledge, 1951), p. 183. 'Paracelsus' (Philipus Aureolus Theophrastus Bombastus von Hohenheim) died in 1541. His voluminous writings (some apocryphal) covered a wide variety of philosophical and medical topics and exerted considerable influence in the late Renaissance. See further B. P. Copenhaver and C. B. Schmitt, *Renaissance Philosophy* (Oxford: OUP, 1992), p. 306.

11 For the incomprehensibility of the divine will in Descartes, see J. Cottingham, 'The Cartesian Legacy', *Proceedings of the Aristotelian Society*, Sup.Vol. LXVI (1992) 1–21.

12 '[Ces notions générales touchant la physique] m'ont fait voir qu'il est possible à parvenir à des connaissances qui soient fort utiles à la vie, et qu'au lieu de cette philosophie spéculative, qu'on enseigne dans les écoles, on en peut trouver une pratique, par laquelle, connaissant la force et les actions du feu, de l'eau, des astres, des cieux et de tous les autres corps qui nos environnent, aussi distinctement que nous connaissons les divers métiers de nos artisans, nous les pourrions employer en même façon à tous les usages auxquels ils sont propres, et ainsi nous rendre comme maîtres et possesseurs de la nature': *Discourse on the Method* (1637), part vi. See *The Philosophical Writings of Descartes*, ed. J. Cottingham, R. Stoothoff and D. Murdoch (Cambridge: CUP, 1985), Vol. I, pp. 142–3.

13 Psalm 100, verse 2 (Authorized Version).

14 See J. Cottingham, 'Partiality and the Virtues', in R. Crisp (ed.), *How Should One Live? Essays on the Philosophy of Virtue* (Oxford: Oxford University Press, 1996).

15 The slogan is reconstructed from connections made explicit in Plato, *Republic*, 353b2–3 and 353c5–7.

16 Source: THE *Independent* (London), 1st February 1995, p. 21.

17 To avoid any possible misunderstanding: the point of the example is *simply* to indicate the limitations on what can logically be within the doctor's proper function; I am *not* of course saying that one who administers euthanasia *on request* is just like someone who executes a convict *against his will*. (It is worth adding, though, that *doing what the patient wants* cannot, as such, be part of the doctor's job. A patient may request all sorts of things – aphrodisiac drugs, bizarre mutilating surgery – which the good doctor should refuse.)

18 It could be objected that it is over-restrictive to insist on health (even broadly defined) as the sole proper goal of medicine. Could not pain relief as such also qualify as one of the goals at which medicine aims (in which case killing a patient to stop the pain could be a medical act)? Reflection reveals, however, that this will not work. A doctor who thought the relief of pain *as such* was his goal would make a very bad doctor. Pain is a monitoring system vital for health (which is why post-operative analgesics have to be so carefully and sparingly administered). Health must be the overriding goal. (It seems to me in general that pain-avoidance and pleasure-promotion cannot be ends in themselves, but only means to other ends, but this is too large a topic to pursue here.)

19 See P. Foot, 'Abortion and the Doctrine of Double Effect', in *Virtues and Vices and Other Essays in Moral Philosophy* (Berkeley: University of California Press, 1978).

20 J. Bentham, *An Introduction to the Principles of Morals and Legislation* (1789), ed. J. Burns and H. L. A. Hart (London: Methuen, 1970), ch. 8. See further G. E. M. Anscombe, 'Modern Moral Philosophy', *Philosophy* 33 (1958) 1–19, and R. A. Duff, *Intention, Agency and Criminal Liability* (Oxford: Blackwell, 1990), ch. 4.

21 'Some extremes seem to bear a greater resemblance to the mean, e.g. rashness seems like courage'; 'Anyone who is aiming at the mean should keep away

from that extreme which is more contrary to the mean... for one of the extremes is always more erroneous than the other': *Nicomachean Ethics*, 1108b30 and 1109b30 (Book II, chs. 8 and 9).

22  *Nicomachean Ethics*, 1106b21–3 (Book II, ch. 6).

23  See Jean-Paul Sartre, *L'Etre et le Néant* (1943), trans. H. Barnes, *Being and Nothingness* (London: Methuen, 1957), Part I, ch. 2.

24  Though even here reflection on how the virtues are acquired suggests that the process begins, for most of us, in early childhood, when the right habits are laid down at a time when we are overwhelmingly influenced by our parents and teachers.

25  'It does not follow that the unjust man can stop being unjust and be just if he wants to – no more than a sick man can become healthy, even though (it may be) his sickness is voluntary, being the result of incontinent living and disobeying his doctors. There was a time when it was open to him not to be ill, but when he had thrown away his chance it was gone, just as when one has let go of a stone it is too late to get it back': *Nicomachean Ethics*, 1114a13–19, trans. J. A. K. Thomson (Harmondsworth: Penguin, revised ed. 1978).

26  In Godwin's famous example, if two people (a philanthropic archbishop and a chambermaid) are trapped in a burning building, and I can rescue only one, then I should rescue the one who can do more good for mankind as a whole. Given that this is the archbishop, then it is he who should be rescued; I should resolutely set aside the fact that the chambermaid happens to be my mother, for 'What magic is in the pronoun "my" that should justify us in overturning the decisions of impartial truth?': William Godwin, *An Enquiry Concerning Political Justice* (1793), Bk II, ch. 2.

27  *Nicomachean Ethics*, Book VI, ch. 5.

28  See B. Hooker, 'Practical Reason and Impersonal Good – The Indirect Connection' (unpublished).

29  See J. Cottingham, 'Partiality and The Virtues'. As I note in the paper cited, justice presents a notable exception, but its place in the Aristotelian table of virtues is highly problematic, and Aristotle has notorious difficulties fitting it into his triadic schema of good dispositions of character flanked by vices of excess and deficiency.

30  There are, of course, a number of what may be called 'official' or 'adjudicatory' virtues (those of the magistrate, the examiner and the tax collector, for example) which require impartiality by reason of the job specification; but it would be quite wrong to take these as a model for the virtues generally. It is worth noting that even within the class of public servants, not all are required to be impartial: the immigration officer, for example, is typically instructed to give preference to certain 'favoured nations'.

31  See J. Rawls, 'Two Concepts of Rules', *Philosophical Review* 64 (1955) 3–32.

32  For the consequentialist to be able to make such a move presupposes that the inculcation of Hippocratic values could indeed be shown to maximize global utility – something which seems open to doubt.

33  The rule consequentialist may resist the elitist or 'Government House' approach, insisting instead on the public promotion of rules for all, subject to conditions of open debate about the consequences of their adoption. But then the objection raised in the first half of this paragraph simply recurs.

34 'He who would do good to another must do it in Minute Particulars. General Good is the plea of the scoundrel, hypocrite and flatterer': William Blake, *Jerusalem* (1805), f.55 1.54.

35 I am grateful to Brad Hooker and Jim Stone, and to the editors of this volume, for helpful comments on an earlier draft of this paper.

# 8  On Not Destroying the Health of One's Patients

*Lance Simmons*

Suppose a professional golfer learns that having one of her breasts removed would improve her swing.[1] After consulting at length with her doctor and reflecting with care on the full range of values at stake in her deliberations, she may conclude that improving her golf swing would make up for losing a normal breast. If she goes on to request the procedure, her doctor must decide whether or not to honour her request. If he honours it, he must either perform the surgery himself or refer her to someone who is willing to perform it. If he does not honour it, he must either persuade her to disregard her own best judgment in this matter or insist that she leave his care. What should he do?

We have here a question in medical ethics: Should the golfer's doctor honour her request or not? The object of the present essay is to construct a philosophically satisfying answer to this question. As a first step toward that goal, we will examine the complex network of philosophical conflicts within which this question traditionally has been embedded. Our final answer will be satisfying only to the extent that it enables us to navigate successfully within this network of conflicts, and for this reason it is important to make clear from the outset the different kinds of objections an answer to our question is likely to encounter.

Let us begin by considering what is surely the most familiar answer to our question.[2] This answer, which I shall not defend here, runs as follows:

1  The primary end of a practice is that end to which the practice's other, secondary ends are subordinated, and which itself is subordinated to no other end of the practice.
2  Health is the primary end of medicine as such.
3  The destruction of health as such is thus contrary to the primary end of medicine.
4  Insofar as one is a doctor (that is, qua doctor), one must not undertake acts contrary to the primary end of medicine; to do so would be to cease functioning as a doctor.
5  Therefore, insofar as one is a doctor (that is, qua doctor), one must not undertake the destruction of health.

6 Because removing a normal breast damages a woman's health as such, it follows that insofar as one is a doctor (that is, qua doctor), one must not honour requests to remove normal breasts.

Modern medical ethicists have articulated two distinct objections to this answer. The first objection arises from disputes about medical teleology: health no longer is widely agreed to be medicine's primary end. Dan Brock reports that, 'at least in the developed countries,' the 'common view' is that

> medicine's goal should be to provide treatment that best enables patients to pursue successfully their overall aims and ends, or life plans. It is the relative value of health, and of different aspects of health, as compared with other ends, that varies for different persons and circumstances.[3]

Some critics of the liberalism characteristic of developed countries believe medicine's primary end should be to promote 'social adaptability' rather than the pursuit of individual life plans.[4] In any case, whether they are liberal or anti-liberal, most modern medical ethicists reject the claim that health is medicine's primary end, and for this reason they also reject the most familiar answer to our question.

The second objection arises from disputes about medical essentialism. The premises of the familiar answer include claims about medicine as such, health as such, and doctors insofar as they are doctors, yet our acceptance of these claims is justified only if we possess essential definitions of all three terms. The rational acceptability of the familiar answer thus appears to be imperilled by arguments that human practices and their objects lack essential definitions.[5] Whatever the final result of the broad debate about practices in general, elaborate historical arguments have been advanced purporting to show that medicine and health in particular have been thoroughly transformed over time and have no essential definition.[6] Some argue that health has been incrementally 'medicalized' over many centuries, so that pre-modern beliefs about health no longer can be justified.[7] Others argue that attributions of health now are subtly determined by modern medical conceptions of pathology and disease.[8] In light of these developments, many regard as naive any argument which assumes medical essentialism.

As well as undercutting the most familiar answer to our original question, these two objections also suggest distinct counter-answers to that question. The objection about teleology leads one to wonder whether secondary ends such as health may not be sacrificed in order to achieve a practice's primary end. If indeed secondary ends may be attacked in this way, and if health is not medicine's primary end, then perhaps doctors should remove normal breasts, or in other ways attack the health of their patients, whenever this would best promote the primary end of medicine. If we adopt the liberal view that medicine's primary end is to promote the successful pursuit of individual life plans, it seems to follow that we should honour the golfer's request. The rejection of health as the primary end of medicine thus suggests a counter-answer to our question.

The objection about medical essentialism suggests a somewhat different counter-answer, for this objection leads one to wonder whether the surgical removal of a normal breast should continue to be reckoned an attack on health. If medicine and health have no stable character, perhaps appropriate revisions in the medical conception of health would allow us to conclude that the golfer's health will be diminished unless her doctor honours her request. This new conception of health admittedly has not yet emerged from those fluctuating ensembles of instruments and procedures which we informally consider medical, but perhaps this development should be encouraged. Even if health is related analytically to medicine as its primary end, the content of the medical conception of health is determined by what doctors actually do to their patients. In light of this fact, the best way for the golfer's doctor to encourage the development of a more agreeable conception of health may be to honour her request now, despite the fact that most other doctors practising today would regard this as an attack on her health. The rejection of medical essentialism thus suggests a second counter-answer to our original question.

Any successful defence of the most familiar answer to our question will either say why objections about essentialism and teleology may be set aside in favor of an ahistorical notion of health as the primary end of medicine as such, or else say why no such response is required. Perhaps in the end advocates of the familiar answer will meet these challenges. Until then, however, perhaps the refusal of doctors to remove normal breasts can be defended without relying upon assumptions about medical essentialism and traditional primary-end teleology, while at the same time undercutting the two counter-answers to our question suggested by the disavowal of such assumptions.

Recent developments in general ethics are instructive in this regard. Familiar arguments for content-full moral claims are routinely criticized for assuming a suspect primary-end teleology which is rooted in an even more problematic essentialism about human nature. In addition, the rejections of essentialism and traditional teleology have served as the basis of counter-arguments against those same claims. In response to this predicament, some ethicists in recent decades have deliberately skirted questions of teleology and essentialism when defending content-full moral claims, while still undercutting the counter-arguments against those claims; by doing so, they have successfully rehabilitated traditional virtue concepts such as 'generosity' and 'courage.' The following discussion will show that content-full claims in medical ethics can be defended in a similar fashion. Without relying upon assumptions about teleology or essentialism, and while still undercutting the two counter-answers to our question suggested earlier, we shall say why the golfer's doctor should not honour her request.

The guiding intuition of our answer will be that good doctors regard the surgical removal of normal breasts much as good people regard acts contrary to the virtues.[9] For example, good people shun stingy and cowardly acts. If through weakness a good person behaves in a stingy or cowardly fashion, even in pursuit of a great good, she soon regrets it and seeks to form her character so as to avoid such episodes in the future. Good people adopt similar attitudes regarding dishonest and unfair acts, except that if through weakness a good person behaves dishonestly or unfairly, she may also regard herself as deserving punishment for having offended some law. Good people adopt these attitudes prior to reflection; moral theory seeks to explain, justify, and when necessary revise such attitudes. Our answer thus will attempt to establish that good doctors prereflectively dispose themselves in ways which preclude honouring the golfer's request.[10] It also will attempt to establish that removing a patient's normal breast resembles a dishonest or unfair act more than a stingy or cowardly one, and hence that a good doctor who through weakness honours the golfer's request is likely to regard himself as deserving punishment, such as revocation of his medical licence.

Since our answer will be only as plausible as its guiding intuition, a brief presentation of the recent retrieval of traditional virtue concepts into general ethics is in order. Bernard Williams's account of thick concepts and Alasdair MacIntyre's treatment of goods internal to practices are notable attempts to discuss traditional virtue concepts such as 'generosity' and 'courage' apart from disputes about teleology and essentialism, so we shall consider each in turn. Taking the central points of their accounts seriatim, we shall see whether the intuition governing our answer withstands scrutiny.

Williams characterizes traditional virtue concepts as thick concepts, and by so doing he intends to distinguish them from two other kinds of concept.[11] First, thick concepts such as 'generosity' and 'courage' are unlike concepts used in evolutionary biology, the neurological sciences, and other modern sciences which explain psychological and social phenomena.[12] Whereas virtue concepts are used to express distinctively human beliefs and attitudes, scientific concepts such as 'mutation' and 'stimulus' are used to explain those same beliefs and attitudes, but themselves are (or rather approximate to being) non-perspectival.[13] In other words, thick concepts are not fit for use in the modern sciences, because thick concepts are perspectival.

Second, thick concepts are distinct from many other perspectival concepts, such as perceptual concepts (let us call these thin concepts).[14] Even though both thick and thin concepts are perspectival, our rational justification for using thick concepts such as 'generosity' and 'courage' is inherently unstable, whereas our rational justification for using thin concepts such as 'grass' and 'green'[15] remains quite secure. There exist widely agreeable explanations of our use of thin concepts which tend not to subvert our justification for continuing to use those concepts. In contrast, the most widely agreeable explanations of our use of thick concepts tend also to subvert our justification for using those concepts, while those explanations by appeal to which one might hope to justify the use of thick concepts tend not to be widely agreeable.[16]

Williams identifies five distinctive traits of thick concepts; let us consider each in turn to determine whether medical concepts such as 'health' may plausibly be regarded as thick concepts. First, the use of a thick concept always expresses a valuation of an act, person, or situation. There may be personal qualities more morally significant than generosity or courage, but the characterization of someone or something as generous or courageous expresses a valuation, and is never merely an impartial report regarding a state of affairs about which any evaluative attitude whatsoever might be adopted.[17] Likewise, we find that philosophers of medicine for the most part agree that use of the concept 'health' also expresses a valuation; health is considered valuable in its own right, even though many goods are prized more highly than health.[18]

Secondly, although it expresses a valuation, the use of a thick concept also tracks objective states of affairs and does not merely express subjective preferences. In other words, the use of a thick concept expresses a speaker's grasp of the facts of the matter, and competent auditors readily discount arbitrary or inept uses of thick concepts. For example, a speaker who characterizes paradigmatic instances of generosity or courage as stingy or cowardly risks alienating her audience.[19] In a similar way, use of the concept 'health' is generally agreed to be world-guided. One sign of this is that the aptness of particular uses of the concept 'health' is (ordinarily) determined by states of affairs outside the speaker's immediate control. Although a speaker may subjectively prefer to apply the concept 'health' to a particular act, person, or situation, competent auditors freely discount uses of 'health' which appear to stray from the facts.

Thirdly, as well as being guided by the world, the use of a thick concept guides action. This is so not primarily because such use conveys emotive force from the speaker to her audience, but rather because the use of a thick concept such as 'courage' or 'generosity' offers a reason for action. Acknowledging the applicability of a thick concept to a particular act, person, or situation puts one in possession of a reason for acting in certain ways rather than others.[20] In like fashion, use of the concept 'health' also offers a reason for action, even if not always a decisive reason. Opaque patterns of behaviour are revealed to be intelligible human actions when they are justified as being undertaken for the sake of health. (In contrast, thin concepts and scientific concepts are not commonly used to offer reasons for action. Only in somewhat specialized contexts does the use of 'green', 'grass', 'mutation', or 'stimulus' offer a reason for action.)

Fourthly, thick concepts characteristically lack scientific equivalents.[21] In order to predict how native speakers will apply a thick concept to non-paradigmatic cases, one ordinarily must first have grasped the concept's narrow evaluative point by locating it in relation to the larger network of evaluative interests shared by the natives.[22] In other words, before being able to predict how a thick concept such as 'courage' or 'generosity' will be used in unfamiliar contexts, one first must have learned to navigate within the intricate web of evaluative interests which motivate native speakers to construct and preserve that particular concept rather than some other, less complex concept.[23] Constructing a scientific (non-perspectival) concept with the same extension as a thick concept is thus exceedingly difficult. Likewise, despite the best efforts of modern scientists, it is now widely agreed that 'health' lacks (or perhaps merely does not yet have) a scientific equivalent,[24] that widespread use of the phrase 'health science' risks misrepresenting the perspectival character of medical knowledge,[25] and that the social enterprise of medicine is in important ways irreducible to the biomedical sciences.[26] Modern science has not yet offered compelling equivalents of medical concepts.

The fifth and most important trait of thick concepts is that those who do not share the evaluative perspective (or network of evaluative interests) in relation to which the narrow evaluative point of a particular thick concept makes sense ordinarily cannot use that concept themselves.[27] Attempts to import thick concepts into alien evaluative perspectives thus typically fail, in either of two distinct ways. The first kind of failure transpires when particularly enterprising aliens learn to navigate within an unfamiliar evaluative perspective. For example, by their protracted efforts to learn how natives use thick concepts such as 'generosity' and 'courage,' aliens may eventually acquire the ability to use such expressions as 'what those others would call "generosity" or "courage" '.[28] In itself this is a significant achievement, but often it is mistaken for something more, namely a genuine translation. Reports are not translations, any more than 'what the French would call "la plume de ma tante" ' is a translation of 'la plume de ma tante.' When this point is forgotten, it becomes easy to imagine that one has successfully glossed a thick concept merely by offering a detailed description of its use by others.

Failed consequentialist accounts of virtue concepts such as 'generosity' and 'courage' illustrate the second way in which efforts to import thick concepts into alien evaluative perspectives typically miscarry.[29] Such accounts usually culminate in a systematic revision of criteria for applying the original concepts. In itself this is unobjectionable, but the revisionism typically (and it seems necessarily) extends even to those paradigm cases by which the virtue concepts traditionally have been acquired in their original setting. This 'rejection of ordinary intuitions'[30] regarding paradigmatic instances of generosity or courage results in a failure of translation between the old virtue concept and the new consequentialist concept. For this reason, the revisionist should withdraw any claim to have provided a consequentialist gloss of 'generosity' or 'courage'. Those who seek to import thick concepts into alien evaluative perspectives thus seem to face a dilemma: it seems they must either settle for a report in place of a translation, or else construct a new concept the extension of which differs significantly from the extension of the thick concept it is meant to gloss.

These two patterns of translation failure (report mistaken for translation, arbitrary revisionism) recur throughout modern ethics. For example, modern moral philosophers generally adopt one of two attitudes regarding injustice.[31] Some deny that what those others would call 'injustice' is always wrong. Others so alter the paradigmatic instances of injustice as to render tautological the claim that injustice is always wrong. In the former case, modern moral philosophers do not use the concept 'injustice' themselves, but merely report on its use by others. In the latter case, they display their failure to grasp the evaluative point of the original concept. If the claim that injustice is always wrong turns out to be tautological (as typically happens when the extension of the complex concept 'injustice' is revised arbitrarily), then the behaviour of those who constructed and preserved the original concept becomes opaque, for the new concept which is meant to gloss the original concept has no evaluative point worthy of note. Modern moral philosophers for the most part have failed in one of these two ways when they have attempted to import the thick concept 'injustice' into modern moral theories.

In much the same way, those who do not share the evaluative perspective (or network of evaluative interests) in relation to which the narrow evaluative point of the concept 'health' makes sense ordinarily cannot use that concept themselves. Efforts by modern medical ethicists to justify attacks on health characteristically fail in one of the two ways just mentioned: either 'health' is supplanted by 'what doctors would call "health"', and we no longer can say why attacking what doctors would call 'health' is wrong; or else the paradigmatic instances of health and its destruction are so thoroughly revised that (typically) 'health' is transmuted into the moralizing concept 'what doctors must not attack.' (As in the case of the thick concept 'injustice,' this second outcome drains all content from the claim that doctors must not attack health, leaving behind only an emotionally charged residue.) Both outcomes ensure a failure of translation when the content-full concept 'health' is imported into modern theories of medical ethics. For example, removing a normal breast (which all good doctors presently recognize as an attack on a woman's health) comes to be defended either as a justified attack on what doctors (but not theorists) would call 'health', or as a justified attack on something other than what (theorists say) doctors must not attack. Removing a normal breast has never yet been defended as a justified attack on health.

As in modern general ethics, these two patterns of translation failure also recur throughout modern medical ethics. Failures of the second kind (in which thick concepts are arbitrarily revised) are perhaps easier to recognize and discount in medical ethics than in general ethics: it is difficult to take seriously the proposal to construe medical concepts as having extensions which differ significantly from the extensions acknowledged by doctors. In contrast, failures of the first kind (in which reports are mistaken for translations) are more subtle and often go unchecked. Consider, for example, Brock's claim that modern medical ethicists 'need not reject the functional account of health as a biological norm defended by [Leon] Kass and others'.[32] Brock claims that, for Kass, 'health is a biologically determined, objective matter of fact' which doctors know in virtue of 'their impressive body of scientific knowledge concerning human biological functioning and the impact of therapeutic interventions on diseases...'[33] Brock's report of Kass's use of the con-

cept 'health' is actually quite misleading, for according to Kass, health is
even more fundamentally

> a high good, which... is *capable of calling forth devotion*, because it is
> both good and high, but which... *requires such devotion*, because *its
> service is most demanding and difficult, and... thereby engages one's
> character*, not merely one's mind and hands.[34]

On the basis of the consensus among liberal medical ethicists that the
primary end of medicine is to enable patients to pursue their life plans,
Brock contends that doctors must be willing to attack the health of their
patients upon request.[35] According to Kass's account of health, however,
no doctor willing to follow Brock's counsel in this regard could at the
same time possess the thoroughgoing ('professional' in the etymological
sense) devotion to health required of those who would know and serve
that high good.[36] On Kass's account, this professional devotion plays a
greater role in doctors' knowledge of health than do particular bodies of
scientific belief about biological function and disease. (Kass's belief that
professional devotion plays a central role in doctors' knowledge of health
allows him to regard himself as participating in the same practice as Hip-
pocrates, Galen and countless others whose knowledge of biological
function and disease was little more than what any ordinarily reflective
human being can acquire in nearly any historical setting.[37]) Thus, while
Kass indeed regards health as an objective matter of fact, he also holds
that those who seek knowledge of health must satisfy rigorous subjective
conditions before acquiring it. In particular, aspiring doctors must dispose themselves in ways which preclude their undertaking the destruction of health.[38] Brock's claim that modern medical ethicists need not
reject the account of health maintained by Kass and other practising
physicians is thus false; theorists who would counsel doctors to attack
the health of their patients show that they already reject that account.
Brock's claim appears plausible only insofar as one mistakes his misleading report of Kass's use of the concept 'health' for a genuine gloss of that
concept. The result is familiar: a failure of translation.

On all five counts, then, 'health' appears to be a thick concept. Turning
to another recent treatment of traditional virtues, we find MacIntyre
contending that virtues are initially best understood as acquired qualities
'the possession and exercise of which tends to enable us to achieve those
goods which are internal to practices and the lack of which effectively
prevents us from achieving any such goods'.[39] Three features of this account demand our attention. First, a good internal to a practice can be
adequately specified only in terms of and by means of examples taken

from that practice, or from some practice or set of practices closely enough related to it to make comparison fruitful.[40] Evaluative perspectives are thus situated within practices. Returning to medicine and health, we find that in each culture for which we possess the requisite anthropological data, the practice of medicine (or some relevantly medicine-like practice) has fixed a set of examples which have been used to specify the good of health. Especially helpful for establishing this connection are historical accounts of how changes in medical practice have transformed conceptions of health. For example, statistical models of pathology and disease developed in this century now determine which conditions of human beings fall within the range of biological normality and thus are healthy.[41]

Secondly, identifying and recognizing a good internal to a practice requires active participation in that practice (or in a closely related practice or set of practices).[42] Thus, not only are evaluative perspectives situated within practices, but access to evaluative perspectives requires active engagement in those practices. Turning again to medicine and health, we find that merely possessing a broad stock of medical examples does not of itself enable one to identify and recognize health. One's degree of mastery of these two tasks is determined rather by the depth of one's experience in adapting medical examples to non-paradigmatic cases. That this experience can be acquired only through active participation in medicine (or closely allied practices) justifies the convention by which doctors are required to undergo lengthy apprenticeships before practising on their own authority. It thus seems reasonable to hold that health is a good internal to medicine.[43]

Finally, echoing Aristotle's account of special justice, MacIntyre distinguishes between virtues the lack of which prevents us from achieving goods internal to practices, and virtues the lack of which destroys practices and the goods internal to them.[44] For example, misers and cowards fail to achieve the goods internal to practices and may accidentally destroy them, but liars and cheats sabotage practices together with the goods internal to them, and for that reason deserve to be punished. Good doctors likewise distinguish between two kinds of medical virtues.[45] The lack of certain medical virtues, such as courage and patience, prevents a doctor from successfully promoting the health of his patients and may cause him to destroy the health of his patients accidentally. In contrast, the lack of other medical virtues, such as justice and discretion, causes a doctor to transgress the limits which otherwise would constrain her use of therapeutic means and regulate her interpersonal conduct. Such offences damage the health of patients and sabotage the practice within which sick people hoping for a return to health request help from doctors, and for these reasons doctors who misbehave in these ways merit punishment within the medical community. It thus seems reasonable to hold that those acquired qualities are virtues the possession and exercise of which tends to enable doctors to heal and the lack of which effectively prevents them from healing.[46]

In its present form, then, the answer we have been constructing runs as follows:

1  Good people regard acts contrary to the virtues in the following ways: they shun them before the fact, regret them after the fact, and for acts (such as lying and cheating) which attack rather than merely fail to achieve goods internal to practices, they are willing to suffer punishment. Those who do not share the evaluative perspective within which these attitudes make sense characteristically fail when they attempt to import the relevant thick concepts into their own moral theories.

2  'Health' is a thick concept.

3  Removing a normal breast is presently recognized by doctors as a paradigmatic instance of an attack on a woman's health.

4  Health is a good internal to the practice of medicine, and those acquired qualities the possession and exercise of which tends to enable doctors to heal and the lack of which effectively prevents them from healing are thus virtues.

5  Good doctors therefore regard acts which attack the good of health (acts such as removing normal breasts) in the following ways: they shun them before the fact, regret them after the fact, and, because such acts attack rather than merely fail to achieve the good of health, they are willing to suffer punishment for them. Those who do not share the evaluative perspective within which these attitudes make sense characteristically fail when they attempt to import the thick concept 'health' into their own theories of medical ethics.

6  More specifically, such theorists typically adopt one of two stances regarding health: either they deny that what doctors would call 'health' must not be attacked, or else they so alter the paradigmatic instances of health and its destruction as to render tautological the claim that doctors must not attack health. In the first case they mistake a report for a translation, while in the second case they fail to grasp the evaluative point of the original concept.

This answer to our question assumes neither a primary-end teleology nor medical essentialism. It thus evades the objections most commonly raised against the familiar answer considered earlier. Nonetheless, because this answer remains at the level of dialectics, it cannot compel assent to a content-full moral conclusion. It merely poses a dilemma: either good doctors should deny requests to remove normal breasts, or health is not an end of medicine. Perhaps medicine one day will become a practice which no longer counts health among its ends. If that ever happens, good doctors will be at liberty to honour requests like that of the golfer in our example. Until then, however, such conduct cannot be justified by claiming that health may be attacked in the name of some other end because health is not the primary end of medicine, or by claiming that the removal of normal breasts need not be reckoned an attack on health because medicine and health have no essential definition. As we have seen, doctors should not attack the health of their patients even if health is a secondary end of medicine, and the medical examples by which doctors acquire the concept 'health' cannot be revised for reasons which are not internal to the practice of medicine, even if medical essentialism is false.

The points we have considered may be summarized as follows. Grasping the evaluative point of a content-full moral concept requires learning to navigate within an intricate web of evaluative interests shared by those who use the concept themselves. In addition, actually using a content-full moral concept (as opposed to reporting on its use) requires disposing oneself in ways which preclude undertaking the destruction of the goods specified by that concept. The proposal to revise the extension of a content-full moral concept according to criteria which are not internal to the concept's native evaluative perspective is thus fatally flawed, as is the proposal to attack the goods specified by a content-full moral concept. Those who embrace the former proposal must first release their grasp on the evaluative point of the concept, whereas those who embrace the latter proposal must first renounce any claim to use the concept themselves. I have argued that the concept 'health' conforms to this pattern.[47]

NOTES

1 See Leon Kass, *Toward a More Natural Science: Biology and Human Affairs* (henceforth *TMNS*) (New York: The Free Press, 1985), pp. 187–210.
2 See, for example, Kass, *TMNS*, pp. 157–86.

3 Dan Brock, 'Quality of Life Measures in Health Care and Medical Ethics,' in M. Nussbaum and A. Sen (eds.), *The Quality of Life* (Oxford: Clarendon Press, 1993), pp. 95–132, 101–2.

4 For example, Igor Smirnov, 'Human Health: From Theory to Practice,' *The Journal of Medicine and Philosophy* 14 (1989) 251–9.

5 For a discussion of the ways in which the familiar answer assumes practice essentialism, see Janet Coleman, 'MacIntyre and Aquinas,' in J. Horton and S. Mendus (eds.), *After MacIntyre: Critical Perspectives on the Work of Alasdair MacIntyre* (henceforth *After MacIntyre*) (Notre Dame: University of Notre Dame Press, 1994), pp. 65–90, esp. pp. 80–4.

6 The most challenging historical arguments against medical essentialism eschew the presumption of Kuhnian discontinuity; rather, they expose to view a continuous process of transformation which achieves radical difference only cumulatively. So long as historians of medicine narrate dramas of discontinuity, medical essentialism can be defended by first isolating discrete medical epochs or paradigms and then evaluating them as better or worse instances of medicine as such in virtue of possessing more or less adequate conceptions of health as such. This strategy has become less viable as more historians of medicine have adopted a methodological preference for continuity, for it has become increasingly difficult to isolate discrete medical epochs or paradigms. (See, for example, Harold J. Cook, 'Physick and Natural History in Seventeenth-Century England,' in P. Barker and R. Ariew (eds.), *Revolution and Continuity: Essays in the History and Philosophy of Early Modern Science* (Washington, D. C.: Catholic University of America Press, 1991), pp. 63–80.)

7 See, for example, Ivan Illich, *Medical Nemesis: The Expropriation of Health* (New York: Random House, 1976), chs. 3–5.

8 See, for example, Georges Canguilhem, *The Normal and the Pathological* (New York: Zone Books, 1991).

9 The condemnation of acts directly contrary to the virtues traditionally has been justified by claiming that the exercise of the virtues fully or partially constitutes the primary end of practical life. The more recent retrieval of the virtues which we shall examine does not rely upon a primary-end teleology in order to exclude such acts from the consideration of good people. For a presentation of rival Aristotelian accounts of the relationship of the virtues to the primary end of practical life, see Richard Kraut, *Aristotle on the Human Good* (Princeton: Princeton University Press, 1989), esp. chs. 4–5.

10 The fact that the dispositions which preclude removing normal breasts are characteristic of good doctors rather than doctors in general may help explain why a practising physician writes that 'no physician *worthy of the name* would... lop off a breast to improve a lady's golf swing' (Kass, *TMNS*, p. 198, emphasis added): some physicians fail to be worthy of the name.

11 Bernard Williams, *Ethics and the Limits of Philosophy* (Cambridge, Mass.: Harvard University Press, 1985), chs. 7–8.

12 Williams, *Ethics*, p. 140.

13 A non-perspectival (or properly scientific) concept is one 'that might be arrived at by any investigators, even if they were very different from us.' Williams believes this ideal of 'the absolute conception' articulates 'the possibility of a convergence characteristic of science, one that could meaningfully be said to

be a convergence on how things (anyway) are' (Williams, *Ethics*, p. 139). Note that in proposing the absolute conception, Williams asserts neither practice essentialism nor essentialism about human nature, but only that modern science converges on how things are. Depending on what account of explanation is accepted within the absolute conception, Williams may not be asserting essentialism of any kind.

14  Williams, *Ethics*, p. 149.

15  Williams, *Ethics*, pp. 138–9. Perceptual concepts such as 'grass' and 'green' are perspectival because they are used to express distinctively human beliefs and attitudes. There may be competent (non-human) observers who cannot use the concepts 'green' and 'grass,' whereas any competent observer can use scientific (non-perspectival) concepts such as 'mutation' and 'stimulus.'

16  Williams, *Ethics*, pp. 149–52. Williams insists on the distinction between thick and thin perspectival concepts primarily because he regards the Kantian ideal of public reason as the element of our Enlightenment heritage most worth preserving, yet he also hopes to save perceptual concepts such as 'green' and 'grass' from being relegated to the private realm, where traditional virtue concepts such as 'generosity' and 'courage' are widely agreed to reside. Since no principled account of the distinction between public and private reason can permit perspectival concepts to remain public, Williams relies instead upon an empirical distinction between more and less widely agreeable explanations of the use of concepts.

17  Williams, *Ethics*, p. 129.

18  A vast literature catalogues normative elements of the concept 'health'. In addition to such familiar aspects as function, adaptation, and capacity, recent work explores the concept's aesthetic elements (for example, John Ladd, 'The Concepts of Health and Disease and their Ethical Implications', in B. Gruzalski and C. Nelson (eds.), *Value Conflicts in Health Care Delivery* (Cambridge, Mass.: Ballinger, 1982), pp. 21–39; and B. Stafford, J. La Puma, and D. Schiedermayer, 'One Face of Beauty, One Picture of Health: The Hidden Aesthetic of Medical Practice', *The Journal of Medicine and Philosophy* 14 (1989) 213–30).

19  Williams, *Ethics*, p. 141.

20  Williams, *Ethics*, p. 140.

21  Williams, *Ethics*, p. 141. Williams presents as historical rather than conceptual the claim that thick concepts lack scientific equivalents, so as not to beg the question against reductionists. If any reductionist program is ever completed, then a scientific equivalent finally will be constructed for each thick concept. Modern science has established its power to offer compelling reductions of thin perspectival concepts such as 'green' and 'grass.' It is characteristic of thick perspectival concepts, in contrast, that no scientific equivalent has yet been constructed, and that no adequately determinate proposal for performing such a reduction is presently on the table. Nonetheless, it would be rash to rule out in advance the possibility of such reductions.

22  Although Williams holds that the property of being a thick concept is anatomic, this alone does not commit him to denying the possibility of fully punctate languages. At most it commits him to translation holism, and that only with regard to languages which contain thick concepts. See Jerry Fodor and Ernest Lepore, *Holism: A Shopper's Guide* (Oxford: Basil Blackwell, 1992).

23  Williams, *Ethics*, pp. 141–5.
24  See, for example: Joseph Margolis, 'The Concept of Disease', *The Journal of Medicine and Philosophy* 1 (1976) 238–55; H. Tristam Engelhardt, 'Ideology and Etiology', *The Journal of Medicine and Philosophy* 1 (1976) 256–68; and Julius Moravcsik, 'Ancient and Modern Conceptions of Health and Medicine', *The Journal of Medicine and Philosophy* 1 (1976) 337–48.
25  See, for example, R. John Bench, 'Health Science, Natural Science, and Clinical Knowledge', *The Journal of Medicine and Philosophy* 14 (1989) 147–64.
26  See, for example, Ronald Munson, 'Why Medicine Cannot Be a Science', *The Journal of Medicine and Philosophy* 6 (1981) 183–208. Although Munson regards health as the primary end of medicine, his argument against the reduction of medicine does not require this strong thesis. While many hold that the biomedical sciences can be reduced to purely biological sciences, no detailed proposals remain on the table for reducing medicine to a set of biomedical sciences. (See Kenneth F. Schaffner, 'Philosophy of Medicine', in M. Salmon, J. Earman et al. (eds), *Introduction to the Philosophy of Science: A Text by Members of the Department of the History and Philosophy of Science of the University of Pittsburgh* (Englewood Cliffs: Prentice Hall, 1992), pp. 310–45.)
27  Williams, *Ethics*, p. 144. Williams distinguishes between predicting how others will use a thick concept and using it oneself. Accurate prediction requires locating a concept's narrow evaluative point in relation to the network of evaluative interests which constitutes the evaluative perspective shared by the native speakers. Use typically requires membership of the native culture in virtue of having come to share its distinctive evaluative perspective.
28  Williams, *Ethics*, p. 142.
29  See, for example, Michael Slote, 'Utilitarian Virtue', *Midwest Studies in Philosophy* XII (1988) 384–97.
30  Slote, 'Utilitarian Virtue', p. 396.
31  See G. E. M. Anscombe, 'Modern Moral Philosophy', in her *Ethics, Religion and Politics* (Minneapolis: University of Minnesota Press, 1981), pp. 26–42, 40–1.
32  Brock, 'Quality of Life Measures', p. 102.
33  Brock, 'Quality of Life Measures', p. 101.
34  Kass, *TMNS*, pp. 215–6; emphasis added.
35  Brock, 'Quality of Life Measures', pp. 102–3.
36  Kass, *TMNS*, p. 215.
37  Kass, *TMNS*, pp. 224–45, esp. p. 228. Although Kass is an essentialist regarding medicine and health, his claims about the role of professional devotion in the acquisition of medical knowledge can be understood and assessed without reference to essentialism.
38  Kass, *TMNS*, pp. 232–6.
39  Alasdair MacIntyre, *After Virtue* (Notre Dame: University of Notre Dame Press, 1984, 2nd ed.), p. 191.
40  MacIntyre, *After Virtue*, p. 188.
41  'The consciousness of biological normality includes the relation to disease, the recourse to disease as the only touchstone which this consciousness recognizes and thus demands... The menace of disease is [that is, has become] one of the components of health.' Canguilhem, *The Normal and the Pathological*, pp. 285–7.

42  MacIntyre, *After Virtue*, p. 189.
43  David Miller denies that health is a good internal to medicine (David Miller, 'Virtues, Practices and Justice', in *After MacIntyre*, pp. 245–64, 250–5). He claims that the healing of the sick is medicine's 'external purpose' (p. 250) and as such is adequately specifiable without reference to any good internal to medicine, such as the good of being an excellent doctor. Miller, however, neglects to consider that MacIntyre defines the excellence of the products of a practice as itself a good internal to that practice (MacIntyre, *After Virtue*, pp. 189–90). For MacIntyre, as for any Aristotelian, the excellence of the products of a practice cannot be specified apart from the excellence which perfects participants in that practice (Alasdair MacIntyre, 'A Partial Response to My Critics', in *After MacIntyre*, pp. 283–304, 284–6). Health as an excellence produced in the sick by doctors thus cannot be shown to be a purpose external to medicine as long as health (1) is adequately specifiable only by means of examples taken from medicine and (2) can be identified and recognized only by those with the experience of participating in medicine. Any attempt to criticize the claim that health is a good internal to medicine must focus on these two points, rather than on the distinction between artisan and product. (Miller also identifies external purposes of architecture, farming, and physics, but in each case he ignores MacIntyre's distinction between the products of a practice and the excellence of those products.)
44  MacIntyre, *After Virtue*, pp. 151–2, 187–8.
45  Kass, *TMNS*, pp. 221–3, 232–40.
46  MacIntyre's full account of the virtues defines them with reference to their role in sustaining both those social and cultural traditions and those traditions of inquiry within which individuals seek the good of their whole lives and specific practices are sustained and enriched (MacIntyre, *After Virtue*, p. 223). Before concluding that the acquired qualities characteristic of good doctors are indeed virtues, we first would need to show that, in addition to enabling good doctors to heal, these qualities also enable them to achieve both the good of a whole life and the goods of community. In other words, we would have to show that these qualities help good doctors live good lives in good communities. Our present purposes, however, do not require these extra steps, for the proposal to attack goods internal to practices is fatally flawed. This is true even if the goods in question are internal to bad practices. When one concludes that participation in a particular practice (such as medicine) is incompatible with the good of a whole life or the goods of community, one is not thereby put in a position to attack the goods internal to that practice. Rather, one simply stops seeking those goods while continuing to seek other goods internal to practices participation in which one now regards as compatible with a good life in a good community. Good people sometimes must destroy institutions which place external goods such as money and prestige at the service of bad practices, but this never involves attacking goods internal to those practices. Interactions between internal goods, external goods, virtues, practices, and institutions are often quite complex, but the proposal to attack goods internal to practices remains fatally flawed (MacIntyre, *After Virtue*, pp. 194–5). The limited purposes of the present discussion thus require us to conclude only that health is a good internal to medicine and that the qualities which enable doctors to heal therefore function much like virtues. If

in fact these qualities are not virtues because medicine is a bad practice, this does not affect the answer we have been constructing.

47 I am grateful to Scott Crider, William Frank, Alfred Freddoso, Robert Kugelmann, Mark Lowery, Mark Smillie and Janet Smith for their comments on an earlier draft of this paper.

# 9 Intentions in Medical Ethics

## J. L. A. Garcia

### INTRODUCTION

In Western medical ethics, the centre has not held and things are fast falling apart. Some practices long recognized as barbarous in themselves and opposed to the nature and aims of medicine are now routine; others are fast winning acceptance, and even those still beyond the pale have an air of inevitability. Abortion is now one of the most common medical procedures; assisted suicide enjoys broad public support and has won some contests in legislatures and popular referenda; infanticide and passive euthanasia are widespread practices for which some demand legalization and moral legitimation. Flood tides of social change erode our long-held conception of medicine and its associated restraints and pull us into a sea of medical homicide. A new ethic, really a reinvigorated ethic from the Enlightenment, has emerged to grant its moral and intellectual *imprimatur* to medicine's lethal new agenda. In it, medical technology is to proceed largely unconstrained by any fear that we degrade humanity when we consider the sick and dying merely as providers of recyclable organs, or when we treat people as objects of manufacture and their parts as commercial goods, or when we experiment on embryos *in utero* or in test-tubes or on the terminally ill. Indeed, in the emerging ethic, modern medicine's technological imperative increasingly meets its match only when it runs afoul of the new agenda of death and dehumanization. For these 'ethicists' technology systematically loses out only to the fear that it might be used to preserve life our elites deem unworthy, nonautonomous, or undignified, especially the lives of those relegated to their new, Orwellian category of human 'unpersons': the brain-damaged, the irreversibly comatose, the unborn, and so on.

The Hippocratic tradition famously deplored several of these now accepted, even fashionable, practices, most notably euthanasia and abortion. However, it acknowledged that some medical procedures it deemed legitimate could sometimes go wrong, prematurely ending a patient's life or pregnancy, while others were known to cause pain or loss of function as side-effects of measures taken to restore health or preserve life. The medical code came to limit its condemnation to the 'intentional termination of life', a formulation still sometimes employed. One reason

161

for this is straightforward. Medicine is, as we say today, a part of *health care*. Its primary goal, and that of its practitioners, is the patient's health, understood as the integrated functioning of her systems as an organism. Dying is the comprehensive breakdown and dissolution of this functioning. You do not get any less healthy, any worse off as an organism, than by dying. So, as the tradition recognized, it perverts medical skills to turn them to the pursuit of death, whether as means or end, as happens when physicians become executioners, suicide assistants, or – assuming the unborn are human beings – abortionists.[1] Those 'ethicists' who celebrate the emerging medical order have made this restriction their preferred target, identifying the traditional claim that life is sacred with endorsement of just such a moral principle against the intentional termination of human life.[2] Thus, Helga Kuhse labels 'the [Q]ualified Sanctity-of-Life Principle' the thesis that 'it is absolutely prohibited either intentionally to kill a patient or intentionally to let a patient die, and to base decisions relating to the prolongation and shortening of human life on consideration of its quality or kind; it is, however, sometimes permissible to refrain from preventing death'.[3] She directs her book's arguments chiefly against this thesis. The self-declared enemies of life's sanctity insist the stricture against medical personnel acting with the intent that a patient's life end stems from religious faith and lacks all justification outside that context.[4]

In my view, these hostile critics of this element of traditional medical ethics deeply misunderstand or ignore reasons supporting it. In other essays, I have tried to defend traditional moral absolutism against general philosophical attacks, especially its emphasis on the crucial moral role of the agent's intentions. Here I wish to rebut some of the criticisms salient in the medical ethics literature, concentrating on Kuhse's discussion, which is, as far as I know, the most detailed and sophisticated attack on the moral importance of intentions in medical ethics. I will defend what we can call 'intention-sensitivity' in medical ethics. More specifically, I will try to show: (i) that there is a genuine psychological difference between intending something to result from one's behaviour and merely expecting it to; (ii) how it can matter to whether a health-care worker acts in ways morally permissible that she intends (and does not merely foresee) certain aspects or results of her behaviour; and (iii) that we can often have reasonable beliefs about whether an agent acted with an intention that should disqualify a course of action. I will also sketch the beginnings of an approach to medical ethics in which the reasons for the critical importance of intentions become clearer. My approach here will be secular in James Rachels's sense: I will not treat morality simply 'as a matter of faithfulness to abstract rules or divine laws', but rather will treat 'the point of morality [one of the chief objectives of moral agents, as I should put it] as the good of creatures on earth'.[5]

## 1. MUST SOMEONE INTEND TO DO ALL SHE EXPECTS TO DO?

Kuhse worries about efforts to limit the scope of the agent's intentions so that a physician might intend to turn off a patient's life-sustaining respirator without intending to kill her. She thinks there is no principled way of keeping this restricted notion of intention from contracting to the point where blatant malefactors are exonerated. If the physician can say she meant only to turn off the respirator but not to kill, why cannot the greedy and impatient heir say she did not mean to kill her rich uncle but only to shut his body down long enough for the authorities to think him dead and award her the inheritance? What Kuhse calls the Qualified Sanctity of Life doctrine requires some limitation in the scope of intentions, but then how do we keep things that common sense and traditional medical ethics classify as intended from turning into mere side-effects? If intended means can turn into side-effects so easily, is there a real difference between them?

I think Kuhse exaggerates the problem here, misled perhaps by misinterpreting a line of argument defenders of intention-sensitive ethics offer. It is true that in order to show that the physician injecting a medicine does not intend the pain she causes her patient, defenders sometimes point out that the physician's objective derives no advantage from the pain itself but only from the injection. This is true, but by itself it is not sufficient to show that the physician does not intend the pain. The physician may hate the patient, who has been uncooperative and rude, say, and may not only delight in the latter's pain but inject the medicine motivated in part by her desire for such revenge. The traditionalists who made this point relied on the fact that they were discussing a *physician*, presumed to be a person of goodwill, not ill will. Their point was that this injection did not itself compromise that goodwill. They were not imagining an agent motivated by hate or revenge. The injection need not involve any intent to cause pain and they assumed that nothing else in the agent committed her to such an intention. Once this is seen, fears like those of Kuhse can be shown to be immaterial.

She points out that in certain kinds of abortion motivated by concern to save the pregnant woman's life, the foetus's death is not a 'necessary means' to the medical end.[6] That is correct. However, the relevant psychological issue is not what an agent rationally *has to* intend in acting to achieve her end, but what she *does* intend. Even if foetal death is not a 'necessary means' in many abortions, it may be true that it is an *actual* means, what the agent does intend, even if she could have acted similarly with other intentions. Where Kuhse talks about what needs to be included within the scope of the agent's intention on 'any plausible interpretation of what the agent intends', what we need is not merely a 'plausible' interpretation of her intention but an accurate one.[7] There is no reason to suppose that agents always intend only the bare minimum necessary to achieve their goals. Normally, people leave themselves a little margin for error in what they intend. Oftentimes, if we aim to attain the result X+Y, then we are more likely to ensure it is at least X. So often we set ourselves the wider aim. The detective detains all eyewitnesses to ensure the one who killed does not escape. The frightened infantry soldier decides to kill all civilians in a village to make sure that no members of the guerrilla movement survive. The baseball manager has the relief pitcher warming up early so he will be ready if and when needed later on. The physician removes extra tissue beyond that known to be cancerous to make it more likely she gets all the diseased tissue. In all these cases, an agent, sometimes permissibly, sometimes not, intends more than she minimally needs for her goal.

This fact provides a response to Kuhse and others.[8] They maintain that the restricted conception of intention employed to exonerate the physician from the charge of intentionally harming when she gives the injection will similarly exonerate from any intention to kill the greedy heir who need only intend that her victim be judged dead long enough for her to collect, the terror bomber who need only intend that her victims look dead long enough to demoralize the enemy leaders, as well as the physician who need only intend to reduce or remove the foetus's head to save the woman's life. These thinkers tend to welcome the last conclusion and to deplore the others, but their main point is that the distinction between what is intended and what is merely foreseen becomes unstable, even incoherent, thereby undermining its use in any acceptable ethics. However, it should now be clear that the question is not whether the greedy heir, the terror bomber, and the physician *need to* intend death but whether *in fact* they do. There is good reason to suppose so. First, few real-life agents are likely to have framed their practical deliberation and their decision making in such sophisticated terms as those the enemies of intention-sensitive ethics place in the minds of their imaginary agents. For familiar Humean, associationist reasons, not every distinction of propositions the mind can be brought to recognize is one that it does (or is likely or able to) observe or utilize in actual practical deliberation and decision making. Secondly, it is not the case simply that each agent has a certain limited objective and takes action to achieve it. Each must also adopt some scheme for connecting action to objective. To identify that we need to determine, as best we can, each agent's plan of action. We need to find out how these agents mean their actions to get them to their objectives. Surely, even if they are so sophisticated (indeed, sophistical) that they adopt such rarefied objectives as those of making it appear that their chosen victims are dead, nevertheless the most likely, secure, and attractive scenario for getting from dropping the bomb on a city to demoralizing enemy leaders with the thought that its inhabitants are dead is to have the bomb actually kill them. That an agent adopts an artificially narrow objective does not preclude her also adopting a wider instrumental one as a way of securing it. Indeed, as we see, the broader objective is quite likely to be part of the intended path from the action to the narrower objective, just as the baseball manager may ask two pitchers to warm up as a way of ensuring that one will be ready when needed. That separates the imaginary, sophistical agents of the critics' examples from the familiar ones the tradition describes, whose sensibly narrowed intentions (to heal but not to hurt, for example) are related to ordinary, recognizable human planning.

We should note another difficulty as well. Both Kuhse and her opponents may have mislocated the more important moral issue for an intention-sensitive ethics. I think that in such cases as those of abortions to spare the woman's body physical traumas from pregnancy – as distinct from those to save her (or others) from the difficulties of birth or child-rearing – the major question may lie elsewhere: not in whether the agent intends the death, but whether the intention she does act with (even if not to cause or allow death) is comparably illicit, as in intentionally crushing or removing someone's head. Philippa Foot claimed that occasionally two possible contents of intention, $p$ and $q$, are so 'close' that when someone intends $p$ she intends $q$. Kuhse asks what this talk of 'closeness' of possible intentional contents means and how it can matter to what an agent intends.[9] I think Foot's point is that $p$ is *sometimes* so connected to $q$ that it is either silly to claim (i) that an agent intended $p$ but did not intend $q$, or (ii) that the difference between her intending $p$ and intending $q$ is morally important.

'Closeness' can matter to what an agent intends ('psychological closeness') because, as we noted, the fact that the mind can be brought to recognize a certain distinction of possible intentional contents does not imply that, on a given occasion, it utilizes that distinction in its actual practical deliberation and decision making. Closeness can matter to the moral permissibility of what the agent intentionally does ('moral closeness'), because sometimes $p$ and $q$ will be so connected that intending $p$ will be vicious for largely the same reasons that intending $q$ is. Consider a much- discussed example from Foot, in which spelunkers use dynamite to blow up the body of an overweight comrade who has gotten himself caught in the cave's entrance and his company trapped inside. Perhaps they do not mean to kill him but 'only' to destroy his body. However, it is reasonable to think that, given the nature of bodily integrity as a component of human well-being, the latter intention, like the former, will suffice to rule out the action as vicious. So, too, for the abortionist's intention to remove someone's head. There will, of course, be different accounts of what makes acting on one intention immoral in a way comparable to that of acting on a closely connected one. I think the best way to understand such matters is to say that each intention is about equally distant from the standard of some relevant moral virtues. Whether or not that is correct, intention-sensitive ethics is committed neither to the claim that absolutely every difference in intention matters morally nor to the claim that an agent's intentions must be in the clear morally if she does not intend anyone's death.

## 2. DISTINGUISHING INTENDED RESULTS FROM SIDE-EFFECTS

Even if there is in principle a relatively stable difference between intended results and side-effects, is it a difference sufficiently discernible to be of use to us in our moral deliberation or assessment? Can we *know* what we intend to do (as distinct from what we merely expect to do)? In general, there are several questions we can ask to help determine what we or others intend in action and, specifically, to determine whether a medical care-giver intends someone to die. (i) Does the patient's death figure in the agent's plan not just as a presupposition, or a probable result, but as an *objective* (an interim or ultimate goal), a thing to be attained? (ii) Is she *trying* to attain the patient's death? (iii) Does she do anything *in order to* attain death? (iv) Does she perform the lethal action *in order to* derive some result (perhaps only an interim goal) *from the death itself*? (v) Does the death make her and her behaviour at least a partial *success*? (vi) Would survival make her and her behaviour at least a partial *failure*? When the answer to any of these questions is affirmative, the agent intends the death, for any affirmative answer places the death within the agent's plan of action in the special sort of place only what is intended occupies.[10]

Other tests for distinguishing intended results from side-effects have sometimes been proposed, but they have misled some people. So, it is said that we must welcome intended results but not expected side-effects, and must regret it when an intended result does not occur but not when a merely expected one fails to materialize. However, this is open to the argument that since the high-minded mercy-killer need not rejoice over the death of her victim/beneficiary and might even be cheered if the patient not only miraculously escaped death but fully recovered, then perhaps the mercy-killer does not intend to kill.[11] I suppose the mercy-killer might be pleased by a miraculous cure, but what matters is that, in the event of such a miracle, she and her action would have been *failures* in the effort to achieve the patient's death. Welcoming the recovery involves abandoning and repudiating her plan to kill, and that distinguishes her mental stance from that of someone who expected to shorten life but did not intend to. (Of course, she can still stand ready to reactivate the homicidal plan should the patient relapse, but she renounces the plan for the time being.)

Similarly, some defenders of intention-sensitive ethics have relied upon what is called the counterfactual test for intention. According to it, on Kuhse's formulation, the key question for the agent is: 'If you had believed your action would not have resulted in the patient's death, would you still have acted in the way you did?'[12] Partisans of intention-sensitive medical ethics have wanted to say that the physician who legitimately prescribes high doses of painkiller to a patient for whom lesser doses would be ineffective, even though they may shorten the patient's life, can answer this question affirmatively. Similarly, a doctor can answer affirmatively who withdraws what are usually deemed 'extraordinary means', such as dialysis and artificial respiration machines, from an irreversibly comatose patient for the sake of 'avoiding "the investment of instruments and personnel... disproportionate to the results foreseen"'.[13] However, according to traditional defenders of intention-sensitive medical ethics, the mercy-killer cannot 'act the same way'. The mercy-killer needs the patient's death for her plans for pain-relief to succeed, and must change her plans if she loses her belief that the patient will die from her conduct. The plans of the first two physicians, in contrast, do not depend on the patient's dying, so they need not change them and can continue to act 'the same way', even if they think their patients will survive the high dosage of painkiller and the withdrawal of treatment, respectively.

Problems attend this test as well. Kuhse rejects the usual interpretation of the test question, according to which only the expected results of the patient's death ('causally downstream factors'), but not its causes ('causally upstream factors'), are changed in the situation where we imagine that she will not die.[14] She argues that this interpretation is unfair and 'misleading because it makes it easy to ignore causally upstream factors that are relevant to letting die but not to killing: whether, because of causally upstream factors, the agent's action or omission is under particular circumstances sufficient to bring about a patient's death. If it is, as it is in the cases mentioned, then we cannot leave out the causally upstream factors that make the agent's action what it is: an instance of letting die, or of refraining from preventing death, rather than an instance of "turning off an iron lung" '.[15]

To the extent that I follow Kuhse's reasoning, it appears to me that she has misunderstood the point of the test. The relevant issue is what is part of the agent's actual plan. What the proponent of intention-sensitive medical ethics wants to show is that death is not part of the agent's plan in permissible instances of letting die. The test helps to show this because changing her expectation of death tends to change the mercy-killer's behaviour because it forces a change in her plans to end her patient's pain; while it tends not to change the behaviour of the other physicians (i.e. the ones who discontinue extraordinary means or who prescribe high dosages of painkillers to relieve discomfort even at the risk of hastening death) because it forces no change in their plans, since their patients' deaths were not planned in the first place. These latter physicians 'act the same way' even if they know their omissions will not now constitute instances of letting die. However, the mercy-killer has no reason to 'act the same way' when she finds her action will not be a killing, since she acts as she does inter alia in order to kill. To accept Kuhse's interpretation of the test is to beg the question by rigging things so that the agent's changes of plan track death.[16]

Kuhse thinks 'incoherent' common sense's moderate conception of intention, according to which an agent intends all her ends and means (objectives) but not the side-effects of her actions (the ones she merely foresees). We have seen that there is no basis for such a judgment. We intend what we plan to do and the tests proposed can usually identify what we intend, especially when the question is whether someone acts with a homicidal or other seriously evil-minded intention. Hence, we can reject both disjuncts in the dilemma with which Kuhse confronts defenders of intention-sensitive ethics and the Qualified Sanctity of Life thesis: 'accept the broad conception of the intentional, according to which the agent terminates life intentionally whenever she could by an act or omission, prevent a foreseen death and refrains from doing so; or . . . accept the narrow conception of the intentional, according to which an agent terminates life intentionally only when she intends the death in question as her end, for its own sake.'[17]

It is absurd to think I intend to terminate your life even though I do nothing whatever aimed at making sure you are dead, so any broad conception of intent is unacceptable. It is counter-intuitive on its face and in its implications, and it goes contrary to our best current understandings of intention, which conceive intention as what one plans, aims, or tries to do whether as end or means.[18] Kuhse and others who support such an excessively broad conception of intention at least owe us some general and persuasive account of intention to make such a view plausible. This is missing. Likewise, the extremely narrow conception of intention that includes only what the agent pursues 'for its own sake' and excludes the agent's chosen means is absurd. There is little in life we pursue for its own sake. Many philosophers have thought there was only one such end, though they disagreed on what it was. The narrow conception of the intentional, whether meant to apply (quite arbitrarily) only to cases of intending death or as a general account, implies that we do almost nothing intentionally, depriving the notion of its crucial role in the explanation of human action. Thus, quite apart from their implications for morality, these extremely broad and narrow views of the intentional, at least insofar as they imply (as Kuhse's argument requires) comparably broad and narrow conceptions of what is *intended*, are unacceptable simply as theses in philosophical psychology, independently of their implausible implications for ethics.

## 3. CAN AN ACTION'S MORALITY DEPEND UPON WHAT THE AGENT INTENDS?

Even if there is a coherent and moderate notion of intention, according to which an agent intends her means and ends but not the side-effects of what she does, does the morality of behaviour ever hang on what the agent intended? More specifically, can it make a difference to whether an agent acted permissibly whether she intended a certain result or merely expected it as a side-effect? This is what proponents of intention-sensitive ethics affirm and its opponents deny. Let us consider some grounds offered for this denial.

Rachels charges that any theory that makes the morality of an agent's conduct thus depend on the agent's intentions must violate the principle of rationality and morality that similar cases be treated alike. To show this, he invites us to consider Jack and Jill, both of whom visit their 'sick and lonely grandmother' – Jill in order to ingratiate herself to win inclusion in the old woman's will, Jack simply from the compassionate desire to cheer her up. 'Jack's intention was honourable and Jill's was not. Could we say on that account that what Jack did was right, but what Jill did was not right? No; for Jack and Jill did the very same thing, and if they did the same thing, in the same circumstances, we cannot say that one acted rightly and one acted wrongly. Consistency requires that we assess similar actions similarly.' He concludes, 'The traditional view says that the intention with which an act is done is relevant to determining whether the act is right. The example of Jack and Jill suggests that, on the contrary, the intention is not relevant to deciding whether the act is right or wrong, but instead is relevant to assessing the character of the person who does it, which is another thing entirely'.[19]

I return below to the relevance of intentions to character assessment. What should we make of Rachels' argument for his thesis that intention is irrelevant to whether conduct is right or wrong? Not much, I think. Such arguments blatantly beg the question. Consistency does not require that things in *any* way similar be treated alike, only that things *relevantly* similar be treated alike. Proponents of intention-sensitive ethics maintain that the intention with which an action is done is relevant to its moral permissibility. Rachels' argument merely presupposes that this is not true, it offers no reason to reject it. One could as easily 'prove' that consistency rules out any moral theory, e.g. act utilitarianism. Suppose that, out of affection, Joe and Jane both visit their sickly and rather grumpy grandfather. Since the old man loathes Joe but loves Jane, Joe's visit brings about less pleasure than his staying home would, but Jane's act brings more pleasure into the world than anything else she could have done. The act utilitarian judges Joe's action impermissible but Jane's right. However, they did 'the very same thing' (visit their grandfather) in the same circumstances (viz. sickness), and so the utilitarian's judgment violates consistency. Obviously, this argument merely *presupposes* that the acknowledged difference in the effects of Joe's and Jane's actions makes no moral difference. This consistency argument against utilitarianism does not prove false the utilitarian thesis that effects are relevant; it simply assumes it is false. In just the same way, Rachels' consistency argument assumes that the acknowledged difference in the intentions behind Jack's and Jill's actions makes no moral difference. It presupposes that the thesis of intention-sensitivity is false, instead of showing it to be false.[20]

The charge of inconsistency fails without support, but it may suggest a better argument against intention-sensitivity in ethics. If the rightness or wrongness of what I do can depend on my intentions, then will not an intention-sensitive ethics normally be unable to answer the ordinary request for moral advice: Is it permissible morally for me to do $V$? Will not the intention-sensitive theorist have to duck any such straightforward question, and reply weakly, 'Well, it depends (on what intentions you would have)'? And is this not a serious weakness inasmuch as a moral theory is supposed to guide practice? These worries are less blatantly without merit, but on examination they pose no serious difficulty. Again, this can be brought out by comparing intention-sensitive ethics with other approaches to moral theory. Intention-sensitive medical ethics is no more at fault here than is either (direct or indirect) consequentialism or Kant's theory. All demand further information before answering such a question as 'May I morally do $V$?' Before it can offer its own answer to the request for moral advice, each must await the answer to its special question: With what intentions would you do $V$? With what total results? From what 'maxims'? Indeed, the answer to the question that intention-sensitive medical ethics asks is likely to be contained in the term '$V$', at least, if '$V$' is a term from our familiar, ordinary moral vocabulary, such as 'lie', 'rape', or 'kidnap', or from specialized medical ethics terminology such as 'directly kill' or 'directly abort'.[21] The application of any of these terms requires that the agent have certain intentions, and these are precisely the kinds of intentions (to deceive, to coerce, etc.) to which intention-sensitive ethical theories have traditionally assigned morally determinative import. This is not the case for total results or 'maxims'. I cannot know that what I do would be a lie without knowing some of the morally pertinent intentions with which I would be acting, but I can know it would be a lie without knowing its total effects or the 'maxim' on which I would be acting. When it comes to giving a non-evasive response to a request for moral guidance couched in the terms of our ordinary moral discourse or in suitably specialized vocabularies, intention-sensitive ethical theory is at a considerable advantage over its chief rivals.

Now consider a different, stronger argument against intention-sensitive ethics. Many have rejected intention-sensitivity in ethics on the grounds that it threatens to evacuate moral norms of power and invites hypocrisy, because an agent can, it is said, always evade an intention-sensitive norm against what she wants to do simply by tinkering with her intentions but otherwise acting the same and to similar effect. Glanville Williams considers it 'altogether too artificial to say that a doctor who gives an overdose of a narcotic having in the forefront of his mind the aim of ending the patient's existence is guilty of sin, while a doctor who gives the same overdose in the same circumstances in order to relieve pain is not guilty of sin, provided that he keeps his mind steadily off the [inevitable] consequence...' He concludes that if intention-sensitivity 'means that the necessity of making a choice of values can be avoided merely by keeping your mind off one of the consequences, it can only encourage a hypocritical attitude towards moral problems'.[22]

Must intention-sensitivity make norms of action vacuous and encourage hypocrisy? I think not, though it seems to me that Williams and other critics of intention-sensitivity have a legitimate concern when they raise the danger of easy changes of intention by the mere 'redirection' of one's will. We cannot plausibly maintain that intentions play a decisive moral role if they are so shallow in the person, phenomena so readily manipulable that they may, like some internal flashlight, be turned on or off, directed this way or that, with only the slightest and easiest of adjustments. The sorts of changes of mind and conduct that respectable norms of moral action must require of an agent inclined toward evil-doing must be real, and they must be *substantial*.When I say that changes of intention must be something real, I mean that they cannot consist solely in redescription, nor in pretence (lies), nor in self-deception. When I say that they must be substantial, I mean that they cannot consist simply in the agent's keeping this or that at the 'forefront of his mind,' and that they cannot be merely ceremonial (e.g. repeating to oneself 'I'm only trying to do X, not Y').

Fortunately, there is little basis for regarding intentions as shallow phenomena. A real change of intention is a genuine change in one's actual plans. It requires adopting a different set of objectives and instruments. It is to launch oneself on a different path to one's destination, at least, if not to set off for a different destination itself. This is not a mere linguistic matter, dressing things up in finer language, let alone concealing them behind a false front. Yet this is the picture Williams offers. Tellingly, he contrasts an agent's putting 'in the forefront of his mind [one] aim' with 'keep[ing] his mind off the consequence.' However, if we examine it, we shall see that this passage runs together two contrasts, and runs them together in a way designed to make the discredit of the merely ceremonial difference, which is a difference of emphasis, to rub off on and bias us against the other, which is important and substantive. The first contrast in the passage is that between what I keep at the mental forefront and what I manage to distract myself from. The second contrast is between what the agent aims to achieve and what she merely expects as a consequence of her action. This latter is an important psychological difference.

Indeed, it contrasts two *types* of psychological stance, since expectation is a doxastic state and intention a volitional, and thus, conative, state. Doxastic states are evaluated for truth value; the way the world is constitutes the standard against which they are assessed. Conative states normally are not evaluated for truth value. Rather, we tend to treat them as standards against which we assess the way the world is to determine which parts of it to change.[23]

Williams, of course, may think that the difference between something's being my aim and its being a consequence is the same as the difference between my having it in the forefront of my mind and my keeping my mind off it. However, this is a highly implausible account of intention, and I can see no advantage it has over the more sophisticated accounts we have today, which understand intention in terms of what plays a certain peculiar role in one's practical planning. While it is highly implausible to maintain that it makes an important moral difference what I keep telling myself (or otherwise maintain at the front of my mind) as opposed to what I distract myself from, that is very different from the thesis of intention-sensitive ethics that it matters morally what I do or do not treat as good, that is, what I aim at, strive after, and favour as an agendum, a thing to be attained or done. Whether I keep something at the forefront or the background of my mind is a matter of no evident moral importance and seems quite a fishy business in any case, an empty psychological ceremony or – worse – an opportunity for self-deception. However, whether I adopt something as a good, as a thing to be attained or, on the other hand, merely accept it as a probability that I make no special plans to oppose, is a matter of different responses to possible situations. Moreover, since some of these are desirable or undesirable, this distinction marks a difference between two contrasting forms of value-response. Modes of value-response constitute a long-acknowledged and highly plausible source of morality.

Although Williams et al. have, as we saw, a valid (though overstated) point here, we should note something ugly and disturbing in the criticism itself: the critics seem to assume a merely instrumentalist picture of human relationships. Hobbes provides a negative model of instrumentalism, in which other persons confront one primarily as rivals, dangers. Bentham and Epicurus perhaps provide a more positive model, in which others matter to one as potential sources of new benefits, not just as threats to the benefits one could acquire alone. What is important is that no such instrumentalism about human relationships is either appealing or plausible. People matter to one another not merely as potential *causes* of welcome or unwelcome results, but as *subjects*. I care about you as such, independently of and prior to my interest in what you can do for me (and of my fear of what you may do to me). I care about how you feel about me, irrespective of whether you bring me additional benefits or burdens. Because of this, the contents of your heart – your desires for me, hopes, fears, and aims – take on human significance independent of their causal impact on me.

An appealing and human moral theory should assign such contents of the human heart and aspiration moral importance in their own right. One of the places where these critics go wrong is in their implicitly instrumentalist assumption that no 'mere' change of heart can really matter to morality, let alone be its focus. I think a human morality makes what matters centrally in morality the same things that matter centrally to us as people. Those are not merely the probable effects on us of people's actions, but the contents of their hearts in their attitudes and aims (instrumental or ultimate) toward us. This is the essence of a properly intention-sensitive ethics, and it suggests that such a theory should be part of a broader theory centred on what people want, enjoy, aim at, and oppose – in short, on the virtues. I will return briefly to this question of wider moral theory at the end. At this point, let us pursue the question of how intentions have moral significance in what I have called a genuinely human morality.

Intentions seem to matter both in their own right and as bridges connecting actions with the other personal contents (i.e. attitudes of heart) that have central moral significance: desires, hopes, fears, likes, dislikes, and so on. Intentions matter morally in their own right, because intention is a form of morally significant favouring, a form of response to something – such as life or death – that has positive or negative value. Intentions matter morally, then, whether or not, as some have maintained, intending also involves wanting in a special way that merely expecting does not.[24]

However, I think that intentions also matter morally because they are bridges connecting actions (especially physical actions) to other motivational inputs (desires, hopes, fears, etc.) that give moral significance and status to actions. Thus, I think the tradition is correct that the mercy-killer must in a certain way want and prefer the patient's death, while the physician permissibly providing a large dose of analgesic (to a patient who requires that much to lessen her pain) need not. We can see the difference this way. The latter physician adopts an aim to change a certain temporal period (call it Time One) from one in which the patient experiences painful life to one in which she has painless (or, at least, less intensely painful) life, in spite of her expectation that the action will also bring on an earlier death. In contrast, the mercy-killer aims to change a temporal period (call it Time Two) from one in which the patient experiences painful life to one in which she is dead and thus has neither pain nor life. So considered, it becomes clearer that the physician offering legitimate pain-relief, even at life-shortening levels, need have no preferences at all about the patient's death. She prefers the behaviour of providing relief during Time One, despite its shortening life, to the behaviour of maintaining a longer life, despite its being filled with pain. However, I cannot see a preference for death over (even painful) life anywhere in that state of mind.[25]

This morally important psychological difference between the mercy-killer and the physician providing a medication to relieve pain (even at dosages expected, but not intended, to shorten life) can be brought out in another striking way. The mercy-killer cannot rationally take simultaneous measures to make the patient's death less likely. In contrast, the physician who legitimately provides medication to relieve pain, even at what she expects will be a life-shortening dosage can, at the same time she provides this probably lethal dose, without any irrationality or inconsistency, also take measures to make the patient's death less likely. The motivational input to the mercy-killer's behaviour renders that conduct rationally incompatible with her simultaneously making efforts to preserve her patient's life. This shows that the mercy-killer's frame of mind puts her at a very great distance from any intent to preserve the patient's life. The motivational input to the palliating physician's behaviour does not similarly preclude the latter's rationally and simultaneously trying to preserve her patient's life. The latter is thus less distanced from the good-hearted intent to preserve life. A moderate account of what is intended nicely explains this difference. The mercy-killer intends her patient's death, and it is a familiar truth of philosophical psychology that one cannot rationally intend not to do what one simultaneously intends to do.[26] Thus, she cannot also rationally take steps attempting (and, thus, intended) to preserve that life or to render it less likely that the patient die. In contrast, the physician who legitimately prescribes high doses of palliatives, but only to give the patient a less painful life (not the dubious relief of the painlessness of death), can, without irrationality or inconsistency, still take measures to preserve the patient's life. That is because there is nothing rationally inconsistent in an agent's attempting (and intending) to avoid a result she regards as probable but does not intend. So, the mercy-killer, but not the other physician, intends the patient's death and thereby objectionably distances herself from the aims of medicine.

## 4. WHY SHOULD MEDICAL ETHICS BE INTENTION-SENSITIVE?

I will conclude with some reflections on a conception of medicine and a
conception of the moral life that help us see why medical ethics is best
understood as intention-sensitive. As we observed, medicine is increasingly seen as a part of the wider institution of health care. Health *care*, as
the term suggests, comprises the *caring* professions. Such positions have
their meaning in care. It is tempting to see 'care' merely as a synonym for
'treatment', but I think it instructive to reflect on the terminology of care:
taking care of patients is a notion derived from the deeper concept of caring *for* them. Whereas taking care *of* somebody is an activity, caring *for*
them is not. Primarily, it is an orientation of the heart toward them, a response to them. Ideally, this response is a response of one self to another
as a fellow and as a bearer of value. It derives from the more general and,
as I urged above, not-merely-instrumental interest each of us has in being
the recipient of others' goodwill. Admittedly, the patient's interest in her
physician may, when securing treatment at a moment of crisis, be largely
instrumental and results-oriented. However, this is a time of emergency
and is a matter of selecting a *particular individual care-giver*. The larger
human interest behind the patient's desire is not strictly instrumental.
The morality of medicine is best understood as emerging from the other,
broader, inner-focused part of interpersonal interest. It is an interest in
being cared for because we are cared about.

This does not imply that the actions we judge are entirely 'interior'
mental acts of wanting, hoping, intending, and so on. They need not be;
we judge ordinary physical, publicly observable actions as well.[27] However, what is true is that such actions are properly judged on the basis of
the interior acts that inform them. Intention-sensitive ethical theory does
not, as Kuhse and Rachels charge, 'confuse' the 'nature' (permissibility)
of actions with the goodness of agents and their character.[28] Rather, such
an understanding of the moral life theoretically derives judgments about
the permissibility of actions from more basic moral judgments about the
virtue of subjects and the exercise of their agency. For such reasons, I
think it best to conceive of an intention-sensitive account of the moral
permissibility of actions as part of a virtues-based moral theory that focuses on the roles we need people to play in our lives if we are meaningfully to flourish as human beings. I think these are also role-relationships
that it is mere human nature to want others to fill for us and that it is no
part of healthy human nature to be averse to filling for others. I do not
claim that the health-care professions and occupations are themselves

morally fundamental role-relationships. It is clear, however, that these medical relationships emerge from the specialization of particular elements of such roles – as do such other professions as that of teacher – and that their moral structure is best understood on the model of such non-professional, morally fundamental roles as those of friend, fellow citizen, sibling, confidante, spouse, and 'neighbour' (in the broad sense employed in the Christian Scriptures, where it picks out any human being qua fellow traveller on life's way).

## CONCLUSION: 'THOU SHALT NOT KILL; BUT NEED'ST NOT STRIVE/OFFICIOUSLY TO KEEP ALIVE.'

A final observation. Glover, Kuhse, and other proud opponents of life's sanctity pour scorn on naive defenders of the tradition who have quoted A. H. Clough's satiric line from his 'The New Decalogue', as if it were meant straightforwardly. They are, of course, right to remind us of the poet's irony. However, we should not be misled into assuming the poem is best interpreted as an endorsement of Rachels's thesis that killing and letting die are morally equivalent. The poem makes little sense read as bestowing a moral *imprimatur* on killing, especially medical killing, as today's ethicists are wont to do. Rather, Clough seems to satirize the legalistic abuse that looks for moral loopholes and supposes we are automatically in the clear if we can just avoid the behavioural extreme explicitly condemned. Intention-sensitive ethical theory, especially if virtues-based, nicely avoids that legalism while preserving the spirit, ground and letter of the moral condemnation of typical killings as wrong because vicious in the attitudes toward human life they express. Letting die, like killing, can but need not also embody such vice. Whether it does will depend on the motivational inputs that inform the relevant behaviour. An ethical theory that is insensitive to what, we must admit, are sometimes subtle matters of intention, is condemned to insensitivity to the human heart and thus to the heart of medical ethics and of any genuinely human morality as well.

## NOTES

1  See Garcia (1993) and responses in following numbers of that periodical.
2  See, especially, Rachels (1986), chs. 2, 6; Kuhse (1987), chs.1, 3; Singer (1995), *passim*. 'Celebrate' is not too strong a word. Singer, for example, sees medicine's

recent turn toward death as great news, 'a period of opportunity, in which we have a historic chance to shape something better... an ethic that is more compassionate and more responsive to what people decide for themselves.' By this last, he means less fussy about killing those who despair or who are deemed unworthy of protection. Singer offers five 'new commandments' to replace the old ones and enthusiastically heralds 'another Copernican Revolution', this time in ethics (Singer (1995), pp. 6, 189).

I should make it clear at the outset that throughout I presuppose that an agent intentionally does only what she intends to do. This is sometimes denied both by defenders and opponents of intention-sensitive ethics, but I think it true, have defended it elsewhere, and since Kuhse (whose work I treat in some detail) also seems to presuppose it, it is best to work with it here. On the dispute, see especially Garcia (1990).

3  Kuhse (1987), p. 23.
4  '[T]he absolute prohibition of the intentional termination of life has its source in theology, and makes little sense outside that particular framework' (Kuhse (1987), p. 15). Discussing some 'assumptions' of traditional Western moral thought, including the principle 'that we are responsible for what we intentionally do in a way that we are not responsible for what we deliberately fail to prevent', Singer writes: 'Taken independently of their religious origins, both of the crucial assumptions are on very weak ground' (Singer (1995), p. 221).

The critics tend to remain silent on whether they think it justified even *within* a religious context, perhaps because they find such thinking too unfamiliar. Not all the apologists for medical homicide are so circumspect, however. Rachels writes, 'We have now looked at three arguments (against the morality of euthanasia) that depend on religious assumptions. They are all unsound, but I have *not* criticized them simply by rejecting their religious presuppositions... The upshot is that religious people are in the same position as everyone else. There is nothing in religious belief in general, or in Christian belief in particular, to preclude the acceptance of mercy-killing as a humane response to some awful situations' (Rachels (1986), p. 165).

5  Rachels (1986), pp. 6, 38. This secular approach frees me from the need to show how what I say squares with any religious or ethical tradition, let alone recent interpretations or extensions of it. On the other hand, I do not deny that such fidelity can be a useful corrective to our tendency to go astray when we try in Singer's terms to 'rethink' complex matters ab initio. I suspect that Kuhse gets confused by taking the innovations of a dissident theologian such as Fr. Gerard Hughes as amply representative of his tradition, and that Rachels makes a similar mistake in relying upon Daniel Maguire. I hope my approach here will also free me from that sort of danger. Of course, as Rachels notes, my taking a secular approach does not commit me to a generally anti-theistic understanding of morality.
6  Kuhse (1987), p. 96.
7  Kuhse (1987), p. 108.
8  See Bennett (1981); Holmes (1989); and the discussion of David Lewis' objection in Quinn (1989), p. 343, note 16.
9  Foot (1967); Kuhse (1987), p. 100ff.
10  These are discussed a bit further in Garcia (1991). On intentions and plans, see Bratman (1990).

11  See Kuhse (1987), secs. 3.43 and 3.44, esp. p. 126.

12  Kuhse (1987), p. 131.

13  Kuhse (1987), p. 124ff.

14  Kuhse prefers to interpret the question as requiring us to suppose that everything causally connected to the death either as effect or as cause changes. She maintains that, so interpreted, not just the mercy-killer, but also the physicians whose conduct partisans of intention-sensitive ethics have traditionally defended, would answer the test question negatively. On her preferred interpretation of the test question, she says, the doctor in the 'extraordinary means' case we mentioned, no less than the mercy-killer, 'would also answer "no" if asked the test question, because he too believes that there is no death, and hence must believe there will be no saving of disproportionate resources (for he believes the resources are needed to keep the patient alive).' She concludes that 'the test question will not allow us to distinguish between the intentions of the doctors' (Kuhse (1987), p. 132ff). I confess that I cannot follow Kuhse's reasoning here. Presumably, Kuhse should be understood as toying with different understandings of the metaphysicians' proposal that counterfactuals be understood as claims about what obtains in those possible worlds 'closest' to the actual. If we imagine that the patient will not die, and we change everything causally connected to her death, either as cause or as effect, then what seems to follows is not that the medical equipment is 'needed to keep the patient alive', but that she does not have a life-threatening illness. After all, the equipment is needed to keep her alive in the situation where she would die without it. If we suppose that she does not die when it is turned off, then it must be that it was not needed for life. Given that, I see no basis for Kuhse's insistence that the physician in the extraordinary means case would not 'act the same way', that is, would not turn off the equipment.

15  Kuhse (1987), p. 134.

16  Note that the test question Kuhse discusses constitutes only a rough criterion for intention anyway, because a relevantly changed plan might involve the same action. If Crook pulls a human shield in front of her, Cop may not abandon her original plan to shoot Crook. But even if she does not, she must nonetheless alter her plan, for now Cop plans to shoot *through* the human shield. The external behaviour is identical, but it is performed with different intentions, ones whose difference is quite important morally.

17  Kuhse (1987), p. 147.

18  See Bratman (1990), Harman (1986), or Anscombe (1957) for some current views that support a moderate conception of the intended. Unlike Kuhse and I, several of these authors allow what the agent intentionally does to extend beyond what she intends to do. Thus, they may support a broad conception of the intentional, but not in a way that helps Kuhse's case against intention-sensitive ethics. What an attack on the latter requires is a broad view of the intended. The allies Kuhse needs, then, have to support not just a broad view of what the agent intentionally does but of what she actually intends. On this, all the thinkers cited reject her position.

19  Rachels (1986), pp. 93, 94.

20  For additional arguments against intention-sensitivity, some of them similarly question-begging, see Thomson (1991) and Holmes (1989). For criticism of Thomson's reasoning, see Garcia (1995); of Holmes', see Garcia (forthcoming).

21  I suspect that technical talk of 'direct killing' and 'direct abortion' entered ethi-
    cal discussions because it is useful to have a term to pick out the types of kill-
    ing that are always intentional. Notice that, unlike lying, rape, kidnapping,
    etc., killing need not be intentional. (See Kuhse's discussion of 'direct' killing
    at Kuhse (1987), sec. 3.3, especially pp. 103, 124.)
        Incidentally, Kuhse is wrong if (as is apparent) she thinks that traditional
    Christian medical ethics permits direct killing of innocents in tubal pregnan-
    cies or self-defence. I will not discuss self-defence here: the topic is not within
    the realm of medical ethics, and efforts to understand some medical quand-
    aries as instances of self-defence (as in cases where pregnancy endangers the
    woman's life or health) have generated absurd, sophistical claims (e.g. the fan-
    tasy that one might profitably think of a foetus as a kind of aggressor). In ecto-
    pic pregnancies, suffice it to say that, in my limited understanding of the
    medicine, the mother's blood vessels are normally damaged, so the arteries
    leading to the tubes may properly be clamped to stop haemorrhaging there
    with no intent to deprive the foetus within of life. The diseased tube can like-
    wise be licitly removed with the foetus inside in what clearly counts as an indir-
    ect abortion. (See Kuhse (1987), p. 107ff.)
22  Williams' complaint is explicitly directed against what he calls the 'Doctrine
    of Double Effect', but he is concerned only with that so-called 'doctrine's'
    embrace of intention-sensitivity, not its other elements. So, like similar philo-
    sophical treatments of double effect reasoning, it is relevant to our discussion.
    (See Williams (1958), p. 286.) By the way, I should acknowledge that Tom Ca-
    vanaugh convinced me that, since double effect is too complicated to be con-
    sidered a single principle, and seems never to have been explicitly taught in
    its entirety by highest religious authority, it is best conceived of as a special
    form of reasoning rather than as a 'principle' or 'doctrine'.
23  See Anscombe (1957).
24  See the discussion of Boyle at Kuhse (1987), pp. 126–130.
25  At most, perhaps, the physician offering the high dosage of pain medication
    must prefer the conjunction no-pain-during-Time-One-plus-early-death to
    the conjunction later-death-plus-pain-during-Time-One. However, this pre-
    ference for one conjunction over another is not one that simply distributes by
    any valid logical mechanism to a preference for each conjunct in the preferred
    conjunction over its complement in the other conjunction. That is to say, it
    does not commit one to preferring the patient's being dead during a certain
    period to her having painful life during it. Hence, such a physician, unlike
    the mercy-killer, has no *necessary* preference for death. It follows that we need
    to be given some special reason to think she has an *actual* preference for the
    patient's death.
        I see no such reason to attribute that kind of preference to a decent-hearted
    and right-thinking physician. In short, it is doubtful that the physician's legiti-
    mate preference to combat pain in the short term ($A$) despite its life-shortening
    effect ($B$) is adequately captured by attributing to her a conjunctive preference
    for $A\&B$. Even if it were, it is additionally doubtful that her conjunctive prefer-
    ence for lessened pain plus shortened life ($A \& B$) over longer life but more
    pain (not-$B$ & not-$A$) distributes so as to entail that she simply prefers not only
    less pain to more pain (not-$A$ to $A$), but also shorter to longer life ($B$ to not-$B$).
26  See Bratman (1990).

27 Compare Kuhse (1987), p. 136.
28 See Kuhse (1987), p. 90; Rachels (1986), p. 93.


## REFERENCES

Anscombe, G. E. M. (1957) *Intention* (Ithaca: Cornell University Press).
Bennett, Jonathan (1981) 'Morality and Consequences', in Sterling McMurrin (ed.), *Tanner Lectures on Human Values, Vol. 2*, pp. 47–116 (Salt Lake City: University of Utah Press).
Bratman, Michael (1990) *Intentions, Plans, and Practical Reason* (Cambridge, Mass.: Harvard University Press).
Fischer, John Martin, et al. (1993) 'Quinn on Double Effect: the Problem of "Closeness"', *Ethics* 103, pp. 707–25.
Foot, Philippa (1967) 'The Problem of Abortion and the Doctrine of Double Effect', *Oxford Review* No. 5, pp. 5–15; reprinted in Foot, *Virtues and Vices* (Berkeley: University of California Press, 1978), ch.1.
Garcia, J. L. A. (1990) 'The Intentional and the Intended', *Erkenntnis* 33, pp. 191–209.
—— (1991) 'On the Irreducibility of the Will', *Synthese* 86, pp. 349–60.
—— (1993) 'Better Off Dead?', *American Philosophical Association Newsletter on Philosophy and Medicine* 92:1, pp. 85–8.
—— (1995) 'Intention-Sensitive Ethics', *Public Affairs Quarterly* 9, pp. 201–13.
—— (forthcoming) 'Intentions and Wrongdoing', *American Catholic Philosophical Quarterly.*
Glover, Jonathan (1977) *Causing Death and Saving Lives* (Harmondsworth: Penguin).
Harman, Gilbert (1986) *Change in View* (Cambridge, Mass.: MIT Press).
Holmes, Robert (1989) *On War and Morality* (Princeton: Princeton University Press).
Kuhse, Helga (1987) *The Sanctity of Life Doctrine in Medicine: a Critique* (Oxford: OUP).
Quinn, Warren (1989) 'Actions, Intentions, and Consequences: The Doctrine of Double Effect', *Philosophy and Public Affairs* 18, pp. 334–51.
Rachels, James (1986) *The End of Life* (Oxford: OUP).
Singer, Peter (1995) *Rethinking Life and Death* (New York: St. Martin's Press).
Thomson, Judith J. (1991) 'Self-Defense', *Philosophy and Public Affairs* 20, pp. 283–310.
Williams, Glanville (1958) *The Sanctity of Life and the Criminal Law* (London: Faber and Faber).

# 10  The Pre-eminence of Autonomy in Bioethics

## Janet E. Smith

Upon reading case books on medical ethics or simply news reports in the media, one cannot escape noticing that the medical professions are currently involved in practices that some few decades ago would have been unthinkable, not only because of the level of technology involved, but because of the then prevailing moral evaluation of the practices. One reads of Dr. Kevorkian and his death machine; of a sixty-one-year-old woman having a baby conceived with another woman's ovum in a petri dish; of embryos created solely for experimental purposes; of vital organs taken from living anencephalic infants; of millions of abortions yearly. Clearly a revolution of some kind, beyond the merely technological, has taken place.

Again, some few decades ago all of these procedures would have horrified most individuals for there was a widespread consensus that such practices violated some fundamental good, such as the laws of nature, or the dignity of persons, or God's laws, or that they were indicative of bad character – that those who performed them were venal or malicious. Perhaps there is not yet a consensus that these practices are morally good. Many factors, beyond a favourable moral evaluation, undoubtedly contribute to the growing acceptance and legalization of such practices. Certainly a major contributing factor is the importance that our culture and bioethicists in particular have come to put on respect for autonomy.

There seems to be a growing consensus that respect for the autonomy of individuals disallows the prohibition of practices previously thought morally objectionable – even were there to be a widespread consensus that such practices are wrong. Abortion may be a good example of this phenomenon; some studies show that most Americans oppose abortions done for the reasons most women put forth to justify their choice, yet despite this opposition, most Americans support a woman's 'right to choose'.

Although the growing primacy of the value of autonomy in bioethics has not gone unchallenged,[1] virtually no bioethicist denies that the increasing respect for the autonomy of patients has been a very salutary development in medicine.[2] The debate rages largely over what other principles, if any, compete with and might limit the principle of respect for autonomy (PRA). What I would like to do in this essay is to show how, in spite of claims to the contrary, respect for autonomy has begun to eclipse all other values in bioethics. I will show that advocates of the PRA have come to promote it no longer as the prima facie primary principle of bioethics, but as an absolute value that trumps all others.

The importance of respect for an individual's autonomy can be seen in a shift in the issues that dominated bioethical discussion: whereas bioethical texts and journals used to be occupied largely with assessing the moral pros and cons of procedures, an increasingly large proportion of bioethical literature now focuses on determining means to ensure competency, protection of confidentiality and privacy, informed consent, and voluntariness. In discussion of cases, bioethicists will often argue in a way that suggests that once it is ensured that the patient's choice is autonomous, the work of the bioethicist has been done. A bioethicist concerned that a patient make a good moral choice would be attempting to explain the principles which have led the bioethicist to judge a choice to be moral, and finding ways to persuade the patient to accept these principles and then to make the moral choice. Less and less of bioethical literature argues the morality of procedures and practices; more and more is directed towards finding means to ensure that choices are autonomous. The autonomous choice has supplanted the good moral choice as the primary concern of bioethics. What explains this dominance of the PRA and related concerns in bioethics?

It might be supposed that the ascendancy of the PRA is best explained by a growing respect for the self-determining powers of the human person. I will argue, however, that moral pluralism and scepticism have in fact been the forces pushing us in the direction of a nearly unfettered respect for autonomy. And I will suggest that scepticism in particular threatens the very enterprise of bioethics. Whereas ethical debate may be possible – though frustrating and perhaps ultimately indecisive – in a climate of moral pluralism, scepticism eliminates the need for debate about the moral acceptability of different practices and policies. I shall propose that efforts to justify the PRA by appeal to moral scepticism, the view that universal standards for ethical judgment cannot be known, have seriously eroded the capacity of bioethics to assess the moral acceptability of different practices and procedures.

Bruce Miller's much-cited article 'Autonomy and the Refusal of Life-saving Treatment' offers a core definition of autonomy: 'the right to autonomy is the right to make one's own choices, and ... respect for autonomy is the obligation not to interfere with the choice of another and to treat another as a being capable of choosing.'[3] As he describes four senses of 'autonomy', he sketches criteria that are generally considered requisite for a choice to qualify as an autonomous choice: autonomy considered as 'free action' requires that the choice be voluntary and intentional; autonomy as 'authenticity' requires that a choice be consistent with a patient's 'attitudes, values, dispositions, and life plans'; autonomy as 'effective deliberation' requires that the patient was 'aware of the alternatives and the consequences of the alternatives, evaluated both, and chose an action based on that evaluation' and that the patient 'rationally weight' the alternatives; autonomy as 'moral reflection' means that one has personally appropriated the values that govern one's choices.[4]

The emphasis on the PRA is relatively new in bioethics.[5] Paternalism is generally recognized as the historical rival value to autonomy and the one that the PRA has dethroned. Beauchamp and Childress define paternalism as 'the intentional overriding of one person's known preferences or actions by another person, where the person who overrides justifies the action by the goal of benefiting or avoiding harm to the person whose will is overridden.'[6] Many have observed that while it can be and has been abused, the principle of paternalism seems quite well-suited to medicine, given the concern that medicine has with health and given that doctors are likely to know better than patients what is conducive to their health. Many speak of illness as a condition of reduced autonomy, in which it is quite proper that a patient submit to the authority of others. The necessity of paternalism for at least the incompetent, or those deemed incapable of exercising autonomy either because of age or condition (known as 'weak paternalism'), is recognized even by the strongest advocates of the PRA.[7]

The importance of the PRA to medicine is perhaps not as obvious as the suitability of paternalism. Few would argue that the PRA is invoked to promote the health of patients. Given the complexity of medicine, and the dependency of patients, it should be no surprise that in the clinical setting paternalism still reigns; patients want to trust their doctors.[8]

The PRA clearly challenges paternalism by making patients responsible for choosing what care they receive. Whereas paternalism has been advocated as a means to ensure the best medical care for a patient, the widespread acceptance of the PRA stems from quite different concerns. It is advocated not so much as a means of restoring health, but rather as a means of ensuring good medical ethics. But it is no longer simply a means to good medical ethics; the PRA has assumed such centrality to the practice of bioethics, that some bioethicists now believe that the very goal of medicine should be changed 'from restoring health or reducing suffering' to 'restoring the autonomy of the patient'.[9]

The literature on the topic of autonomy suggests many reasons for the elevation of the PRA as the reigning principle in bioethics. Several have to do with developments within the health professions:

1 Exposés of the treatment of the subjects of medical research and experimentation brought about an interest in autonomy. Subjects of experiments were exposed to risks about which they had no knowledge. It was thought it would be minimally decent to inform them of what risks they were undertaking when they volunteered to undergo experimental treatment.[10]

2 Many medical procedures have been introduced which, while offering some chance of cure or prolongation of life, are burdensomely painful or expensive. Patients facing horrendously painful procedures should have the option of declining such treatment.

3 Medicine is no longer considered an art, the physician no longer an artist. Medicine has become a contractual enterprise with patients as consumers and the doctor as a technician for hire.[11]

4 Some proponents of the PRA are reacting against utilitarianism, which tended to override the wishes and good of the individual in favour of the good of the community.[12]

5 Given the complexity of medical options today, many doctors invoke the PRA in order to 'avoid traditional responsibilities'.[13]

6 At one time the curative power of medicine was greatly dependent upon the authoritativeness of the physician who actually had little genuine scientific knowledge. Advancing medical knowledge as well as the corresponding advance in education of the patient, permits the involvement of the patient in decision-making.[14]

The reasons cited above for the elevation of the PRA are largely historical and situational. That is, developments in medicine have made it possible and necessary to give greater respect to the choices of the patient.

Until recent years, however, the PRA has not been treated as a principle that 'trumps' all other principles. Certainly, two limitations to the PRA are perhaps obvious, uncontroversial, and ineluctable. There are certain biological limitations to the range of choices that a patient has,[15] even if those limitations might eventually be overcome; for instance, Arnold Schwarzenegger films notwithstanding, as yet males cannot gestate foetuses. Medical resources and cost containment also necessarily limit a patient's choices; for example, not all those wanting to conceive babies through in vitro fertilization will be able to afford the procedure. These limitations seem more a function of practical considerations than moral ones.

The primary moral reasons generally given for limiting a competent individual's exercise of autonomy are threefold. First, a patient's choice must not do clear and serious harm to the patient himself (the first principle of medicine being 'do no harm'). Secondly, the community may have values the violation of which it does not wish to tolerate; for example, it may forbid abortion should the large majority of the citizenry consider abortion to be the killing of human beings. Thirdly, a patient's choice may endanger public health, and when the good of the whole is valued above the good of the individual, autonomous choice may be limited: for instance, it may be necessary to override the reluctance of some people to be tested for AIDS.[16] Some evidence suggests, however, that these constraints against the exercise of autonomy are losing their strength.

The loosening of these constraints is probably attributable more to social factors than to developments within medicine itself. That is, the values of a democratic society contribute to the growing ascendancy of the PRA:

7 The PRA comports well with the values of a democratic society which elevates individualism and freedom over community and authority. The rebelliousness of the sixties catapulted individualism and anti-authoritarianism to new heights.[17]

8 Democratic society is highly tolerant of pluralism. Fear that the doctor and patient may not share the same moral commitments is one of the chief factors undergirding the interest in autonomy.

Recognition of the moral pluralism of modern society drives H. Tristram Engelhardt, Jr's advocacy of autonomy.[18] His advocacy is based not on the claim that autonomy is a premier value in itself. Rather, he argues that in a pluralistic society in which consensus about moral matters no longer exists and no mechanism exists for adjudicating moral disagreements, the PRA is the best means for ensuring that one group of individuals does not impose its views on another. While it is not right to say that Engelhardt's advocacy is solely political, the respect he gives to individuals who adhere to an ethical tradition and who allow that tradition to guide their choices indicates that he is not an unrestricted advocate of the PRA. Moreover, he seems to hold out the possibility that rational individuals could come to some agreement about the morality of actions, even though it has not happened. He advocates the PRA as a peace-keeping measure, not as an ideal. Acknowledging that many morally objectionable choices will be made in the name of the

PRA, Engelhardt accepts this as the price to be paid for the peaceful coexistence of adherents of incompatible moral traditions.

Yet, in a context of moral pluralism, the PRA may achieve ascendancy for more than practical reasons. In fact, in a context of moral pluralism, pluralism itself may become a value, and this development may enhance the status of autonomy. The motivations behind the liberalization of laws against abortion may be of such a kind; that is, although the majority of a community may disapprove of abortions, the value of pluralism and the value of choice may supersede the community value.

We can also see autonomy overruling a community value in the well-known cases of a Jehovah's Witness refusing a blood transfusion. The community believes blood transfusions to be normal medical care and the refusal of such to be tantamount to suicide. Yet, the wishes of Jehovah's Witnesses have routinely been honoured, initially, one suspects, because of respect for the sovereignty of religious belief, but now more probably because of the desire to respect autonomy. The respect for the sovereignty of religious belief may have contributed to a climate of moral pluralism and made autonomy more attractive. At any rate, autonomy can clearly supersede community value.

Although moral pluralism does not entail subjectivism, relativism, and scepticism, the inability to resolve moral disputes that customarily results from debates in a context of moral pluralism quite readily leads to scepticism. Daniel Callahan, a vigorous opponent of the pre-eminence of the PRA in bioethics, argues that scepticism explains the commitment to autonomy 'on the streets':

1 As moral agents, we are essentially independent of each other and isolated; we are not social animals, but morally self-enclosed, self-encompassing animals.

2 There can be no moral truth or wisdom about individual moral goods and goals and few if any about communal ends; morality is inherently subjective and relativistic.

3 The ideal relationship among human beings is the voluntary, contractual relationship of consenting adults; the community has no standing to say what is good or bad in such relationships.

4 In any weighing of the relative interests of individual and community, the burden of proof is always upon the community to prove its case for restricting the liberty of individuals.

5 The only moral obligations I have toward others are those I voluntarily undertake; there can be no such thing as involuntary moral obligation.

6 The only moral obligations that others have toward me are those
  that I autonomously allow them to have; all I am owed by others is
  respect for my autonomy.
7 Respect for the autonomy of others is sufficient for overriding my
  own conscience.[19]

These 'on the street' justifications for the pre-eminence of autonomy have
some roots or at least parallels in the philosophical justification of autonomy, a justification that is sometimes difficult to unearth.

The philosophical deliberations of Kant and Mill are frequently invoked to justify the PRA. What moderns find appealing about Kant's
view of autonomy is, first, his position that rational beings are always to
be treated as ends and never as means, and secondly, his contrasting of
autonomy, or the ability to be self-legislating, with heteronomy, or being
subject to the laws of another. What is entirely absent from the modern
employment of the PRA is Kant's insistence that all choices of rational
beings must be subject to the categorical imperative; that all moral
choices are subject to universal norms. Freedom, for Kant, is actualized
properly only through a life of duty.[20] Moderns, on the other hand, understand 'autonomy' or 'self-legislation' to be largely a principle of 'preference': 'I do what seems good to me to do – *not* what is dictated by
universal norms, the community, natural law, etc., unless I so choose to
make these *my* moral principles.'[21] The modern view finds some covert
support in Kant, however. For although Kant believed in a universal
morality, binding on all, his nonrealistic metaphysics is arguably more
compatible with subjectivism. If one can have no certain knowledge of
the external, objective world (the noumenal world), the subjective world
or the phenomenal world begins to take precedence. While surely the
transition to a highly individualistic, subjectivistic ethic has many
sources, Kant's philosophy, in spite of its inherent incompatibility with
such an ethic, contributed to this transition.

Mill's ethics exhibited nearly no concern that ethical norms be universal. Mill largely wanted to give man free reign to actualize his individuality within the limits of harming others or harming his own ability to
make free choices. In fact, for Mill, one major source of man's happiness
is his autonomous pursuit of self-defined goals. Mill's exaltation of freedom was based largely on scepticism, on the view that since certainty
about the nature of reality and about morality is impossible, individuals
should be free to shape their lives in accordance with their own views.

The fact that two such disparate philosophies as those of Kant and
Mill are invoked willy-nilly to support commitment to the PRA suggests

that the justification of the PRA does not rest upon the strength of the philosophical argumentation of Kant, Mill or any other philosopher. It is not their philosophies that validate commitment to the PRA; it is the compatibility of their philosophies with scepticism.

The close alliance between the recent ascendancy of the PRA in bioethics and scepticism can be seen in the work of Beauchamp and Childress. They somewhat gingerly propose that truth is not possible in the moral realm:

> Yet it is far from settled that this treatment of moral truth is adequate. It is doubtful that a successful body of coherent beliefs, no matter how stable, yields truth. For one reason, it is doubtful that moral statements have truth values and that truth is a category that should appear in moral theory. For another reason, we would need a theory of *truth*, itself a complicated and controversial subject. We are content to conclude here that justification successfully occurs in ethics and that the right approach to justification is the coherence account...[22]

While Beauchamp and Childress do not straightforwardly deny that truth is possible in the moral realm, their firm expression of doubt about this possibility and their approach to bioethics qualify them, in effect, as sceptics.

The 'coherence theory of justification' advocated by Beauchamp and Childress requires 'starting with considered judgments that are settled moral convictions in a broad expanse of ethics, and then casting the net more broadly in specifying, testing, and revising those convictions'.[23] All convictions are ultimately revisable; they depend upon no fundamental unchangeable principles, nor is one seeking to establish any unchangeable principles.

Although Beauchamp and Childress cite Kant and Mill as possible sources for a philosophical justification of the PRA, they ostensibly ground their commitment to the PRA in common morality: 'Respect for the autonomous choices of other persons runs as deep in common morality as any other principle...'[24] Furthermore, they find the grounding of this (and their other principles) in common morality to be more secure than a grounding in philosophical theory:

> If we could be confident that some abstract moral theory was a better source for codes and policies than the common morality, we could work constructively on practical and policy questions by progressive specification of the norms in that theory. But fully analyzed norms in

ethical theories are invariably more contestable than the norms in the common morality. We cannot reasonably expect that a contested moral theory will be better for practical decision making and policy development than the morality that serves as our common denominator. Far more social consensus exists about principles and rules drawn from the common morality (for example, our four principles) than about theories.[25]

Beauchamp and Childress do not explore the reasons why 'common morality' values autonomy so highly. While in the understanding of Beauchamp and Childress, 'common morality' is not identical with public opinion,[26] it seems fair to note that, as Callahan observes, the reason that the public values the PRA is largely scepticism. Thus, in my view, it is largely scepticism, their own and that which seems to characterize our age, that undergirds the commitment of Beauchamp and Childress to the PRA.

Beauchamp and Childress have claimed that the PRA is a prima facie principle that in some circumstances must yield to other values.[27] Yet, the shift in Beauchamp and Childress's treatment of voluntary euthanasia reveals that in spite of their denials, the PRA has begun to assume the status of an absolute value in their account. The question of voluntary euthanasia is a good test of the moral limits of the PRA, since voluntary euthanasia seems to violate what we identified earlier as generally recognized limits of the PRA: (1) that the patient not be doing clear and serious harm to himself; (2) community values; and (3) the common good.

In the third edition of their *Principles of Biomedical Ethics*, Beauchamp and Childress seemed to agree that voluntary euthanasia did not fall within the limits of what is permitted by the PRA. They certainly saw it as a reversal of the values of the medical community ('do no harm') and of the larger community, and that it threatened the common good as well:

[W]e need to ask which side in the debate [on voluntary euthanasia] has the burden of proof – the proponents or the opponents of a practice of selective killing. One prominent view is that supporters of the current practice of prohibiting killing bear the burden of proof because the prohibition of voluntary euthanasia infringes liberty and autonomy. However, a policy of voluntary euthanasia, based on either a negative right to die (a right to noninterference) or a positive right to die (a right to be killed), would involve such a change in society's vision of the medical profession and in medical attitudes that a shift in the burden of proof to the proponents of change seems to us essential. We have argued that the prohibition of killing expresses important moral principles and attitudes whose loss, or serious alteration, could have major negative consequences. Because the current practice of prohibiting killing while accepting some 'allowed deaths' has served us well, if not perfectly, it should be altered only with the utmost caution. Lines are not easy to draw and maintain, but in general we have been able to respect the line between killing and letting die in medical practice. Before we undertake any major changes, we need more evidence than we now have that the changes are needed in order to avoid important harms or secure important benefits and that the good effects will outweigh the bad effects.[28]

In this passage Beauchamp and Childress place the burden of proof on supporters of voluntary euthanasia, since the widespread acceptance of this practice would require undesirable changes in society's views of the medical profession and would be harmful to society. In elaboration of their opposition to voluntary euthanasia[29] they state that 'a policy that authorizes killing in medicine – even in a few cases – stands to violate the obligation of nonmaleficence by creating a grave risk of harm in many cases'.[30] They speak of a likely erosion of trust between patient and doctor: 'The prohibition of killing is an attempt to promote a solid basis for trust in the role of caring for patients and protecting them from harm. This prohibition is both instrumentally and symbolically important, and its removal could weaken a set of practices and restraints that we cannot easily replace.'[31] They invoke the principle of the slippery slope and summarize their position in this way:

> The main reservation expressed in this argument is the following. If rules permitting mercy killing were once introduced, society might gradually move in the direction of nonvoluntary and perhaps involuntary euthanasia – for example, in the form of killing handicapped newborns to avoid social and familial burdens. There could be a general reduction of respect for human life as a result of the official removal of barriers to killing. Rules against killing in a moral code are not isolated fragments; they are threads in a fabric of rules, drawn in part from nonmaleficence, that support respect for human life. The more threads we remove, the weaker the fabric becomes.[32]

By the fourth edition of their text, published only five years later, Beauchamp and Childress argue that the burden of proof against voluntary euthanasia now lies with opponents. Their shift in view does not seem to

be based on an argument that there has been a change in community values outlined in their third edition. Now the harm that comes to a patient
through denying the patient's autonomous choice outweighs all other
goods:

> If a person desires death rather than life's more typical goods and pro-
> jects, then causing that person's death at his or her autonomous re-
> quest does not either harm or wrong the person (though it might still
> harm others – or society – by setting back their interests, which might
> be a reason against the *practice*). To the contrary, not to help such per-
> sons in their dying will frustrate their plans and cause them a loss,
> thereby harming them. It can also bring them indignity and despair.
> Furthermore, if *passive* allowing to die does not harm or wrong a pa-
> tient because it does not violate the patient's rights, then assisted sui-
> cide and voluntary active euthanasia similarly do not harm or wrong
> the person who dies. Those who believe it is sometimes morally accep-
> table to let people die but not to take active steps to help them die must
> therefore give a different account of the wrongfulness of killing per-
> sons than the one we have suggested. The burden of justification, then,
> seems to rest on those who would refuse assistance to those who wish
> to die, rather than on those who would help them.[33]

Note, again, that the reason offered for shifting the burden of proof to
the opponents of voluntary euthanasia is not the potential harm to the
community, but rather the harm that refusing wishes does to the moral
agent. In another statement justifying placing the burden of proof on opponents of voluntary euthanasia, Childress combines the concern for
the community with a concern for autonomy:

> Other communitarian concerns may also outweigh the principle [of re-
> spect for autonomy] in some contexts. Consider the debate about relax-
> ing the societal and professional rules against physician-assisted
> suicide and active euthanasia. The principle clearly establishes a prima
> facie case for changes in these rules as a way to respect patient autonomy.
> However, the debate rightly focuses on whether over time the commu-
> nity as a whole, including its most vulnerable members, would be best
> served by a change in the rules – for example, would such a change *pro-
> mote or threaten patient autonomy* under conditions of serious illness?[34]

Here the community value that would need to offset the goodness of
honouring a patient's wish to die is no longer the need to protect doctor/
patient trust or the life of the patient, but the value of patient autonomy.

The implications of the growing pre-eminence of the principle of autonomy, and the shifting grounds for its justification, have serious implications for bioethics. Both deontological and utilitarian arguments seem now without place in bioethics. Neither bioethicists, nor doctors, nor patients need to justify their choices in terms of moral principles: the overriding concern is whether or not a patient's autonomy is being respected. This turn from considering the moral acceptability of issues to ensuring the autonomy of choices renders the discipline of bioethics vacuous.

It would require another essay to argue that moral pluralism need not lead to the unfettered primacy of autonomy or to the evacuation of the substance of bioethical discussions. Bioethicists could be helping patients understand the implications for their decisions of their own moral traditions; they could be helping patients without a tradition to identify what principles of moral discernment are acceptable to them; they could be helping patients to learn how to respect their own principles, the values of the communities in which they live, and the values of the doctors who serve them. A respect for patient autonomy would clearly be a driving force behind such activity but would retain bioethics as a discipline that is concerned with evaluating the moral status of medical practices. It is time for bioethics to reconsider the value it places on the PRA.

## NOTES

1 An exhaustive bibliography of articles challenging the primacy of autonomy will not be offered here. But see, for instance, Douglas N. Husak, 'Paternalism and Autonomy', *Philosophy and Public Affairs* 10 (1980) 27–46; Mark S. Komrad, 'A Defence of Medical Paternalism: Maximising Patients' Autonomy', *Journal of Medical Ethics* 9 (1983) 38–44; Harry Yeide, Jr., 'The Many Faces of Autonomy', *The Journal of Clinical Ethics* 3 (1983) 269–74; Onora O'Neill, 'Paternalism and Partial Autonomy', *Journal of Medical Ethics* 10 (1984) 173–8; Daniel Callahan, 'Autonomy: A Moral Good, Not a Moral Obsession', *The Hastings Center Report* (October 1984) 40–2. Especially valuable is Edmund D. Pellegrino, M. D. and David C. Thomasma, Ph.D., *For the Patient's Good: The Restoration of Beneficence in Health Care* (New York: OUP, 1988; hereafter FPG). For a very challenging criticism from the clinical perspective see Stephen Wear, 'The Irreducibly Clinical Character of Bioethics', *The Journal of Medicine and Philosophy* 16 (1991) 53–70.
2 Edmund Pellegrino has done some of the most interesting work on the role of autonomy in medical ethics. He was pioneering in his description of disease as a state of reduced autonomy ('Humanistic Base for Professional Ethics in

Medicine', *New York State Journal of Medicine* 77 (1977) 1456–62). In FPG, he situates autonomy within a system of ethics that holds beneficence to be the pre-eminent value.

3  Bruce L. Miller, 'Autonomy and the Refusal of Lifesaving Treatment', *The Hastings Center Report* (August 1981) 22–9, at p. 24.

4  Miller, pp. 24–5.

5  A good history of the emergence of the value of autonomy is to be found in Ruth R. Faden and Tom L. Beauchamp, *A History and Theory of Informed Consent* (New York: OUP, 1986) and J. Katz, *The Silent World of Doctor and Patient* (New York: The Free Press, 1984). See also FPG.

6  Tom L. Beauchamp and James F. Childress, *Principles of Biomedical Ethics* (New York: OUP, 1994, 4th edition; hereafter PBE(4)), p. 274.

7  See, for instance, PBE(4), pp. 271–84.

8  Stephen Wear, 'The Irreducibly Clinical Character of Bioethics'.

9  See, for instance, Eric J. Cassell, 'The Function of Medicine', *The Hastings Center Report* (December 1977) 16–19 and Komrad, 'A Defence of Medical Paternalism: Maximising Patients' Autonomy.' Even Edmund Pellegrino accepts the restoration of autonomy as the proper goal of medicine (FPG, p. 6).

10  Robert S. Morison, 'The Biological Limits on Autonomy', *The Hastings Center Report* (October 1984) 43–9.

11  Leon R. Kass, *Towards a More Natural Science: Biology and Human Affairs*, (New York: The Free Press, 1985).

12  Miller, 'Autonomy and the Refusal of Lifesaving Treatment'.

13  Morison, 'The Biological Limits on Autonomy', p. 45.

14  See Pellegrino, FPG, p. 12ff.

15  See Morison, 'The Biological Limits on Autonomy.'

16  Beauchamp and Childress, PBE(4), p. 126.

17  Paul Ramsey, *The Patient as Person* (New Haven: Yale University Press, 1970).

18  H. Tristram Engelhardt, Jr., *The Foundations of Bioethics* (New York: OUP, 1986).

19  Daniel Callahan, 'Autonomy: A Moral Good, Not a Moral Obsession', p. 41.

20  As one author observes: '. . . we have come to interpret "autonomy" in a sense very different from Kant's original use of the term. It has come to mean simply the patient's freedom or right to choose the treatment he believes is best for himself. But as Kant knew well, there are many situations in which people can achieve autonomy and moral well-being only by sacrificing other important dimensions of their well-being, including health, happiness, even life itself': John Hardwig, 'What About the Family', *The Hastings Center Report* (March/April 1990), p. 8.

21  Beauchamp and Childress insist that '[m]orality is not a set of personal rules created by individuals isolated from society and moral principles have authority over our lives by virtue of a social and cultural setting that is independent of any single autonomous actor. That we share these principles in no way prevents them from being an individual's own principles': PBE (4), p. 124. Callahan observes, concerning Beauchamp and Childress's insistence that autonomy need not entail subjectivism: '. . . in our culture, the gap between the notion of autonomy they espouse (solidly based, I might add, in the philosophical literature) and that which is more pervasive in daily life is large; as

actually used, I believe autonomy is tantamount to subjectivism': ('Autonomy: A Moral Good, Not a Moral Obsession', p. 41).

22  PBE(4), p. 27. I do not find a similar passage in the 3rd edition of their *Principles of Biomedical Ethics* (New York: OUP, 1989), hereafter PBE(3).

23  PBE(4), p. 24.

24  PBE(4), p. 120.

25  PBE(4), p. 102.

26  Beauchamp and Childress state that 'common-morality ethics relies heavily on ordinary shared moral beliefs for its content, rather than relying on pure reason, natural law, a special moral sense, and the like', but also deny that it is synonymous with 'customary morality': PBE(4), p. 100.

27  PBE(4), p. 126.

28  PBE(3), pp. 146–7.

29  They make it clear that their opposition is not based upon some deontological principle: 'we . . . maintain that rules against killing, including mercy killing, are important in order to protect vital social practices and to maintain attitudes of respect for life, even if it is difficult to determine the degree of risk. This argument is not meant to suggest that mercy killing is always wrong' (PBE(3), pp. 142–3).

30  PBE(3), p. 138.

31  PBE(3), p. 139.

32  PBE(3), p. 141.

33  PBE(4), p. 236.

34  James F. Childress and John C. Fletcher, 'Respect for Autonomy', *The Hastings Center Report* (May/June 1994), p. 35; emphasis added.

# 11 Innocence and Consequentialism: Inconsistency, Equivocation and Contradiction in the Philosophy of Peter Singer

*Jacqueline A. Laing*

'Ubi innocens formidat damnat iudicem' – Sententiae No. 709[1]

The dictum of Publilius Syrus expresses a central idea of traditional morality. When we say an action is gravely wrong because it betrays the innocent, we assume that morality addresses, at least in part, questions of justice, and further that these questions of justice are inextricably linked with the concept of innocence. The concept of innocence however is as broad as it is multifaceted. An agent may be innocent (of an act, say) or she may be *an* innocent (a child, perhaps). Condemning an innocent human being is ordinarily considered an evil and abusing or harming the innocent is regarded as a disgraceful thing. Innocence is often seen as finding its opposite in guilt, so that the term necessarily involves a determination of an agent's liability. But in fact the concept extends far beyond questions of liability and culpability into realms that are not ordinarily discussed by contemporary moral philosophers.

Traditional morality has always regarded the concept of innocence as central to right conduct. Indeed many principles of traditional morality are precisely principles which safeguard the innocent. Accordingly, it is traditionally taught that where innocence is concerned, the desires of third parties must be reasonable. Threats of violence or destruction if an innocent is not executed cannot alter the wrongness of killing that innocent. Again, according to traditional morality, it is not merely those who have the actual and actuated characteristics of the mature human being who are properly accorded respect and protection. Traditional morality has always acknowledged the need to protect the vulnerable, for example the sleeping, the comatose and the very young, as well as healthy, mature human beings.

Contemporary utilitarians deny these principles of traditional morality. Talk of innocence is all but non-existent in their work. One influential commentator writing on the subject of bioethics in this vein is Professor Peter Singer. Among his recommendations for society are infanticide of the severely disabled (or in his own words 'euthanasia for defective infants') and the destructive use of human embryos for scientific experiment. To arrive at these conclusions Singer takes seriously the proposition that the stuff of ethics is precisely the maximization of good consequences. He also promotes the doctrine of personism,[2] the view that a human may have more or less of a claim to life according as he or she displays certain defined characteristics (like rationality and self-consciousness). Furthermore, he insists that the desires of third parties may affect a person's claim to life. But the principles of traditional morality which safeguard the innocent present Singer with cases which threaten the logic of his arguments. Equivocations, inconsistencies and contradictions emerge in his writing. My aim here is to point out in his work certain instances of these kinds of irrationality.

## 1. INNOCENCE THREATENED OR SINGER MISUNDERSTOOD? PROPOSALS FOR 'NON-VOLUNTARY' KILLING

Peter Singer's espousal of the cause of what he calls 'non-voluntary euthanasia' is well known in philosophical circles. He was the longtime director of the Centre for Human Bioethics, a government-funded organization connected to Monash University in Victoria, Australia, and is the author of several influential books and papers on human bioethics.[3] Whereas some consider his notions respectable, disabled people in some European countries have disrupted his lectures. On occasion, his seminars have been cancelled owing to protest. At other times he has been disrupted or shouted down by disabled people in the audience who presumably felt threatened by his proposals. There is considerable public revulsion over his repudiation of long-accepted norms. However, Singer himself believes he has been misunderstood.[4] On the one hand he characterizes the protests by the disabled at his lectures as a peculiarly German thing, even comparing them with the growing tide of German Nazism in the latter days of the Weimar Republic.[5] On the other, he claims that the disabled have nothing to fear from his proposals. He also suggests that those who boycotted his lectures were in fact members of a small group of feminists, anarchists and left-wingers. Whether the reaction he encountered was the result of dictatorial thinking, or the consequence of genuine fear of discrimination, together with a collective conscience sensitized by relatively recent experience of totalitarian attacks on the innocent, is itself an intriguing question. These issues are not, however, the subject of this paper. What is of concern here is first, whether Singer has been misinterpreted and secondly, whether his arguments are self-contradictory, equivocal or inconsistent precisely where rationality is crucial. Singer's recommendations are self-confessedly practical. They counsel the killing of innocent human beings. It is therefore important to be clear about the foundations of his scheme and to understand the principles he applies to arrive at his revolutionary conclusions. The common notion that it is wrong to attack the innocent seems to make no appearance in his work. I want to show to what extent various principles of traditional morality, explicitly rejected by him, must explain certain of his positions. If flaws in his argument are apparent, we may want to think twice before embracing his justification of the killing of the very young, the disabled and the very old. Let us see how this is so.

## 2. THE LANGUAGE OF UTILITY AND RESPECT FOR ONE ANOTHER

### 2.1 'Defective'

It is worthwhile making some preliminary observations about the very language Singer uses. The first edition of *Practical Ethics* is replete with references to 'defective infants' and 'euthanasia for defective infants'.[6] In the second edition Singer becomes coy about using the adjective 'defective' and systematically drops the reference to 'defective infants'. Instead he talks about 'Life and Death Decisions for Disabled Infants'[7] and 'disabled infants' more generally. He is right to make this modification. The very language of the first edition (prior to his experience of the boycott of his lectures and publications by disabled people) indicates how we are asked to regard the vulnerable. Disabled infants are indeed doubly vulnerable where Singer's proposals are concerned: first in virtue of their youth, and second in virtue of their disability. We ordinarily speak of goods, products, artefacts and material objects as defective if they are not fit for their purpose. Singer was initially content to apply this language to infants who are handicapped or disabled. The very use of this terminology is repugnant. Ordinary language, it could be pointed out, does not apply the language of products to humanity. There is, however, a serious objection to this kind of response to Singer. It is not enough to demonstrate that ordinary language does not support the usage Singer would advocate. The fact that certain language is not 'ordinary' is no argument against its rightful use. Discourse that is unacceptable at one time might be acceptable in another. Furthermore, were the language of products liability to become the language of bioethics, for example, it would still be open to doubt that such use was appropriate. If we are examining substantive moral issues, then, we will need to do better than to appeal to ordinary language. In any case, in the interests of a fair and faithful interpretation of Singer's approach, it will be necessary to have recourse to the terms he actually uses – language which we ourselves might balk at using. Moreover, it might well appear repugnant or disgraceful that the powerful in society should turn on the most vulnerable and needy by defining them out of the moral universe or by, quite simply, attacking them. That fact alone is however no argument against such attacks and their justifications. Philosophy is not built on the tastefulness of propositions. What appears repugnant to me might seem virtuous or even saintly to you. Gut reactions need to be articulated in rational terms before they can be understood. We need only note for the time being that Singer, in the first edition and prior to his experience in Europe, applies the word 'defective' not simply to products and objects but to infants with disabilities.

## 2.2 Persons and *persons*\*

Singer also applies the term 'person' in a way that is at odds with ordinary language. For him, a person is anything that answers to the description 'rational and self-conscious'.[8] What of autonomy (the capacity to choose)? On this he is unclear. He does not reject the idea that autonomy is part of the concept of personhood but denies that it has any bearing on the wrongness of killing. 'The classical utilitarian might have to accept that in some cases it would be right to kill a person who does not choose to die on the grounds that the person will otherwise lead a miserable life'.[9] Again 'preference utilitarians . . . must allow that a desire to go on living can be outweighed by other desires'.[10] He also holds that it might be better to encourage the belief that autonomy matters even though it does not: 'This is true [that autonomy does not matter] only on the critical level of moral reasoning . . . utilitarians may encourage people to adopt, in their daily lives, principles that will in almost all cases lead to better consequences . . . The principle of respect for autonomy would be a

prime example of such a principle.'[11] So Singer's favoured morally significant description of a person, the description which is the criterion when
it comes to killing, seems to be a 'rational and self-conscious' being.
Much could be made of the arbitrariness of his chosen definition of a
'person', his lack of interest in qualities like humour, musicality, artistry
and spirituality. But I do not propose to enter into a debate about the
meaning of 'person'. I will assume Singer's definition for the purposes
of argument.

Singer's use of the term is still at best technical, understood largely
only by philosophers familiar with his work. Ordinary language, however, does not place use of the term 'person' under the strictures that
Singer employs. In ordinary parlance it is roughly equivalent to 'human
being'. And in our ordinary dealings with one another we do not detach
moral significance from human beings and attach it solely to 'persons'
(in Singer's sense). Nevertheless, that it is a technical term in contemporary philosophy is not yet any reason to reject it outright. In order to mark
the difference between ordinary language and the use urged by Singer I
shall speak of persons (as we ordinarily understand them) and *persons**
(as Singer understands the term).

## 3. RIGHTS-BASED FEMINIST ARGUMENTS DISTINGUISHED

There is a distinction between *rights-based* arguments for the killing of
human beings on the one hand and *consequentialist* and *personist* arguments on the other. Among the rights-based arguments I count those
which analyse the rightness or otherwise of killing in terms of the *threat*
that the proposed victim poses to another human being. Judith Jarvis
Thomson,[12] for instance, uses a memorable example to argue by analogy
that it is not always obligatory to refrain from killing others. She asks us
to consider someone, A, who wakes up to discover himself in a hospital
connected to an unconscious man, B, in the nearby bed. The man B, it
transpires, is a famous violinist with a kidney disease. His survival depends upon his circulatory system's being plugged into the system of another of the same blood type. A society of music lovers has kidnapped A
because he is the only one with the requisite blood type. If A chooses to
be disconnected from the violinist B, B will certainly die. If B remains
connected for nine months, he will have recovered and will be able to
be unplugged without injury. Thomson argues that A is not obliged to
act as a life support system. Such a choice would be supererogatory, or
beyond the call of duty. She uses the analogy as an argument in favour of

abortion. Her argument is directed to the special position of the woman qua life support system and mother of the gestating infant. The example stresses the threat posed by the unborn to the mother, upon whom the former is altogether dependent. Unlike Singer, Thomson accepts a system of rights and duties which allows for justifications and excuses on the basis of the threat that is posed by the putative victim. It is non-consequentialist in that it allows that an agent may act for less than the best outcome. It operates, for all intents and purposes, on non-personist assumptions in that it does not rest on the idea that a human being becomes more or less significant or valuable according to the degree to which she satisfies the description of a *person**. I do not propose to discuss rights-based defences of abortion here. Suffice it to say that these defences are entirely different from Singer's in that they do not repudiate the claims of innocence. On the contrary, a theory like Thomson's gives content to the notion of innocence by elucidating its meaning. For her, a human being who is a threat to another (in the case of abortion, her mother) and dependent on that other, might cease to be an innocent properly understood. In such a case, according to Thomson, it would be permissible for the threatened party to retaliate against the aggressor. Moral debates would, given these assumptions, centre on what it is to be an innocent and what constitutes a threat or form of aggression.[13]

## 4. THEORIES OF CULPABILITY DISTINGUISHED

Altogether different again from Singer's defence of killing are theories which analyse the culpability of human behaviour. We often say that some killings are not murderous because the person who causes the death in question is not *acting* in the fullest sense of that term. When a person is thought to be acting involuntarily, as an automaton, or in her sleep, or even under the influence of drugs or alcohol, there are often thought to be grounds for exculpation or reduction in blame because the accused person in question is not altogether in control. Debates in these contexts may centre around the question of the degree to which a person is thought to lack control when she deliberately drinks or takes drugs, and then kills someone. What is not doubted in these contexts is that there is a class of cases in which it would clearly be wrong to blame or punish someone for causing death. A person who through no fault of his own falls from a great height onto an innocent below and kills him ought not be blamed or punished for the resulting death of the innocent. Again, one who has an epileptic fit whilst holding a knife slicing his bread cannot be held responsible for the death of the innocent who is stabbed in the neck whilst trying to assist him. Loss of control explains why it is wrong to blame these people who cause death. There are different ways in which a person may lose control. It is at least arguable that provocation and duress constitute forms of loss of control. But in all these kinds of cases the killing is not justified but excused. Here it is not the victim who is the problem (there is no question of the victim 'having a life not worth living') but the kind of action or behaviour that causes the victim's death. Consequentialist and personist arguments are not of this kind. They are not assessments of culpability based on the degree to which the agent of the resulting death may be thought to be 'in control' of his or her actions.

## 5. PERSONISM AND CONSEQUENTIALISM: PRINCIPLES REJECTED BY SINGER

Among the concepts and principles that Singer rejects as having any relevance to the morality of actions are these:

*(i) Potentiality.* According to traditional morality, the potentiality of a thing or species is a matter of moral significance. A noteworthy feature of Singer's ideology is his *actualism.* For him the only thing that matters ethically are occurrent properties. A favourite technique of Singer's is to compare infants with animals like snails, and the intellectually disabled with more intelligent animals. He points out that if it is rationality and self-consciousness that matter to the rightness or wrongness of killing, then there is nothing except unwarranted bias ('speciesism') to justify our favourable treatment of these disabled humans. Accordingly, a day-old infant should, ceteris paribus (e.g. in the absence of parents who desire her existence) be considered as having the same kind of claim to life as a non-human animal with like characteristics. A human embryo, needless to say, would have very few claims indeed. Its claims would be the same as those of any animal with the same occurrent properties. Its parents presumably would be wrong in thinking they had any special obligations (qua parents) in respect of it.

*(ii) Commonness of kind.* Singer uses the term 'speciesist' to condemn as biased one who discriminates in favour of human beings. There are two aspects of his argument. First, he rejects moral generalizations on the basis of class or species. Secondly, he sees no moral relevance in origins. He appears to reject the idea that special obligations flow from parenthood or common ancestry. I do not propose an elaborate discussion of the 'speciesism' point within the confines of this paper. It is an inde-

pendent topic and deserves analysis in its own right, but some important allied points will be made below (5.2).

*(iii) The reasonableness of third-party desire.* Where an innocent victim is concerned, the desires of third parties must be reasonable. The fact that parents desire the abuse of their young infants (too young to know what is happening to them and powerless to object) in no way alters the fact that the desires are unreasonable and the abuse wrong. Only reasonable third-party desires have any moral significance where the innocent are concerned. Singer, by contrast, espouses a preference utilitarian foundation for his ethic. It is the main feature of preference utilitarianism that maximization of preference satisfaction is the standard by which the rightness and wrongness of actions are judged. There is no independent standard which discounts the satisfaction of some preferences as distinct from others. All preferences, then, are thrown into a philosophical melting pot in order to get the 'right' answers about the morality of particular actions.

Having seen then some of the principles that govern traditional morality, we must now consider Singer's own position for it is within his own work that contradictions appear. Furthermore, unless Singer is prepared to adopt some principles of traditional morality, he is forced to accept conclusions which he himself acknowledges to be grossly unpalatable.

## 5.1 Actuality and potentiality

The traditional moralist often points out that it is insufficient simply to protect those who have the actual and actuated characteristics of the adult (e.g. rationality, autonomy, artistry, musicianship, etc.). Even the most talented musician must sleep. The most honoured among us were once dependent foetuses and infants. In the course of a lifetime many of us will suffer serious illness. Accordingly, traditional morality acknowledges that protection is due not merely to adults but to the sleeping, the young and the sick. Moreover, traditional morality usually points out that it is central to a proper understanding of beings and their treatment that we consider not only an individual's occurrent characteristics nor even its occurrent abilities (to the extent that an ability might be thought to be occurrent at all). It is necessary to consider its potentialities, since these potentialities identify treatment that is proper to it qua member of a kind or species. Singer is fond of pointing out similarities between snails and day-old infants.[14] Indeed they might be thought to be alike as far as *occurrent properties* are concerned. But snails and humans thrive in entirely different conditions and immature snails and immature humans survive in distinct circumstances. Their potential characteristics are unalike, though their actual characteristics might be very similar. One distinction between snails and human infants is that the former have the ability to withstand cold, wet conditions in the garden while the latter do not. It is such distinctions, expressed in generalizations about species and the potentialities of various species, that inform the proper analysis of how they should be treated. Another difference between snails and immature humans is that the latter have human parents, a matter which ipso facto raises the question of parental affection and obligation.

The consequentialist denies these claims, arguing that it is actualized characteristics like rationality and consciousness (these are Singer's preferred criteria) that we value. This proposition I call moral actualism, because it values that which is actual and not that which is potential. It is this proposition combined with a stated belief that it is 'speciesist' to discriminate on the basis of our common humanity that does the moral work for Singer. We must then examine whether in fact Singer abides by his moral actualism.

Before proceeding to this question, however, it is important to make plain some simple errors in Singer's work. These errors take the form of misinterpretations of the opposing position. In *Practical Ethics*[15] Singer considers the question of the potential of the human foetus and announces that the opposing camp holds that '[a] human foetus is a potential human being'. This however is not the position of those who deny moral actualism. There can be no doubt that a human foetus is an actual human being – it is tautologically true. Only an immature human being can become a mature human being. Its potentiality lies precisely in capacity to mature as a human being. Accordingly, there is no sense whatsoever to Singer's protracted discussion of whether a potential X has the same rights as an X.[16] First, no one seriously suggests that a human foetus should have the right to vote or equal opportunity in employment – some of the rights of the human adult. A foetus cannot vote and cannot work. He or she can, however, be killed or allowed to live. It is precisely because a foetus can be killed that the question of his or her value arises. Singer's misleading discussion of potentiality begins with the false claim, placed in his opponent's mouth, that a human foetus is only a potential human being (as distinct from an actual human being who is a potential infant, teenager or adult) and then proceeds by making the obvious but irrelevant point that a potential X need not have the rights of an X. Once we accept that a foetus is an actual human being who is a potential infant, child, teenager or adult, we can hardly assert that he or she has no value whatsoever. By the same token, it is that same potentiality which – qua lack of actuality – explains why the foetus does not have the right to vote, to equal opportunity in employment, etc. Although Singer conducts his discussion of potentiality in the context of the term 'human being', it can just as easily be understood in terms of *persons* *. If foetuses are only potential *persons* * it might be argued that they do not have the same rights as *persons* *. With this we may happily agree, since some of the rights *persons* * have are rights to vote, equal opportunity in employment, and so on. *But these are not at issue.* It is the right to live that is in question. Living is precisely what very young unborn humans are doing while they are subject to these moral disputes. They are not potential lives (as, say, human sperm and ova are). They are actual lives, and so to assert that we need not ascribe to foetuses the kinds of rights we do to *persons* * still does not settle the issue.

### (i) The significance of potentiality according to Singer
These misinterpretations of his opposition aside, Singer's argument is susceptible to deeper objections. For whilst denying that there is any moral significance to the potentialities of individual members of particular species, Singer nevertheless later assumes that there is some moral significance to the concept. Singer holds that infants are not *persons* *. He says:

> Self-consciousness, which could provide a basis for holding that it is wrong to kill one being and replace it with another, is not to be found in either the foetus or the newborn infant. Neither the foetus nor the newborn infant is an individual capable of regarding itself as a distinct entity with a life of its own to lead . . .[17]

He also holds that it is a significant factor in the determination of an infant's claim to life that it have a serious defect:

> [I]t is, rather, characteristics like rationality, autonomy and self-consciousness that make the difference [to the wrongness of killing a human being]. Defective infants lack these characteristics. Killing them, therefore, cannot be equated with killing normal human beings, or any other self-conscious beings.[18]

If, however, Singer holds that infants per se are not *persons* * and so lack the features that make them valuable and worthy of protection, then we have to ask what relevance their disability or 'defect' makes to the question of whether they are justifiably killed. If it is permissible to kill any infant on the grounds that it is not sufficiently developed, there is no good reason to think that killing very young (perhaps unborn) human beings

who are also *handicapped* needs *any* justification at all. That Singer de-
votes much energy to proving that 'euthanasia' might be the best thing
for 'defective infants' indicates precisely that he considers the *potentiality*
of non-disabled infants to develop in the *ordinary* way to be of moral significance. That potentiality is recognized as having any moral significance *at all* demonstrates that Singer does not adhere rigorously to his
actualism. Once liberated from the idea that it is only actual characteristics that count towards a creature's worth, we are bound to reject the view
that infants are for the purposes of practical moral decision just like
snails. Accordingly, there is no need to suppose that unborn humans are
for moral purposes just like snails, a favourite personist contention designed to erode respect for the immature.

It may be objected that this argument from potentiality cuts two ways.
Disabled infants have only some of the potentialities that normal infants
do. Why then should we not kill them? It is, however, not the argument
from potentiality of particular members of species that confirms that it
is wrong to kill disabled infants. It is the argument from the potentiality
of species per se that in part demonstrates this. It is also our common
humanity that is the succour of the disabled. I propose no discussion of
Singer's condemnation (as biased) of those who insist that the fact that a
being is human does count in his or her favour. This is an issue in its own
right warranting independent examination. Suffice it to say that, if Singer is wrong to think that generalizations of the moral and practical sort
about species are always discriminatory and he is wrong to think that
our common humanity counts for nought in life-and-death decisions
about disabled infants, then we are bound to respect the immature
amongst us, whether or not they are also disabled.

### (ii)  Potentiality and the sleeping

That Singer both wants and does not want to recognize the significance
of potentialities is evidenced by the concessions he makes to the sleeping.
In 'On Being Silenced in Germany',[19] reprinted as the appendix to the
second edition of *Practical Ethics*, Singer writes that his 'views cannot be
a threat to anyone who is capable of wanting to go on living, or even of understanding that his or her life might be threatened'.[20] Later on in the article, perhaps realizing that this definition would threaten sleeping
adults, since they too while asleep are incapable of wanting to go on living, Singer modifies the claim. The new definition is rather more verbose.
This time it is not those who are 'capable of wanting to go on living' who
are safe, but 'anyone who is, or ever has been, even minimally aware of
the fact that he or she has a possible future life that could be threatened'.[21]

The only reason we respect the sleeping is then, according to Singer, because prior to falling asleep the sleeper lays a claim to her life when later awake. This claim, as it were, protects her, acts as insurance, while she is asleep.

Now the main problem with Singer's 'awareness of a possible future life' criterion of moral significance is that 'awareness' is not the feature that is doing the moral work for him. It is a central part of his position that comatose people who are judged medically to be 'irreversibly comatose' may be killed or allowed to die. The fact that the comatose person was once aware and concerned for her future life prior to falling into a coma matters not at all. It is the objective potential to survive as a *person**\** that matters for Singer – a potential possessed by the sleeping but not by the irreversibly comatose. This is so whether or not he adds that awareness of a possible future life counts in a human being's favour. Once *potentiality* is accepted as the conceptual instrument which demonstrates why, according to Singer, it is permissible to kill the comatose as distinct from the sleeping, he cannot backtrack. He cannot then decide that potentiality has no moral relevance in the determination of a creature's worth.

Once it is allowed that it is potential, and not merely actual, characteristics that count towards a creature's worth, we are free to reject the view that infants and other immature human beings are, for the purposes of practical moral decision, just like snails.

## 5.2 'A morally indefensible preference for members of our own species': 'speciesism' and 'sentientism'

In *Practical Ethics*, Singer says:

> [N]onhuman animals and infants and severely intellectually disabled humans are in the same category... If we make a distinction between animals and these humans, how can we do it, other than on the basis of a morally indefensible preference for members of our own species?[22]

It is this sort of statement that Singer himself admits[23] has generated fear and, he believes, misunderstanding among some disabled people. Although I do not propose an elaborate discussion of the idea that it is discriminatory to make moral generalizations of a practical nature on the basis of species, a few points need to be made. Singer *himself* makes moral generalizations on the basis of kind. Instead of locating interests in species according to their functions, purposes and potentialities, he locates them in *sentience*. If we accept terms like 'speciesism' we ought logically to condemn as discriminatory any theory which denies beings' interests on the basis that they lack sentience. Lest we misinterpret him, this argument is best understood in the context of Singer's own discussion.

In *Practical Ethics*, Singer claims to have discarded the classical utilitarian interest in pleasure and pain. He expressly abandons the ethic of acting to increase pleasure and reduce pain in favour of one which requires that one do 'what, on balance, furthers the *interests* of those affected...'.[24] But his alleged rejection of the pleasure-pain calculus is only apparent because he elsewhere resuscitates the notion of sentience, the capacity to feel pleasure and pain, in order to reject another position. The position in question is the ethical basis of deep ecology.[25] Freya Mathews in *The Ecological Self* locates interests in plants and ecosystems, amongst other things. Singer protests against Mathews's account that we should confine ourselves to arguments based on *sentience*.[26] There are two points to be made here. If it is only arguments based on *sentience* that matter where interests are concerned, he simply has not, in the final analysis, discarded the classical utilitarian pleasure-pain account of morality. Secondly and moreover, the fact that he limits his prescription (to further the interests of all concerned) to sentient creatures suggests that he is himself prepared to make moral generalizations on the basis of kind. For him, in the context of issues surrounding ecology, sentient creatures are the kind whose interests he is prepared to countenance. Now, by applying his own methodology and using his own mode of condemnation, he is 'sentientist'. He discriminates against the interests of plants, for example, whose interests are clearly demonstrated by their potentiality to grow, reproduce and flourish in their own right (in ways that are not merely useful to sentient creatures) by forcing his analysis of interests into the strait-jacket of the requirement of sentience. His location of the boundaries of moral concern in such a way as to exclude the interests of non-sentients is precisely the discrimination on the basis of kind that he abhors. As a matter of contingent fact, I believe that this failure to comprehend arguments for the interests of, for example, trees and plants derives from a faulty metaphysic, one which deprives itself of the conceptual apparatus which would allow an understanding of those interests. The sorts of concepts necessary to the right account are those already mentioned: potentiality, capacity, function and purpose.

Finally, Singer's sentientism in the context of ecophilosophy sits uneasily with his personism in the context of human bioethics. He was, after all, director of the Centre for *Human* Bioethics. If we should confine ourselves to arguments on the basis of sentience in the case of non-human interests, why is the same not true of human interests? Why do we not simply confine ourselves to arguments from sentience in the human context? By demonstrating that he is prepared to distinguish between non-human interests and human interests, Singer acknowledges that there is some morally significant distinction between humans (qua type) and non-humans. When this acknowledgment is taken in conjunction with the failure of his actualism (supra), we begin to understand precisely what is wrong with the idea that it is sheer bias that motivates our distinguishing the severely intellectually disabled from other non-human animals. We are able to see too why disabled people and indeed many able-bodied and intellectually unimpaired people might find the comparison in the context of his argument so threatening.

### 5.3 Desires of third parties and the inviolability of innocence

One feature of traditional morality is that where innocence is concerned, the actual desires of parties other than the innocent are, for all intents and purposes, secondary. Threats of violence and destruction if an innocent is not executed[27] cannot alter the fact that killing the innocent is, according to traditional morality, entirely wrong. Again, the fact that parents desire to abuse their young infants (who for the sake of argument are too young to know what is happening to them and powerless to object) in no way alters the fact that the abuse is wrong. It is a part of the very concept of innocence that it is not susceptible to variation by the desires or consent of others. On the contrary, desires of third parties, to be morally relevant, must conform to the standard of reasonableness. Indeed it is this feature of traditional morality that explains the drama and the tragedy of many real and fictitious predicaments. Innocence cries out for respect. The mob desirous of the punishment of an innocent must cease its bellowing. The parents of the abused child must abandon their desire to dominate and abuse. This position is to be contrasted with one which argues that the desires of third parties are to be taken at face value in determining the morality of actions, even where innocent victims are concerned. According to this argument, the wrongness of punishing or abusing the innocent is not intrinsic nor connected with the innocence of the victim but arises from extrinsic reasons. If it is admitted at all that actions like punishing and abusing the innocent are wrong, it is admitted on extrinsic grounds which balance the desires of the innocent against the desires of the mob or the parents respectively as well as the desires of existing and future communities. So, it is argued, it would be wrong to punish and abuse the innocent because it would threaten people's belief in systems of justice and make them fearful, but *not*, it must be said, because it does violence to an innocent.

Singer equivocates about the role desires play in his scheme. On the one hand he suggests that what parents want for their 'defective' newborn children and the degree to which they are distressed should be taken at face value when considering whether the newborn should be killed. Their actual desires, whether or not they are reasonable, must be taken into account when assessing moral options. On the other hand, he seems to suggest that the kinds of desire that should be taken into account for ethical purposes are not actual desires but reasonable desires. In one passage, quoted earlier, Singer notes that someone's choice, and presumably too his desire to live, may be outweighed where the person will otherwise lead a miserable life:

> The classical utilitarian [whose position Singer accepts in the context] might have to accept that in some cases it would be right to kill a person who does not choose to die on the grounds that the person will otherwise lead a miserable life.[28]

In this sort of case, what a person actually wants is subject to the demands of reasonableness. Where the desires are unreasonable they may be outweighed by other considerations. In the above example, the unreasonable desire to live is subject to the demands of (utilitarian) rationality. Singer nowhere *rejects* this view outlined by him as the classical utilitarian and the preference utilitarian view, though (as we have noted) he equivocates inasmuch as the demands of rationality seem to consist, for a preference utilitarian, *simply* in maximizing the satisfaction of actual preferences. In any case, for present purposes we may assume that the position outlined in the above quotation also reflects his own. It seems, then, that to the extent that he subscribes to the position outlined, Singer wants to maintain the independence of rationality, so that desires may be classified as irrational and consequently irrelevant or outweighed in his moral calculus. At the same time he wants to use the actual desires of third parties (parties other than the innocent) as a factor in his utility equation. But he cannot insist on both a functional definition of desire (that is, desires conceived *as they are*) and an ideal definition of desire (that is, desires conceived *as they ought to be*, rationally considered). The inconsistency becomes obvious when a clear and rational test of a justified killing is sought.

Suppose an infant who has the potential to live happily, say a baby girl living in China, is not wanted by her parents and causes her parents severe distress. Does this severe distress justify her being killed? If the parents' actual desires are taken to be the criteria by which this matter is judged, the baby girl must die. If the parents' reasonable desires are the criteria by which her life is justified, a quite different result might be achieved, depending on the test supplied for the rationality of desires. This same point about Singer is made by Uniacke and McCloskey:

> The 'parental distress' argument is very indeterminate. How much distress and unhappiness to parents and siblings warrants killing an infant who will lead a worthwhile life? Will any noticeable amount suffice if a replacement infant with at least equally good prospects would enhance parental and sibling happiness?[29]

Singer states that '[p]arents may, *with good reason*, regret that a disabled child was ever born. In that event the effect that the death of the child will have on its parents can be a reason for, rather than against killing it'.[30] It is difficult to know what the phrase 'may, with good reason' is meant to signify in this context. Are parents *permitted*, when they have good reason, to regret that their child was ever born and permitted thereby to count these regrets in the calculus against his or her continued existence? Or are all parents of disabled children correct in regretting that their disabled children were ever born and *ipso facto* right in supposing there are good reasons against his or her continued existence? Or are the regrets of the parents of the disabled child *the very reason* why the disabled child in question should be 'helped to die'? If we construe his remarks in the sense that Singer has a kind of reasonableness requirement on the desires and preferences he is prepared to count in his moral calculus, we realize that he is not neutral between the kinds of desire people actually have. On this account he outlaws forms of desire incompatible with his conclusions and he loses the preference utilitarian foundation for his own ethic. The task then for him would be to give an account of the rationality of desires. This enterprise would be an enormous one. Importantly, it would not be preference utilitarian.[31] On a second interpretation of his argument, the parents' desires regarding a particular severely disabled child are not legislated out of the moral calculus but must always be outweighed by other considerations. What the parents want for a particularly severely disabled child cannot ever affect the final decision because their distress and the fact that they do not want the child, or even the fact that they want the child desperately is, in the end, simply not relevant. Other factors determine the issue. On the final interpretation, the parents' actual desires are taken at face value and there is no requirement that parental distress and preference be a reasonable response to an infant's predicament.[32] This interpretation is incompatible with the view that it is wrong to kill the little girl living in China. It is also incompatible with a conclusion which Singer seems to want to allow, that there are some lives that will be just so miserable that the desires of the family (or the self) are not a reasonable ground in the circumstances for allowing the life to continue. As Singer says: 'The classical utilitarian might have to accept that in some cases it would be right to kill a person who does not choose to die on the grounds that the person will otherwise lead a miserable life.'[33] Which the correct interpretation of Singer's text is in the circumstances, remains mere speculation. There are, however, problems inherent in the discussion.

## 5.4 Baby-farming and harvesting unwanted non-*persons**

If it does not matter what species a creature belongs to and if we ought to be doing whatever is necessary to bring about the best outcome (furthering the interests of everyone involved), why should we not grow human beings (perhaps without brains, or at least intentionally damaged ones) for use as spare parts in transplant surgery? Singer himself tackles this thorny question and urges caution over the growing of human embryos with deliberately damaged brains for organ transplant and other uses. Growing brain-damaged children for use as spare parts cannot contravene any prohibition on killing *persons** (where *persons** are, recall, self-conscious beings) because by definition 'embryos [grown] until they resemble normal babies but with brains deliberately damaged so that they are in a permanent coma'[34] are non-*persons**. These human beings have had their capacities for sentience, self-consciousness and rationality removed. Nor can growing brain-damaged children for use as spare parts contravene any consequentialist principle of maximizing good states of affairs (or furthering the interests of everyone involved) since these transplant organs and limbs would certainly further the interests of those patients who needed them and their friends and families. Whatever it is that is wrong with growing them for the greater good must be a powerful moral principle – since it is doing a great deal of work – and it must be independent of the prohibition on killing *persons**. What then could this principle be? Singer replies that to grow human beings for use as spare parts in transplant surgery would do violence to our basic attitude of care and protection for infant human beings. Furthermore, he even seems to suggest that there is, after all, a morally significant distinction between setting up conflicts deliberately and facing situations when they are forced upon one. This is how he puts it:

To face these situations when they are forced upon us is one thing; to set up such conflicts deliberately is another. For the sake of the welfare of all our children, the basic attitude of care and protection of infants is one we must not imperil.[35]

At this claim we should pause.

Singer uses two principles to explain his intuition that this sort of activity against non-*persons*\* is wrong. Both may be used to demonstrate inconsistencies in his own account. Perhaps the clearer of the two principles is that we must not imperil 'the basic attitude of care and protection of infants'. We must consider 'the welfare of all our children'. The second principle seems to insist that there is a morally significant distinction between facing situations when they are forced upon us and setting up conflicts deliberately.

### (i) The attitude of care and protection.

Consider first the content of the first of the two points thus stated: baby-farming does violence to our basic attitude of care and protection and this feature demonstrates that such activity is unacceptable. If our basic attitude of care and protection matters morally even where non-*persons*\* are concerned, then they matter where the lives of the embryonic, the unborn, the disabled, the suffering, comatose and elderly are at issue. It is, after all, precisely this kind of argument that is often relied on to demonstrate the wrongness of killing vulnerable people. Killing the terminally ill or comatose, it may be argued, does violence to our attitude of care and protection for the terminally ill and comatose. It is precisely the terminally ill and comatose who need simple medical care as well as ordinary respect. Killing them, it might be argued, is incompatible with the care and respect that is owed to them. Likewise, killing the unborn does violence to our attitudes of care and respect for immature humanity. Unborn humans very often need medical and other care as well as simple respect. Killing them is at odds with the care that is due to them.

The inconsistency in Singer's work may be elucidated by posing a dilemma. On either horn of the dilemma Singer must contradict an important aspect of his theory. If our basic attitude of care and protection matters morally then the principle which asserts that it does may be used to safeguard other non-*persons*\* like the embryonic, the unborn, the disabled, comatose and elderly. On this horn of the dilemma, Singer must deny his conclusions about these groups. Conversely, if Singer insists that our attitudes of care and respect for one another are not undermined by, for example, creating human embryos for scientific experiment, we may likewise insist that our attitudes of care and respect for infants are not affected by creating non-*persons*\* for use in transplant surgery. On this analysis Singer must deny his conclusions about baby-farming. He is simply wrong to think that it is morally problematic.

If Singer is wrong to urge caution in respect of baby-farming and if he is wrong to think that the prospect of baby-farming is 'repellent', a great many other kinds of 'repellent' cases are permissible according to his own theory. So long as no members of the victim's family have any objection or, better still where the victim is an orphan, comatose patients may be harvested for their organs and tissue, the terminally ill may be used for scientific experiment and foetal tissue may be used for collagen creams. If Singer is forced onto this horn of the dilemma he must acknowledge that his theory lacks the conceptual apparatus which would allow him to urge caution in respect of any of these cases.

If we wanted to help Singer onto this horn of the dilemma so that he was committed to some really revolting kinds of activity, we could protest that loss of the attitude of care and protection for these groups is only contingently related to particular acts of harvesting, experimentation or exploitation. We might use an example. Imagine a society in which the baby-farming activity is conducted by only a few concerned individuals in private. This small team understands practical morality just as it should be understood according to the combined precepts of personism and consequentialism. The group does not practise baby-farming on brain-damaged babies whose parents object, and there are no abuses of theory. Baby-farming is conducted precisely as it should be, that is to say only in cases where there are no additional moral reasons which speak in favour of the disabled baby's being treated with the sort of care due to ordinary babies. Moreover, the team understands rightly that many other individuals are being helped by their activities. In such cases, we might argue, Singer can have no grounds to object to the activity of baby-farming. There are simply no important attitudes of care and protection at stake so he is wrong to suppose that this is a moral reason against it. His intuition that this sort of activity is unacceptable is entirely mistaken. What this example would show is that given that there is no good reason to suppose that basic attitudes of care and concern for *persons*\* would necessarily be threatened by baby-farming, we would have no reason to balk at the prospect of it. Once committed to this kind of case, Singer would have to admit that his theory could not supply any reason against harvesting the comatose and the terminally ill, taking the gold from their teeth for charitable causes and so on.

Singer might, however, want to hold on to his intuition that baby-farming is unacceptable on another basis. He might insist that there is an intrinsic and logical connection between baby-farming and bad attitudes towards infants generally. But this admission would concede too much. It would then be open to those who disagree with his conclusions likewise to insist that there is an intrinsic and logical connection between particular killings of the terminally ill or comatose and bad attitudes towards the terminally ill and comatose generally. In short, if Singer is entitled to help himself to the idea that we should not do violence to attitudes of care and respect for the vulnerable, then so too are those who disagree with his conclusions. If our basic attitudes of care and protection matter then they matter in respect of other vulnerable groups.

Singer is faced with a dilemma. He must either drop his prohibition on baby-farming and admit that he lacks the conceptual apparatus that would allow him to show that the 'repellent' cases mentioned above are morally problematic. Alternatively, he must admit that a great many other activities, like killing the terminally ill, the comatose and the very young are wrong because they imperil important moral attitudes.

### (ii) 'Setting up conflicts deliberately'.

Consider Singer's alternative explanation of his prohibition on growing brain-damaged embryos for use as spare parts. There is, he admits, a distinction between setting up conflicts deliberately and facing them when they are forced upon one. It should be remembered that this explanation is morally significant in the context of his theory because, like the principle considered above (that we should not imperil attitudes of care and protection), it renders impermissible the kind of exploitation and killing which, he argues, is impermissible, but not prohibited by reason of consequentialism or personism. This explanation, unlike the one just considered, however, is somewhat unclear. What does Singer mean by 'forced'? Does he mean that baby-farming would be acceptable if it were 'forced' on a person by reason of duress? Is he claiming that if someone were to use force to get the baby-farming business going, it would be justified and acceptable? Or is the point about one-off cases generally? Is he claiming that if force were applied to achieve the use of only one embryo grown to the appropriate size for his or her organs, this would be acceptable because it was a one-off case? Or is the point about deliberation and intention? Is Singer saying that growing even one baby for use of its organs is morally objectionable because it exploits an infant that has been deliberately and intentionally disabled for the use of its organs? There are many possible interpretations of Singer's words of caution on baby-farming. Since he does not elaborate on the issue we should not put words in his mouth.

We may make one point about some arguments against, for example, arranging health care in such a way as to make killings or aiding and abetting suicide a legal option for medical staff caring for the terminally ill. In the killing of the terminally ill case, for example, a conflict is deliberately and systematically set up. Arranging health care so that it supplies not merely pain relief but execution services for the elderly and terminally ill itself sets up a conflict about the function of health care. Health professionals are no longer concerned with health care but with executions. Nurses and carers become bearers of death warrants and participants in the activity of killing. This kind of 'health care' arrangement, moreover, forces a number of conflicts on the aged and terminally ill.[36] These patients can no longer rely on the idea that the health professionals surrounding them have their care at heart. They are faced with the conflict of killing themselves when they are most vulnerable.[37] Using Singer's own prohibition on setting up conflicts deliberately, doctor-assisted death legislation would be rightly resisted.

I have suggested that Singer is faced with a dilemma. He must either abandon his prohibition on baby-farming and admit that his account can supply no reason for regarding the 'repellent' cases mentioned above as morally problematic. We should not, then, balk at any of these cases. Alternatively, he must admit that a great many other activities, like killing the terminally ill, the comatose and the very young are wrong because they imperil important moral attitudes or set up conflicts deliberately. On one interpretation of his prohibition on setting up conflicts deliberately, systems of medical killing or medically assisted suicide, to use one example appropriate to our times, are properly treated with caution. We can only speculate which path Singer would care to take in this regard. Both routes, however, are equally destructive of certain of his theses.

## 5.5 Problems of Interpretation

Before concluding this section I need to make two important points about the difficulty of interpreting Singer. He often says that 'standard moral principles, for example, telling the truth, keeping promises... and so on'[38] may be departed from when 'it is absolutely plain that departing from the principles will produce a much better result than we will obtain by sticking to them, and then we may be justified in making the departure'.[39] The problem with this sort of declaration is that it must make us wonder whether Singer sometimes deliberately misstates his own position in order to bring about what he sees as (and what might or might not in fact turn out to be) a much better result. Does he say things for their shock value or in order to bring about change? How are we to construe the motivation for his comments on baby-farming and killing those who do not want to die? What might the 'much better result' be when he makes this or that shocking statement? The problem with these sorts of questions is that they are well beyond the ken of philosophy. The discipline of philosophy cannot supply answers to questions about a theorist's motivation. It is not merely improper but also fallacious to inquire into the psychology and motivation of a theory's proponent in this or that context. We must assume for the purposes of argument that a proponent of a given thesis is bona fide and is not using lies or deception to bring about a much better result.

There is a second problem of interpretation that deserves fuller discussion elsewhere. When he gives reasons against killing one person (or *person\**) for use as spare parts for two, or against baby-farming and like activities,[40] is Singer reasoning critically or intuitively? Following R. M. Hare, Singer maintains a distinction between critical and intuitive moral reasoning. This ethical distinction between *intuitive* reasoning (reasoning which, he says, does not admit of 'lengthy'[41] utilitarian calculation – he believes this is something like traditional morality for everyday use) and *critical* reasoning (which is the sort of protracted reasoning which would allow us secretly to kill one innocent victim for a greater good, say, body parts for two others) suffers from a number of problems. One is that the criteria supplied for the application of the distinction (speed and ease of reasoning[42] for the purposes of decision making) do not pick out the kinds of cases that need to be explained. When we theorize about certain cases, the length of time we have to consider the problem is not ordinarily an issue. Further, if the critical level of moral reasoning is not to be rendered entirely void of practical significance for everyday life, Singer will need to dissociate critical reasoning, at least in part, from the notion that it is utterly distinct from the reasoning of real life. Again he argues: 'It may be that in the long run, we will achieve better results – greater overall happiness – if we urge people not to judge each individual action by the standard of utility, but instead to think along the lines of some broad principles'[43] like those of traditional morality. But it is not clear that this does not simply create two utilitarian principles each of which contradict each other. The first could be stated thus: in order to get better results in the long run in this individual case (of killing one for spare parts for two), we should observe the principles of traditional morality. The second might say this: in order to get better results in the long run, it is better in this individual case (of killing one as spare parts for two) to observe the principles of utility. To point out that both principles are stated in terms of maximization does nothing to remove the contradiction. In order to be a truly practical and rational ethic there must be some solution to this problem.

## 6. SOME RED HERRINGS IN SINGER

*(i) Sanctity of life doctrine.* One of Singer's methods of encouraging us to accept his conclusions is the setting up of a false dichotomy between religious ('sanctity-of-life-based') views and 'rational' views. It is argued as follows:

(1) Either sanctity-of-life-based views are true or Singer's personism-cum-consequentialism is true
(2) Sanctity-of-life-based views are irrational and false, therefore
(3) Singer's view is true.

The first premiss is false. One need not enter into any debate about the existence of God to understand the contradictions inherent in personist and consequentialist theories like Singer's. It is a caricature of the debate to envisage 'Holy Rollers' in one corner and the 'Hard-minded Rationalists' in the other. Rationality is by no means incompatible with non-discriminatory respect for human life. It is a part of the logic of some forms of humanism that every human life be given a chance without the threat of attack or destruction.[44]

When it is understood that Singer himself recognizes the moral significance of potentiality whilst steadfastly denying that it has any significance in the context of embryonic and other immature human life, we begin to wonder just how rational and hard-minded his position is. Again, Singer's intuition that it is wrong to produce brainless children for spare parts in transplant surgery is an intuition that is entirely arbitrary in the context of his theory. His personism does not dictate it. Nor does his maximization principle (that we should act in order to further the interests of *persons** affected) prohibit it. When we understand that certain examples are at odds with his theory and rationalizable only on grounds which contradict other of his proposals, we have good reason to want to part company with Singer's brand of thought.

*(ii) The violation of a right to freedom of speech.* Singer insists that his freedom to speak has been violated by those who either disrupted his seminars or prevented him from being given the opportunity to speak.[45] I do not propose to expatiate upon the subject of free speech.[46] What is of interest in this context is that Singer himself is no champion of the right to free speech. Modern consequentialists believe that it is often better to

propagate traditional morality, or at least principles that are non-consequentialist. It may, for example, be 'better, all things considered' for doctrines which cause offence to be kept quiet even if they are true. This
applies as much to consequentialist doctrine as it does to any other. It is,
moreover, straight consequentialist teaching. It is peculiar, therefore, to
demand rights that one does not believe one has. Given the content of
his theory, Singer must do something other than cry out for his right
to speak.

*(iii) 'Human beings treated with less consideration'*. In response to a protester, Singer once claimed that his views do not reduce the consideration
owed to human beings but raise that due to animals.[47] This thought
would be an excellent one if it represented Singer's real position. But it
does not. There are indeed defences of the rights of animals which are
not founded on personist assumptions.[48] The proposal that separates
Singer from these other accounts is precisely that Singer is *not* merely extending our ordinary concern for humans to animals. He is asking us to
disregard our common humanity in any decision making about the vulnerable, the very young and the disabled. It is just this proposal that
makes Singer's work the 'highly provocative' writing it is claimed to be
for the purposes of publication and sale. And it is this proposal presumably that persuades the disabled to secure their wheelchairs to the doors
of newspaper editorial offices for so much as reporting Singer's views on
euthanasia.

## 6. CONCLUSION

The claims of innocence demand respect. A moral theory which cannot
account for them is to that extent inadequate. It is because of his insistence that 'morality' is synonymous with 'the maximization of good
states of affairs' that Singer is forced to equivocate or contradict himself
over the harvesting of non-*persons*\* for the general good. What is wrong
with these kinds of activity and other abuses of the vulnerable is neither
that the activity is not secret enough, nor that there may in fact be some
people somewhere who want the victim to survive. The wrong is intrinsic:
it is an offence against an innocent. The claims of innocence cut across
utility calculations.

There is always something paradoxical about discussing in detail a
work which one considers ethically dangerous. By citing a philosopher's
work we bolster his presence in various citations indexes. Such is the nature of the modern academy that frequency of citation sometimes even

takes the place of reasons for citation in assessing the worth of a particular brand of thought. Singer notes with some satisfaction that his opponents foster a climate of debate[49] about the topic of killing by criticising his views. But this fact should not cause amusement. It is to be expected that his much-publicized opinions on who may be killed with impunity will attract opposition. While there are good reasons simply to ignore a dangerously false work that is neither public nor gaining respectability, this is not so with one that is government-funded and in the service of a burgeoning industry in human fertility and genetic engineering. It may be necessary in some circumstances to fan the flames of a debate that we should not ordinarily even countenance. Bad theory assisted by public funds and the interests of a growing industry requires more than a refusal to countenance the legitimacy of the very debate.

Singer's theory, however, is not altogether spurious. It does appear to matter to him that his theory is not false. He has no truck with relativism. He points out rightly that if we are going to respect immature human life like human embryos we ought in truth to treat with care our reproductive capacity, since there is the chance that a human being will be created with all the parental obligations that flow from that fact. This is particularly obvious now. Where human ovum and sperm have been abandoned to scientific research, there is the chance that a couple will become parents without even knowing it. Possible parental obligations do flow from our reproductive capacities and Singer is right to point out the continuum. (He is wrong however to think that conception, the point at which parenthood is determined, is a morally irrelevant event. He is wrong to think that a reproductive technologist's promise that he or she will kill the developing human life after experimenting with it frees parents and societies of their obligations to it.) He is even correct to point out that, in some cases, there is no moral distinction between the foetus and the infant. (I limit the generalization, though Singer himself does not, because in some cases the very fact of giving birth can threaten the mother. In such a case there is an obvious moral distinction between the born and the unborn.)

Singer, moreover, writes simply and eloquently about some issues. He points out how barbarously battery farm animals, and animals used for research, are treated. At the same time, however, he articulates the underlying rationalizations of the human fertility industry. The danger of Singer's writing is that his compelling defence of the interests and rights of animals is mixed up with the human fertility business and a eugenic agenda. I have suggested that in order to arrive at his false conclusions Singer must equivocate or contradict his own theory. I have also suggested that those who boycott his lectures are not mistaken about his programme. His plans for the eradication of suffering through disability involve the eradication, the systematic killing, of those with disabilities while they are immature, and even in certain cases when they are adult. To support this conclusion and others which counsel the killing of the innocent, Singer uses arguments which he himself does not respect.

## NOTES

1 'When innocence is frightened, the judge is condemned.'
2 Jenny Teichman coined the term in 1992. See J. Teichman, 'Humanism and Personism: The False Philosophy of Peter Singer', *Quadrant*, December 1992, pp. 26–9. See also her 'Freedom of Speech and the Public Platform', *Journal of Applied Philosophy* 11 (1994) 99–105.
3 Within the confines of this paper I discuss in particular two editions of the same book: P. Singer, *Practical Ethics* (Cambridge: CUP, 1979), hereafter referred to as PE(1), and *Practical Ethics* (Cambridge: CUP, 1993), hereafter referred to as PE(2).
4 'On Being Silenced in Germany', *New York Review of Books*, 15 August 1991, pp. 36–42; 'A German Attack on Applied Ethics: a Statement by Peter Singer', *Journal of Applied Philosophy* 9 (1992) 85–91.
5 PE(2), p. 357. Of the boycott by disabled people of his lecture at the University of Zürich in May 1991, he says, 'I had an overwhelming feeling that this was what it must have been like to attempt to reason against the rising tide of Nazism in the declining days of the Weimar Republic.'
6 PE(1), pp. 131, 134, 136, 156.
7 PE(2), p. 181.
8 PE(2), p. 131.
9 PE(2), p. 100.
10 PE(2), p. 99.
11 PE(2), p. 100.
12 Judith Jarvis Thomson, 'A Defense of Abortion', *Philosophy and Public Affairs* 1 (1971) 47–66. For a feminist rejection of reproductive technologies, see Lynda Birke, Susan Himmelweit and Gail Vines, *Tomorrow's Child: Reproductive Technologies in the '90s* (London: Virago, 1990): '[W]hat we are witnessing is a takeover by scientists of women's role in reproduction... moving towards a dehumanised (and defeminised) technological future. The position is one of total resistance to scientific and male control of reproductive processes, by a complete rejection of the new technologies' (p. 19). See also Mara Mies, 'Do We Need All This? A Call Against Genetic Engineering and Reproductive Technology', in Patricia Spallone and Deborah Steinberg (eds.), *Made to Order: The Myth of Reproductive and Genetic Progress* (New York: OUP, 1987). These approaches are quite unlike some of those of the early 1970s which saw the female biological nature, connected as it is to pregnancy and childbear-

ing, as essentially substandard and, as such, perfected and liberated by the new reproductive technologies.

13  For a non-consequentialist rejection of Thomson's argument in favour of abortion see J. M. Finnis, 'The Rights and Wrongs of Abortion: A Reply to Judith Jarvis Thomson', *Philosophy And Public Affairs* 2 (1972) 117–45.

14  PE(2), p. 90: 'Killing a snail or a day-old infant does not thwart any desires of this kind [for the future], because snails and newborn infants are incapable of having such desires.'

15  PE(2), p. 152.

16  PE(2), p. 153.

17  PE(2), p. 188.

18  PE(1), p. 131. See also PE(2), p. 182 (with 'defective' removed).

19  *New York Review of Books*, 15 August 1991, pp. 36–42; PE(2), pp. 337–59.

20  PE(2), p. 345.

21  PE(2), pp. 357–8.

22  PE(2), p. 60.

23  'One protester quoted from a passage in which I compare the capacities of intellectually disabled humans and nonhuman animals': PE(2), p. 347.

24  PE(2), p. 14; emphasis added.

25  See Freya Mathews, *The Ecological Self* (London: Routledge, 1991).

26  PE(2), p. 284.

27  This example was devised by H. J. McCloskey. See 'A Non-Utilitarian Approach to Punishment', Inquiry 8 (1965) 249–63, and *Meta-ethics and Normative Ethics* (The Hague: Martinus Nijhoff, 1969).

28  PE(2), p. 100.

29  Suzanne Uniacke and H. J. McCloskey, 'Peter Singer and Non-Voluntary "Euthanasia": Tripping down the Slippery Slope', *Journal of Applied Philosophy* 9 (1992) 203–19, at p. 213. Uniacke and McCloskey investigate the question of how serious a defect needs to be for Singer before a baby is justifiably killed. They point out that the attitudes of parents are only contingently related to the degree of defect in an infant or adult. Some defects like disfigurements can cause more distress than apparently more serious disabilities. An important feature of the paper is that it demonstrates that killing of the sort favoured by Singer is not euthanasia (i.e. gentle death) since it is motivated by concern for the welfare of *others* or an increase in the *total happiness*.

30  PE(2), p. 183. For 'disabled' read 'defective' in PE(1), p. 132; emphasis added.

31  Bernard Williams addresses this general point in J. J. C. Smart and Bernard Williams, *Utilitarianism: For and Against* (Cambridge: CUP, 1973), p. 131: '[M]odern utilitarianism is supposed to be a system neutral between the preferences that people actually have, and here are some preferences which some people actually have. To legislate them out is not to pursue people's happiness, but to remodel the world towards forms of "happiness" more amenable to utilitarian ways of thought. But if they are not to be legislated out, then utilitarianism has got to co-exist with them, and it is not clear how it does that.'

32  This is the interpretation Uniacke and McCloskey favour: 'Given Singer's position that "euthanasia" need not be "in the infant's interests" and that infants are replaceable, his justification of pseudo-euthanasia infanticide seems not to require that parental and sibling distress be a reasonable response to an infant's defect': 'Peter Singer and Non-Voluntary "Euthanasia"', at p. 213.

33 PE(2), p. 100.
34 P. Singer and D. Wells, *The Reproduction Revolution* (Oxford: OUP, 1984), p. 148.
35 *The Reproduction Revolution*, p. 149.
36 Rita Marker's book *Deadly Compassion: The Death of Ann Humphry and the Case Against Euthanasia* (London: HarperCollins, 1994) is a readable anti-dote to the writings of Derek Humphry. The latter is cited several times with approval by Singer: PE(2), pp. 176, 369, 370. The details of Ann Humphry's last months after being diagnosed with cancer and her callous treatment by her husband and fellow euthanasia campaigner Derek Humphry, and by the Hemlock Society, are chillingly described by Marker. In a law suit against De-rek, Ann claimed among other things that he intended to 'impede and op-press [her] recovery from cancer itself' and to 'induce [her] despair and [her] suicide': *Humphry* v *Humphry, National Hemlock Society, Mero, Hemlock of Washington State*, Circuit Court, Lane County, Oregon, Oct 19, 1990.
37 I have suggested elsewhere that the very business of arranging death services for the vulnerable may well ensure that one of the consequentialist criteria of a justified killing is present: namely, that the victim in question is made to feel a burden and so wants to die. My point is that the very holding of these fatal views may affect in advance the outcome. It is important to the logic of a theo-ry that it be independent of the consequence it seeks to describe and/or justi-fy: 'Assisting Suicide', *Journal of Criminal Law* 54 (1990) 106–16.
38 PE(2), p. 93.
39 PE(2), p. 94.
40 Let us assume, of course, that the complete secrecy condition holds in these cases.
41 PE(2), pp. 92–4.
42 'In real life we usually cannot foresee all the complexities of our choices. It is simply not practical to try to calculate the consequences, in advance, of every choice we make... in many cases we would be calculating in less than ideal circumstances. We could be hurried, or flustered. We might be feeling angry, or hurt, or competitive... Or we might just not be very good at thinking about such complicated issues...': PE(2), pp. 92–3.
43 PE(2), p. 92.
44 See J. Teichman, 'Humanism and Personism' (n.2). For an eloquent popular defence of the unborn disabled from an atheist, see Dominic Lawson, 'A Spe-cial Kind of Baby', *Sunday Telegraph*, 18 June 1995. Speaking of the free NHS tests for abnormalities which are available, with the offer of abortion on discovering any, he writes: 'In the People's Republic of China, the authorities wait until such children are born naturally, before starving them to death. In Hitler's Germany, even before the final solution to the Jewish problem, the Nazis were exterminating wholesale the mentally retarded. In this country the weeding-out process is done before birth, and only with the parents' con-sent. I do not think, however, that this constitutes a triumph for democracy.'
45 He chastises 'Germans and Austrians, both in academic life and in the press' for showing themselves 'sadly lacking in the commitment' to the right to free-dom of speech. He cites with approval Voltaire's dictum: 'I disapprove of what you say, but I will defend to the death your *right* to say it' (emphasis added). He notes that no one has as yet been asked to risk death in order to defend his

*right* to discuss euthanasia in Germany (PE(2), p. 359). He is nonetheless 'not convinced that the notion of a moral right is a helpful or meaningful one' (p. 96), except as shorthand for considerations the utilitarian thinks fundamental, such as preferences, interests and feelings of pleasure and pain. But the notion of a right had better be a helpful and a meaningful one *in itself* (independently of these considerations) if his right to discuss euthanasia in Germany is not to fall entirely prey to the whims of public opinion or public preference. Even if public opinion were entirely against him, his right, assuming he had one, would remain. These utilitarian considerations have very little to do with his right to speak, though they may, of course, affect his actually speaking.

46 See further J. Teichman, 'Humanism and Personism' and 'Freedom of Speech and the Public Platform' (n.2).

47 PE(2), p. 347.

48 See Stephen Clark, *The Moral Status of Animals* (Oxford: Clarendon Press, 1977); Andrew Linzey, *Christianity and the Rights of Animals* (London: SPCK, 1987); Mary Midgley, *Animals and Why They Matter* (Harmondsworth: Penguin, 1983); Tom Regan, *The Case for Animal Rights* (London: Routledge, 1984).

49 PE(2), p. 350.

# 12 Voluntary Euthanasia and Justice

*David S. Oderberg*

1. The question I shall be looking at is a narrowly-defined one. I shall not be looking at euthanasia in general, nor even at voluntary euthanasia in general. I shall only look at one question: Does a person who kills another, at the latter's request, commit an injustice against that person?

In fact, since it is euthanasia I am concerned with, I shall only look at requested killing in that context, which is essentially medical (where this is defined broadly to cover cases where no professional medical practitioners are present and the setting is non-institutional – for example, an accident), and in order to relieve suffering or otherwise spare the patient some burden. However, if it can be established that it is an injustice to kill with consent even in these circumstances, where there is a motive most of us would call noble, then I take it that the broader proposition that any requested killing is an injustice is also established.

Note also that if it can be shown that voluntary euthanasia involves an injustice, it is thereby shown to be morally unlawful, but this may not be the entire reason why it is unlawful. There are all sorts of other considerations which might be used to show it to be wrong, but these are not going to be looked at. Nevertheless, if it involves an injustice it is wrong, and indeed wrong for the most important reason, since justice comes before all other considerations (such as prudence and charity; it might be imprudent if there is a good chance of recovery, or uncharitable if the killer[1] acts secretly out of malice).

2. First, it is necessary to provide some definitions in order to prepare the conceptual background. 'Voluntary euthanasia' has virtually been defined already, since I mentioned a request for killing in circumstances, essentially medical, where the stated purpose is to relieve the patient of suffering or spare them some burden. But something more needs to be said about the voluntariness requirement.

(i) Voluntariness requires actual consent by the patient, though it need not be expressed at the time of killing. It might be expressed in an 'advance directive', which has been much talked about of late, and where nothing has been said by the patient since then to countermand the directive. Still, advance directive cases are enormously complicated for well-known reasons: for example, the directive does not contemplate or advert to the precise circumstances currently obtaining, or is vague, or superseded by a medical advance about which the patient had no knowledge at the time of framing the directive. Hence, for present purposes, I shall assimilate to cases of consent a directive which suffers from none of these difficulties, but is quite explicit in requesting death and applies directly to the circumstances currently obtaining.

(ii) The consent must be completely free. So, the consent is of no effect if there is error, fraud, fear or violence, whether or not the killer is responsible for that lack of freedom. So for instance, if a misdiagnosis by one doctor leads to the request for death, a carrying out of the request by another doctor would still be involuntary euthanasia. The reason consent must be completely free for the act to be characterized as voluntary is that it has the *form* of an abandonment of a right, namely the right to life, and one cannot partially abandon something: either one abandons something or one does not. (The 'totally' in 'I have totally abandoned my plans to go to France this Christmas' is redundant, and in 'I have not totally. . .' is paradoxical.) It will be argued that abandonment of this right is morally impossible, hence that, in a sense, there *is* no voluntary euthanasia, since nothing capable of being ceded *is* ceded; so the effect of the requirement of complete freedom is that the *intention* to alienate one's right to life must be under conditions of complete freedom, even though it is not morally lawful to give away what one intends. There is no great difficulty here; a parallel, though the reason for inalienability is different (maybe not *wholly* different), is the intention to give away someone else's property: it cannot be done, since one cannot give what one does not have, but the intention (arising perhaps from a mistaken belief that the property is one's own), qua intention to alienate, can be formed under conditions of complete freedom. A question arises about necessity here, since necessity can vitiate consent to the yielding of a right: for example, a workman who accepts starvation wages in order to feed his family cannot be said truly to surrender his right to a just wage. It may be that virtually all the conditions under which euthanasia is requested are like this – for example, extreme distress, anguish, emotional pressure of a subtle or not-so-subtle kind: but this will be left to one side, as it is not germane to the primary issue.

3. Now something needs to be said about justice, since the claim is that voluntary euthanasia involves an injustice, more specifically an injustice by the killer against the person requesting death. I take it for granted that it involves no injustice by the person who requests death against himself, since one cannot be unjust to oneself. Now it should be noted, though

this is probably already apparent, that what is being considered is com-mutative, not distributive justice.

Justice being a virtue, commutative justice can be defined as the virtue inclining an individual to accord other individuals their rights. It con-cerns relations between individuals rather than oneself alone, which is the province of charity. In other words, charity can be owed to oneself or another, but even in the latter case one considers the person as at one with oneself, and gives them what one wants for oneself, i.e. one acts out of empathy and compassion; whereas with justice, one considers the other person as distinct from oneself and gives them what belongs to them, whether or not one feels empathy or compassion.

Hence, without wanting to go deeply into the matter, one cannot be just or unjust to oneself, though one can of course love oneself or feel sor-ry for oneself, and the like. To be unjust to oneself one would have, simul-taneously, to consider oneself as oneself and consider oneself as distinct from oneself, which is impossible. So suicide is not an injustice against oneself, though it may be an injustice against one's family, or society, or country, or, if one believes in God, against God.

**4.** So the claim is that voluntary euthanasia is an injustice by the killer against the killed. And the reason for this is that the right to life is inalien-able. Actually, there is an argumentative gap here: a right may be inalien-able without being absolute, i.e. it may be that a right cannot be waived, and yet to infringe it is not necessarily wrongful, or else it may be lost in certain circumstances. So for instance, if there is an inalienable right to liberty (where 'liberty' is appropriately construed, and so whether there is such a right depends on its formulation), this does not mean it cannot be overridden or lost in some cases – for example, by forfeiture in the case of a punishable offence. So to show that inalienability implies the wrongfulness of every requested killing, it would also need to be shown that the right to life cannot be forfeited or otherwise lost or overridden. (If it could be, it would not be qua *voluntary* that voluntary euthanasia was permissible, but qua *euthanasia* simpliciter.) But that is not the con-cern of the present paper, so it will simply be *assumed* that the right can-not be lost or overridden, *not* because this is an uncontroversial assumption, but because this claim has to be held fixed in order to place the microscope on the question of alienability. Hence, if the right cannot be alienated, and if it cannot otherwise be lost or overridden, *then* volun-tary euthanasia is wrongful, as are most other forms of killing. And even if there are types of killing which are justifiable in circumstances not in-volving voluntary euthanasia, it will still be the case that the latter is al-ways wrong, if the right to life can neither be waived nor otherwise lost or infringed in the case of requested killing. So it now needs to be shown why the right to life is inalienable. The question will be approached from several directions. The first involves some observations concerning moral theory in general. Then I shall consider some examples of inalienable rights in order to show that the concept is not peculiar and that it has various instances, and so to forestall an argument from 'queerness'. I shall end by gesturing positively, in all-too-brief outline, at the rationale for an inalienable right to life in the sort of moral theory that ought to be defended.

**5.** It is generally assumed by opponents of the inalienability thesis (the thesis that there are inalienable rights) that it is perfectly possible, if not common, to have a moral theory without rights, and hence without inalienable rights. Thus there is said to be something peculiar or out of the ordinary about proposing the inalienability of some rights, including the right to life. But this assumption is questionable, which can be shown by a brief consideration of consequentialism, which is held up as a form of moral theory in which, par excellence, rights have no place. On various versions of consequentialism people have feelings, or sensations, or desires, or preferences, or even interests, but not *rights*. Perhaps this is the point at which a definition of 'right' is in order, so we can be clear what it is that consequentialists deny.

A right is best defined as a moral power of doing or having something. By 'power' is meant a capacity or potentiality of doing or having something according to law. Thus a physical power is the capacity of doing or having something according to physical law, and a legal power is the capacity of doing or having something according to positive human law. A *moral* power, then, is distinct from these because possession of neither of the others entails *its* possession, and its possession does not entail possession of either of the others, though it is of course desirable that it be *accompanied* by the others, and vice versa: might does not make right (contra Thrasymachus) and man-made law does not make right (contra legal positivism). A moral power, then, is a power to do or to have something according to moral law, and which enables one to act licitly before its tribunal and before one's conscience, and indeed before all right-thinking people. (It might be argued that it is a conceptual truth that powers are divestible, and hence that no right, qua moral power, can be inalienable. That this is not correct is shown by considering, for instance, powers associated with the essential properties of objects, such as the power of water to separate into its hydrogen and oxygen atoms under electrolysis. Such powers cannot be lost without the relevant object's ceasing to be what it is. On the contrary, the proper view is that there is nothing in the concept of power per se which entails its divestibility or otherwise, and hence a right, qua moral power, may or may not be inalienable; to show a given right's inalienability requires, inter alia, a correct moral theory.)

Now, it should be fairly clear to anyone with even a passing acquaintance with consequentialism that rights thus defined are most certainly *not* the sorts of things which are recognized in that kind of moral theory. Act consequentialists go a whiter shade of pale if they hear that sort of talk (not that they hear it often), and there is no need to elaborate here on why they do so. Rule consequentialism is a little more complicated, however. A rule consequentialist might say something like the following: 'Certainly there are rights according to my theory. An agent has a right to do or to have whatever it is that a given rule sanctions.' A rule will sanction a given doing or having if and only if the relevant behaviour falls within or is contemplated by the rule and the behaviour maximizes ingredient X, on the whole, or on balance, or in general, where X might be feelings, sensations, desires, preferences or interests (or something else). It is not proposed to canvass various criticisms that might be made of rule consequentialism thus formulated, but mention should be made of the obvious one (since although obvious, it is so important that one should not forbear to mention it whenever the opportunity arises), that where the relevant behaviour no longer maximizes ingredient X (on the whole, or on balance, or in general), the applicable rule changes and so what was once a 'right' ceases immediately to be a 'right'. But on the definition just given, rights are plainly not the sorts of things that mutate in this way, not because they are backed by maximization rules which do not change (for plainly they *might*), but because the moral entitlements which confer the rights do not change.

Another reason why anything the rule consequentialist calls a 'right' is not a right stricto sensu, is that rule consequentialism simply does not countenance the sorts of rights which are countenanced on a non-consequentialist theory. There might be some *apparent* overlap (though the overlap is indeed apparent primarily because of the first point just made), but there is a huge area of non-overlap which suggests that the rule consequentialist and the non-consequentialist are talking about different things when they discuss rights. One can play around with examples, but here are two. First, one has a right to the peaceful use and enjoyment of one's chattels (subject to law). This is a right, pure and simple, i.e. without qualification. It is hard to see, however, how the rule consequentialist can countenance a rule which is equally plain and simple. The fact is that the circumstances are so vast in which the loss of peaceful use and enjoy-

ment of one's chattels would maximize ingredient X that any suitable rule
would have to be qualified or conditionalized to a greater or lesser degree. Of course, act consequentialist critics of their rule-following breth-
ren, who accuse them of a rule fetish, would say that the qualifications
would have to be *so* large and diverse in number that one would not end
up with anything recognizably like a rule, or at least a rule one could consistently and easily apply. But this is not something that needs to be
claimed for present purposes (though I agree with the criticism). All that
needs to be said here is that a proper theory of rights *must* countenance
the plain and simple right to peaceful use and enjoyment of one's chattels
(subject to law), whereas rule consequentialism cannot. Therefore the
theories are operating with a different conception of 'right'. The rule
consequentialist can *call* the things he recognizes 'rights' if he wants to,
but this does not *make* them rights, any more than calling an apple an 'orange' makes it an orange. Another example to consider is the right to
complain to the government against unfair treatment. This too is a plain
and simple right, but it is hard to see how the rule consequentialist can
countenance an equally plain and simple rule to the same effect. It is left
to the reader's imagination to come up with circumstances in which any
rule would have to be suitably qualified or restricted.

It appears from this discussion that consequentialism does not recognize rights. But this is only partly true. There is a certain type of right
which it seems the consequentialist does and indeed *must* recognize, on
pain of the theory falling into incoherence. This right might be called
the *right to maximize ingredient X*. There would be something incoherent
in the supposition by a consequentialist that an agent had no right to
maximize according to the dictates of the theory. For the theory simply
*requires* agents to maximize, whether it be in particular circumstances
or by following a rule. It might be said in reply that it is otiose to talk of a
*right* here, since it is simply a metaethical requirement; but this will not
do. The consequentialist must recognize a *capacity* to maximize, and this
is not just a physical capacity, but a capacity conferred by the theory,
upon the agent, as an *entitlement* – but this is just what a right *is*. The consequentialist might however say that all of this can be explained in terms
of *consistent moral obligation* rather than of right: the agent is under a
consistent moral obligation to maximize, but this does not imply the existence of any right. But it is hard to make sense of the notion of consistent moral obligation *without* supposing there to be a right to carry out
the obligation. To take an analogy: I am under a consistent moral obligation to keep my contracts; but this entails that I have a *right* to keep my
contracts, which in turn entails that others may not *stop* me from keeping

my contracts. So, if you procure a breach of contract on my part, by preventing me carrying out my part of the bargain, I am entitled to compensation (both at law and in morality) for the loss occasioned by my failure. At what is the compensation directed? The most edifying explanation is that it is directed at the wrongful infringement of a claim I have against you that you not interfere with my carrying out of my obligation, in other words at the violation of my right to honour the contract. Or again, if you procure my breach of contract, I have been stopped from doing what I am morally entitled to do, and should be compensated for any loss flowing from my failure to act.

Consider an example to illustrate the point about maximization directly (a hackneyed case, unfortunately). Suppose A is trying to decide whether to lie to his wife about his having an affair. Lying would maximize ingredient X (hence telling the truth will not). So for the consequentialist (modify as necessary if rules are involved) A should lie. Is B permitted to stop A lying (*not*: make A tell the truth), for example by changing the subject every time A's conversation with his wife turns to adultery? (Assume B is miraculously present whenever this comes up.) The consequentialist says no. Why? The consequentialist will say that by stopping A from lying, B is himself not maximizing ingredient X, since by lying A maximizes X. But this will not do. For suppose that by stopping A lying, B *himself* maximizes X, say by preserving peace and harmony between A and his wife, which brings about more of X than either A's lying (which might still involve suspicions and secret pain on A's wife's part) or A's telling the truth (which is the worst outcome of all, since all hell will break loose). But here is the problem. Not saying anything is not *open* to A. If B stays out of it, A will be regularly questioned by his wife: A has the choice only of lying or telling the truth – he must respond, and since he is a consequentialist he will lie. It is B, however, to whom it is open to ensure a situation of non-response, by changing the subject every time it is brought up. B's choice is between allowing A to lie, and stopping A from lying. And stopping A from lying (or indeed saying anything) maximizes X as opposed to allowing A to lie. So in this situation, B *maximizes* X by stopping A from lying, so it is not open to the consequentialist to say that the reason B must not interfere is that allowing A to lie maximizes X. Rather, the reason B must not interfere is that A has the *right* to lie, because A's lying maximizes X as opposed to telling the truth, which is his only other option. So A has the right to maximize.

The consequentialist *might* respond that B should forge ahead and interfere anyway, since interfering does indeed maximize X. It would be unwise to do so, however. The complications that would need to be added to a theory already rightly criticized for its unwieldiness would be enormous, perhaps such as to bring all moral agency to a halt. Agents would always have to inquire whether they could achieve more in the way of maximizing ingredient X by interfering in the actions of others than those others would do by acting in an X-maximizing way. Situations in which interference would be recommended *might* be rare, but calculations would always have to be made. Presumably the rule consequentialist, who is not impressed by the 'right to maximize' to which it is claimed he is committed, will seek to generate an account based on a rule or policy of non-interference in others' X-maximizing actions, since non-interference is (on the whole, or on balance, or in general) itself X-maximizing. Such an account will still fall foul of the usual (but powerful) act consequentialist criticisms: why *shouldn't* B interfere in *this* case by stopping A from lying?. Moreover, far from according with non-consequentialist intuitions about non-interference (one should not interfere with the good actions of others even if by doing so one can achieve a greater good (where 'greater' is interpreted to include consequences where they are relevant, but is given an essentially non-consequentialist gloss) ), a consequentialist policy of non-interference makes the freedom of agents to act within the moral sphere something of great fragility. The rule consequentialist, however, typically argues for the superiority of his theory over its act-based counterpart by claiming (falsely, for reasons such as those suggested above) that it is *coextensive* with (much of) what might be called, for want of a better term, commonsense morality.

In any case, it seems that a consequentialist recommendation to interfere in the actions of others, when that interference would be X-maximizing, leads to paradoxical results. For consider two agents, A and B. B has to decide whether or not to $\phi$, and A has to decide whether or not to stop B from $\phi$-ing. B also has the option of interfering with A, by stopping A from stopping B from $\phi$-ing, which is itself a way for B to $\phi$. (In other words, of all the ways that B can $\phi$, one of them involves acting in such a way that he both $\phi$s and prevents A from stopping him from doing so.) The two relevant options for B, then, are these: ($B_1$) he can $\phi$ by stopping A from interfering with him; ($B_2$) he can not-$\phi$ by *allowing* A to stop him from $\phi$-ing. The two relevant options for A are these: ($A_1$) he can stop B from $\phi$-ing; ($A_2$) he can *allow* B to stop him from interfering with B. Suppose now that on a consequentialist calculation, $B_1$ is X-maximizing for B and $A_1$ is X-maximizing for A; in shorthand, $val_X(B_1) > val_X(B_2)$, and $val_X(A_1) > val_X(A_2)$. This means that A should stop B from $\phi$-ing, and B should stop A from stopping him from $\phi$-ing, which are logically incompatible recommendations. But since it is a plausible requirement for a moral theory not to issue in recommendations all of which it is logically impossible for agents to carry out, something is wrong with a theory which does so. What is wrong here is the recommendation that where it is X-maximizing for an agent to interfere with another's X-maximizing actions, the former should do so. Now the paradoxical case just described turns on the following stipulation: that B's action in stopping A from stopping him from $\phi$-ing is not equivalent to A's action of allowing B to stop him from stopping B from $\phi$-ing, and that B's action in not-$\phi$-ing by allowing A to stop him from $\phi$-ing is not equivalent to A's action in stopping B from $\phi$-ing. In shorthand, then, it turns on the claim that $B_1 \neq A_2$ and that $B_2 \neq A_1$. This might seem implausible at first glance, but there is no problem here: suppose that A and B live in a society in which people *approve* of interfering in each other's actions where this is X-maximizing, and *disapprove* of any agent's *allowing* another to interfere with them where, if they interfered themselves rather than allowed interference, they would act X-maximizingly. In other words, in this society *everyone* is supposed to interfere with *everyone else* where this is X-maximizing, and merely allowing interference is seen as a blameworthy capitulation. Now there are plenty of scenarios in which this sort of societal attitude is clearly not paradoxical, so it is not as though the society could be convicted of having obviously incoherent beliefs. And we can suppose that such attitudes of approval and disapproval lead to the sorts of distribution of pains, pleasures, desires, preferences, or whatever is the consequentialist's favourite ingredient, to allow the requisite calculations of the maximizing effects of A's and B's actions. Thus, it can be shown that $B_1 \neq A_2$ and that $B_2 \neq A_1$ because in each pair the actions will have different X-maximizing effects: since $A_2$ involves a capitulation, and taking $-\alpha$ as the disvalue of capitulating (for simplicity let us suppose the disvalue of capitulating to be constant across all actions, though it need not be), we can say that $val_X(A_2) = val_X(B_1) - \alpha$; and since $B_2$ involves a capitulation, we can say that $val_X(B_2) = val_X(A_1) - \alpha$. Hence $val_X(B_1) > val_X(A_2)$ and $val_X(A_1) > val_X(B_2)$, which means that on this scenario it does not follow from the fact that B is required to interfere with A, that A is required to *allow* B to interfere with him.

Therefore, the moral of the story for the consequentialist is that agents should let each other maximize, even if it means forbearing from carrying out an alternative which would itself maximize as opposed to letting others maximize, i.e. interfering. But this is all very well, since agents have a right to maximize anyway, which consequentialists must recognize.

Furthermore, this right to maximize ingredient X must be inalienable. Would it be at all rational for a consequentialist to say, 'I renounce my right to maximize'? This would mean opting for not maximizing, which for the consequentialist is doubly morally wrong: it is wrong because it is irrational, and it is wrong precisely because it involves choices not to maximize. Anyone who made such a statement would have ceased to be a consequentialist. So, without going into this in even more detail than has been necessary so far, the conclusion that has been reached is that consequentialism recognizes inalienable rights, or at least *one* inalienable right.

6. The object of the above discussion was to demonstrate that there is nothing peculiar about inalienable rights as far as moral theory is concerned: even the theory most hostile to rights has them (or one). This should remove the moral theorist's discomfiture about inalienable rights, and allow a more even-handed appreciation of what a non-consequentialist theory has to say about them. Our next task is to look at some examples of inalienable rights. The problem here, though, is that in trying to think of examples that would command unanimous assent it becomes clear how much what might be called the doctrine of the *paramountcy of the will* has come to dominate moral thinking. Every time one tries to think of an example, one is faced with the 'little voice' which has come so much to influence moral thinking: 'Why? Why is that right inalienable? Why *cannot* [with a special inflection on 'cannot'] you do such-and-such, or allow such-and-such to be done to you?' So the example of masochism, which once would have commanded universal agreement, probably does not do so now. Once upon a time people thought there was an inalienable right to bodily integrity; one simply could not cede one's right not to have one's bodily integrity intentionally assaulted. Of course one could *consent* to an infringement in some cases, for example a surgical operation, but this was not a *cession*, merely an agreement to a limited, well-defined infringement for a stated purpose, namely to heal the patient. Indeed, apart from therapeutic or socially necessary cases, for example bumping into someone on a crowded train, it was thought that one could *not* consent to any old assault on one's bodily integrity; even decorative mutilation, such as ear-piercing, was frowned upon once as far as can be ascertained. So any purported abandonment of one's right to bodily integrity was considered null and void. Were someone to say, 'Here's my body; do what you will with it', and moreover to say that this permission had effect in perpetuity, i.e. was a genuine renunciation, they would probably have been locked up. But today, it seems, many or even most people do not find anything irrational in a similar statement by one who was

such an inveterate masochist that they allowed any and every assault on their bodily integrity. 'Why *shouldn't* they be allowed to do that? As long as they're not obviously mad, what's wrong with that?'

But perhaps this feeling is not so widespread. Perhaps we would think more carefully if someone came up to us holding a syringe and various other paraphernalia, and asked us to inject them with heroin because they had not tried it before and were desperate to get addicted. (Perhaps they ask you because they are too nervous to do it themselves, or are physically incapable.) Now, even viewing that as a purported permission to infringe, we would perhaps balk. But if we would balk at it as a purported permission to infringe, how much more would we think twice if we were told by the person that they had abandoned any right they have to be healthy, and one of the first things they wanted to do after such abandonment was to get themselves addicted to heroin? And would not the reluctance then properly be said to stem from the belief that the right to bodily integrity is not the sort of thing one can simply renounce? Or consider another example, say someone desperate to stay hooked for the rest of their lives on smoking or drinking. They know that every so often they will have second thoughts and want to reform their ways, but it is precisely at those times, they tell you, that you must make sure they have a plentiful supply of alcohol or tobacco at hand so as to ensure they stay hooked. Would you agree to such a request? Probably more would refuse it than would refuse the heroin request, although that is probably a sociological anomaly. Suppose, when you question them on their motive for wanting to stay addicted, they say that they have, quite simply, given up their right to be healthy, for whatever reason. Again, it is proposed that most of us would find the doctrine of the paramountcy of the will coming under extreme pressure here. There are some things, we would (one hopes) say, on which you just cannot give up. If this is so, then perhaps those people who agree with the proposed way of dealing with these cases ought to go back and re-examine their intuitions about cases where they *disagree* about alienability; and perhaps the right to life ought to be one of those cases.

There is, however, a strong argument in favour of the alienability of the right to life, based on the analogy of property. We typically think of our lives as our property, perhaps our most important, but property nevertheless. 'It is my life and I'll do what I want with it.' (Recall the play in support of euthanasia that came out a number of years ago, 'Whose Life Is It Anyway?') And the hallmark of property (an essential property of property) is that it is alienable. So someone commits no injustice if they take apples from another's apple tree while the other stands there happily watching, or says 'Sure, take as many as you like.' And of course property can be sold, given away and bequeathed. Why is not life the same? There are some doubts as to the correct response here, but a possible approach can be suggested. One can certainly alienate one's right to this or that property, for example one's apples, but one cannot alienate one's right to property *in general*, considered apart from any particular piece of property. One cannot validly say, 'I renounce my right as a human being to own property'. Alienating your right to this or that property does not entail alienating your right to property in general, and is thus compatible with retaining that right. On the other hand, a purported alienation of your right to your particular life would entail a purported alienation of the right to life in general, it being metaphysically impossible to have more than one life. So, whereas the alienation of the right to this or that property says nothing about the right to property in general, the purported alienation of your particular life does entail the purported alienation of the right to life in general, so there is a disanalogy. Any *similarity* between the two cases only supports the inalienability of the right to life, since the right to property in general seems inalienable.

I say 'seems' here, because there are still uncertainties. What about someone who renounces their right to property in general when, say, they enter a commune where there is no private property? Here it does not seem that there would be an injustice if the relevant member of the commune were to deprive the new member of his secretly-acquired clock radio. There are, however, two possible interpretations of such a case which point to its dissimilarity with the right to life. They are mutually exclusive, but either one will block the analogy, and in any case they might have separate applications to different cases, so I am content to leave it open which interpretation is correct. One is that there is no alienation of the right to property, only a consent to abide by the laws of the commune, which may forbid private property. Once the new member ceases to be a member, by leaving, and hence ceases to be subject to the laws of the commune, he is free to exercise his right to own property again, a right which never left him. Another interpretation is that there is an alienation, but it is only temporary, and the right is reassumed once the member ceases to be subject to the laws of the commune; whereas any alienation of the right to life is necessarily permanent. The circumstances of the particular case will largely determine which interpretation is correct, but either way there is no permanent renunciation of the right to property, which is evidenced by the fact that the leader of the commune would be acting manifestly unjustly if he chased after the person who ceased to be a member, acknowledging that he had left but still trying to stop him owning any property!

7. I have tried to establish that there are examples of inalienable rights other than the right to life, and that the prime example of alienability used to show that the right to life *is* alienable, namely the right to property, does nothing of the sort. Now a positive account of the inalienability of the right to life is needed.

The right to maximize which was identified earlier in respect of consequentialism might be called a structural moral right, in the sense that its possession is a precondition of all moral decision making for the consequentialist. For the act consequentialist, it is a precondition of decision making in particular cases; for the rule consequentialist it is a precondition of rule formulation and rule following. It forms, as it were, part of the architecture of the theory. Similarly (though not *exactly* similarly), the right to life in the sort of theory defended here, one of a teleological but non-consequentialist nature, forms part of the theory's architecture. In it, the concept of a human good looms large, as do concepts of human fulfilment, virtue, human nature, human dignity and others. In particular, human life is seen as a good which is fundamental to the pursuit of all other goods, or a precondition of their pursuit. As such, human life is the *starting point* for moral theory, or the place from which all moral evaluation begins. It is important not to confuse two claims. One is the claim that human life is necessary for the pursuability of human goods, and the other is that it is sufficient. The latter claim is evidently false, but it is hard not to think that it is this claim which advocates of euthanasia attribute to opponents, since they also attribute the moral claim that if human life has a point, other human goods must be pursuable; but, advocates say, in certain cases a person can be reduced to such a state, for example a persistent non-responsive state, in which they simply *cannot* pursue any other goods – in which case human life has no point. But this is not what opponents claim. Rather, they claim that if human goods are pursuable, then human life is important. They then detach the second part of the implication, and say that human life is important pure and simple, i.e. it is a fundamental good.

It is also important to note that the claim is *not* that human life is merely *instrumentally* good; rather, it is *intrinsically* good, since it cannot be separated in thought from the pursuit of all the other goods which together constitute human happiness; they are all pursuits-by-living-beings, and so to the extent that a given good is not pursued for any other sake than its own, so too the life in which it is pursued is not lived for any other sake than its own.[2]

The fundamental nature of the good of life means that it is not just one good among others. It has been argued[3] that all goods are equally fundamental from the observation that an individual can, with equal reasonableness, regard each one as more important than the others in that individual's own life. Two points should be made in response to this. The first is that the subjective ranking of goods has a restricted place in the evaluation of how well an individual's life goes for them. Factors such as upbringing, temperament, abilities and the like clearly influence the order of priorities a person constructs, and this influence is to be given its due place. But the ranking is always subject to the basic question of whether it does *in fact* contribute to the flourishing of that person. A scholar might well devote his life to the pursuit of knowledge above all else, to the neglect of such goods as play. As far as it goes, this does not merit criticism, especially if the factors just mentioned greatly affect the choice. But such a person can clearly go too far, from the objective standpoint, if (for instance) their neglect of play contributes to a deleterious state of health: it is only a comparatively recent phenomenon, born of Romanticism, that the idea of the tubercular scholar who studies himself to the grave has come to embody a noble ideal. Thus, to the extent that goods are equally fundamental, this derives less from the possibility of different reasonable rankings than from the objective contribution each one makes to a life of well being.

Secondly, concerning the good of life, it is clear that this good can never occupy an inferior place in a reasonable subjective ordering of priorities. To take the case of knowledge and health again, we can see that a person might place more emphasis on knowledge at some cost to health, but this demoting of life (which, as a good, includes health) can never be complete. It would be incoherent to suppose that one's *death* could ever enhance one's pursuit of knowledge, any more than it could enhance one's pursuit of any other good. Examples that seem to indicate the contrary are in fact irrelevant. Consider the artist suffering from a terminal and debilitating illness, who forces himself to keep going for the sole purpose of completing his life's work. We would regard such an attitude as unquestionably admirable, but it would not be an attitude which relegated life to having purely instrumental value. It is not as though the artist has come to see the only *point* of life as its allowing him to finish his work; his illness has been foisted upon him and seeks to *deprive* him of life, with the result that, through no fault of his own (in the sort of case being imagined), the instrumental value of life assumes priority. Compare this with the case of a depressed and suicidal parent, tired of life (for whatever reason), who says that the only thing that keeps her going is her children, whom she wants to see grow up: were it not for that, she says, she would commit suicide. Here other goods are being promoted above life itself, which *is* given purely instrumental value. To that extent the subjective ranking is unreasonable, and we can indeed see that the attitude of such a person does not contribute to a flourishing life. (Note that I am talking primarily about settled dispositions or non-transient ways of looking at the world, not momentary lapses brought on by unhappy circumstances, which may temporarily affect an agent's attitudes toward life and other things of value.)

The good of life, then, is fundamental in a way that other goods are not. It is possible that two individuals should live comparably flourishing lives while having different subjective rankings of various goods apart from life, but it is by no means equally clear that life itself can reasonably or even coherently be demoted. For to do so would be to abandon the only moral framework within which evaluation of action can take place, this being one in which human beings strive, within their natural limits, for a *good life*.

What, then, is to be said about a request for euthanasia? First, it is important to observe that the voluntariness component in voluntary euthanasia is, quite simply, a red herring. Just as we would (one should hope) balk at injecting someone with heroin, so we would (one should hope) balk at any old request to be killed. If a person in no pain, in no distress, perhaps with no more than a bout of influenza, were to ask for death, no doctor would accede to the request. Why? If the request is genuine, i.e. a sincere attempt at alienation of the right to life, why *shouldn't* the doctor accede to the request? Why does an evaluation of the patient's reasons *matter*? The fact that the reasons *do* matter itself indicates that there is no true alienation here, rather a request for infringement. Thus inalienability is something agreed upon by most if not all parties to the debate. The real difference is over whether there can be *good reasons* to infringe. And there are plenty of arguments, none of which will be canvassed here, but all critical of the specious moral theories, specious quality of life judgments, misunderstandings of the concepts of benefit, cure, and so on which are used to justify such requests, which show that there *are* no good reasons.

Secondly, it might be said that the reluctance to carry out any old request for death is only a function of moral squeamishness, and that, strictly speaking, autonomy is paramount. The reply here is that autonomy is never paramount, but always subject to human good. Again, although advocates of euthanasia seek to point out a fundamental conflict over the proper role of autonomy, reflection shows that the restriction of autonomy is accepted on all sides, so for instance autonomy is not equated, except perhaps by extreme libertarians or relativists with flawed theories of their own, with the moral capacity to do anything one likes. The real question is *how* and in what *respects* autonomy is to be limited. For a non-consequentialist teleological theorist, autonomy is limited by the very human goods which it is proper, qua human being, to pursue. The will can have various degrees of freedom in, say, the means chosen to pursue some good, or the weight to be given to one good compared to another, but it must still be directed at the pursuit of the good. But since human life is indeed a good, and the fundamental good, since it is the source of all human dignity and well being, autonomy cannot be exercised with a view to abandoning it. The same goes for human dignity itself. One can live in an undignified way, but one cannot abandon one's fundamental right to live in a dignified way.

In the case, then, of someone in a persistent non-responsive state, the proper response is not to say that, since the person is not flourishing or exercising their humanity to the fullest (whatever the latter may mean), their bare right to life is alienable, say in an advance directive. Of course it would be perverse to say that the person *was* flourishing – plainly they are not. But then neither do any of us flourish in an undiminished way, and it is difficult to see how the person in a persistent non-responsive state is qualitatively different from any of us in that respect; it is only the *degree* of diminution of flourishing which is different. The flourishing or lack thereof is irrelevant to a consideration of whether the last remaining good they pursue, namely bare life, should be eliminated as well.

We should conclude, then, that the right to life is inalienable, in which case the carrying out of a request for death is always an injustice where there are no other reasons why the right can be infringed.[4]

## NOTES

1  Note that I shall use words such as 'kill' and 'killer' not because of a desire morally to load the issue, as it were, but simply because they are the most accurate and convenient terms.
2  Compare the sense of 'precondition' used by John Finnis, which he equates with 'instrumentally valuable': *Natural Law and Natural Rights* (Oxford: Clarendon Press, 1980), p. 92. The term is ambiguous, in that it can be given both an instrumental and a conceptual reading, which latter is the one used here in defending life as a fundamental good.
3  Finnis, loc. cit.
4  A version of this paper was read at the Department of Philosophy's Work in Progress seminar at the University of Reading. The author is indebted to the participants in that seminar for most helpful comments and criticism.

# Index

241